T0330580

HIRING LEGALLY:
A Guide for Employees and Employers

Kurt H. Decker, Esq.

Partner
Stevens & Lee
and
Adjunct Professor
Widener University
School of Law (Harrisburg, Pennsylvania)
and
Graduate School of Human Resource Management
and Industrial Relations
Saint Francis College (Loretto, Pennsylvania)

Routledge
Taylor & Francis Group

LONDON AND NEW YORK

First published 2000 by Baywood Publishing Co., Inc.

Published 2018 by Routledge
2 Park Square, Milton Park, Abingdon, Oxon OX14 4RN
52 Vanderbilt Avenue, New York, NY 10017

First issued in hardback 2018

Routledge is an imprint of the Taylor & Francis Group, an informa business

Copyright © 2000 by Taylor & Francis

Library of Congress Catalog Number: 99-17822

Library of Congress Cataloging-in-Publication Data

Decker, Kurt H.
    Hiring legally : a guide for employees and employers / Kurt H.
    Decker.
        p.   cm.
    Includes bibliographical references and index.
    ISBN 0-89503-197-3
    1. Employee selection- -Law and legislation- -United States.
    I. Title
    KF3457.D433   1999   99-17822
    658.3'112- -dc21   CIP

ISBN 13: 978-0-415-78591-4 (hbk)
ISBN 13: 978-0-89503-197-6 (pbk)

Dedication

For Christian, Allison, and all others
whose unique talents should only be evaluated
at the workplace through job-related
inquiries.

Preface

Today, the hiring process is becoming more complex for employees and employers. In seeking employment, individuals must disclose considerable personal information that may or may not be job-related. This disclosure creates vast information resources that may be abused by employers. Often, the employer must verify this information causing additional disclosure concerns.

Prior to the 1980s, human resource administrators and employment law attorneys infrequently encountered claims concerning issues outside the collective bargaining relationship or areas regulated by federal and state fair employment practice (FEP) statutes. However, as the 1990s end and the new millennium begins, employees are increasingly asserting hiring claims against employers.

Employee hiring litigation against employers is being predicated on a variety of legal theories involving tort and contractual claims. These claims are based on defamation, discrimination, invasion of privacy, intentional infliction of emotional distress, negligent maintenance or disclosure of employment records, fraudulent misrepresentation, intentional interference with contractual relations, public policy, and breach of oral or written contracts, handbooks, and policies.

This book reviews the principles, procedures, and policies applicable to hiring to assist in minimizing litigation risks for employers and acquainting employees with certain employer procedures to protect their disclosures of non-job-related information. Chapter 1 discusses the hiring process. Chapter 2 examines pre-employment screening fundamentals. Chapter 3 covers data verification involving arrest records, credit checks, criminal convictions, fingerprints, immigration, photographs, physical examinations, references, and skill testing. Chapter 4 reviews federal and state statutes affecting the hiring process. Finally, appendices are included for pre-employment disability-related and medical examination Equal Employment Opportunities Commission (EEOC) guidance, reasonable accommodation and undue hardship under the Americans with Disabilities Act (ADA), and employee selection procedures.

The book is intended as an introductory text for use by employees, human resource managers, attorneys, and students as a foundation for further inquiry. Its material should be used only as guidelines. Where legal advice is required, it should be obtained.

Kurt H. Decker, Esq.

Acknowledgments

Little in life is a solitary undertaking. Much is a culmination of other people's thoughts and efforts. The material in this book is no different. Over the years many individuals have either provided opportunities or shared their knowledge to make the information in this book possible.

Those who have participated in shaping my understanding of employment law cannot all be recognized. However, H. Thomas Felix, II, Esquire of Montgomery, McCracken, Walker, & Rhoads, Philadelphia, Pennsylvania and Arbitrator John Skonier of Norristown, Pennsylvania are of special importance. Throughout the years these two individuals have served as mentors, friends, and the ones who have most encouraged my employment law research, writing, and teaching interests.

Others who should not be overlooked are Dr. Robert D. Lee, Jr. in giving hope that a future existed after military service by opening the door for a lifelong interest in employment law at graduate school; Dr. William E. Caldwell for nurturing my interest in employment law while a graduate student; Professor Paul H. Sanders for instilling the recognition of conflict resolution's paramount importance in employment law; Professor Robert N. Covington who provided the initial opportunities to research individual employee rights while at law school and who after law school honored me by co-authoring *Individual Employment Rights in a Nutshell* for the West Group; Dr. Harry Kershen for affording the first opportunity to appear in print and in supporting the idea for *The Journal of Individual Employment Rights* with its publisher, Stuart Cohen; Dr. Edwin M. Wagner and Dr. Philip Benham of the Graduate School of Human Resource Management and Industrial Relations, Saint Francis College for encouraging the sharing of knowledge through teaching; former Dean John Gedid of Widener University School of Law for recognizing the importance of the developing area of individual employment rights to the law school curriculum; Dean Loren D. Prescott, Jr. for continuing that commitment at Widener; and Sidney D. Kline, Jr., Esq. and Joseph M. Harenza, Esq. of Stevens & Lee for their support over the years in pursuing academic interests outside of the law firm's normal client responsibilities.

Finally, I am appreciative of those individuals at Baywood Publishing Company, Inc. who labored over this text's physical preparation. Among these individuals are Bobbi Olszewski, Editorial and Michelle Satchell, Marketing.

Kurt H. Decker, Esq.

Contents

CHAPTER 4
FEDERAL AND STATE STATUTES AFFECTING THE

APPENDIX A
PRE-EMPLOYMENT DISABILITY-RELATED AND
MEDICAL EXAMINATION EQUAL EMPLOYMENT

APPENDIX B
EQUAL EMPLOYMENT OPPORTUNITIES COMMISSION'S
(EEOC's) ENFORCEMENT GUIDANCE: REASONABLE
ACCOMMODATION AND UNDUE HARDSHIP UNDER
THE AMERICANS WITH DISABILITIES ACT (ADA)

APPENDIX C
EQUAL EMPLOYMENT OPPORTUNITIES COMMISSION'S
(EEOC's) UNIFORM GUIDELINES ON EMPLOYEE

Chapter 1

The Hiring Process

Hiring is the process used by employers to determine which applicants should be considered for employment and subsequently employed. To limit employer liability, an overall hiring procedure should be developed that considers advertisements, applications, interviews, and data verification.

The overall hiring procedure should ensure that only relevant or job-related information necessary for employment decisions is collected, maintained, and used. Likewise, this information's sensitivity should be preserved through confidentiality procedures in effect prior to, during, and after employment termination. This should be done to minimize employee claims that may arise out of federal or state fair employment practice (FEP) statutory violations as well as those arising from tort or contractual litigation. [See, e.g., *Toussaint v. Blue Cross & Blue Shield of Mich.*, 408 Mich. 579, 292 N.W.2d 880 (1980) (employer liability for interviewer's statement that the employee would be employed as long as he did his job); *Slohoda v. United Parcel Serv.*, 193 N.J. Super. 586, 475 A.2d 618 (App. Div. 1984), *rev'd on other grounds*, 207 N.J. Super. 145, 504 A.2d 53 (1986) (inquiry by employer into extramarital sexual activities could rise to tort liability if the employee were terminated for that reason).]

The human resource principles, procedures, and policies affecting the hiring process are reviewed in this Chapter. Areas covered include general hiring considerations, special hiring considerations, recruiting sources, hiring and dealing with disabled employees, minimizing risks during the hiring process, checklist before employment, and hiring policies.

GENERAL HIRING CONSIDERATIONS

In developing an overall hiring procedure, the following should be considered:

1. Determine who should be the interviewer
2. Determine who should review records

3. Obtain information only from verifiable sources
4. Obtain information by permissible methods
5. Use only reliable consumer reporting agencies
6. Maintain information confidentiality
7. Use only permissible reference checking procedures
8. Inform applicants what information will be collected, maintained, and disclosed
9. Inform applicants of the uses to be made of collected information
10. Adopt procedures to assure the information's accuracy, timeliness, and completeness
11. Permit review, copying, correction, or amendment of this information
12. Limit internal use
13. Limit external disclosures, including disclosures made without authorization, to specific inquiries or requests to verify information
14. Provide for a regular internal compliance review of hiring procedures

SPECIAL HIRING CONSIDERATIONS

In developing an overall hiring procedure, the following special considerations should be noted:

1. The time required to fill vacant positions varies substantially depending upon what position is being filled
2. Employers use a wide variety of recruiting resources to find their applicants, including:
   a. Internal promotions
   b. Employee referrals
   c. Newspaper advertisements
   d. Walk-in applicants
   e. Employment agencies
   f. The Internet
3. Interviewers should be given special training
4. Employers check a wide variety of applicant information, including:
   a. Employment dates
   b. Reason for leaving a prior position
   c. Employment history
5. Employers confirm a wide variety of information by contacting:
   a. Personal and professional references
   b. Prior employers
   c. Educational institutions
   d. Medical information sources
   e. Licensing sources

RECRUITING SOURCES

The following sources may be used by employers to locate applicants for position openings:

1. Internal sources
   a. Promotion from within
   b. Employee referrals
   c. Walk-in applicants
2. Advertising
   a. Newspapers
   b. Journals/magazines
   c. Direct mail
   d. Radio/television
   e. The Internet
3. Outside referral sources
   a. Colleges/universities
   b. Technical/vocational schools
   c. Professional societies
   d. Community agencies
   e. Unions
4. Employment services
   a. State employment service
   b. Private employment agencies
   c. Search firms
   d. United States Employment Service
   e. Employee leasing firms
   f. Computerized resume service
   g. Video interviewing service
   h. The Internet
5. Special events
   a. Career conferences/job fairs
   b. Open houses

HIRING AND DEALING WITH DISABLED EMPLOYEES

Because all employers compete for skilled employees, it is important not to overlook any talent sources. Recruiting should extend to nontraditional sources, including those who may be physically and/or mentally challenged. Assistance in reaching this talent pool is available from rehabilitative, social service, and educational agencies that counsel individuals with disabilities for careers that could coincide with an employer's needs. **[See Appendices A and B.]** A list of some of these agencies, including the services and programs they provide, can be obtained from the following:

1. Department of Veterans Affairs
2. Local vocational, technical, and general high schools
3. Special education schools and programs
4. Local offices or federal and state employment services
5. National organizations or their local affiliates of:
    a. Disabled American Veterans
    b. Epilepsy Foundation
    c. National Association for Retarded Citizens
    d. Easter Seal Society
    e. Goodwill Industries
    f. United Cerebral Palsy
    g. Multiple Sclerosis Society
    h. Arthritis Foundation
6. Blind centers
7. Bureaus of services for people who are blind
8. Projects with industry
9. Labor unions
10. State agencies for vocational rehabilitation
11. State departments of human services
12. State committees for people who are developmentally disabled
13. Disabilities and aging information and referral services
14. Rehabilitation/sheltered workshops
15. Community colleges
16. Welfare employment centers
17. Private industry councils

Many of the above sources are listed in local telephone directories for easier access. [Adapted from the President's Committee on Employment of People With Disabilities, *Ready, Willing and Available: A Business Guide For Hiring People With Disabilities*, Appendix B (1989).]

When contacting a referral source, the employer should inquire regarding the level of services it provides by asking:

1. Does the agency evaluate their clients' employment potential? If so, how?
2. Does the agency provide skills training? If so, what?
3. Are financial incentives available for hiring the persons that the agency represents, for instance, targeted jobs tax credits, wage subsidies, training grants, etc.?
4. Does the agency provide on-the-job training, coaching, counseling, follow-up, etc.?
5. Does the agency offer awareness training to supervisors and managers?

6. What is the agency's placement record, including the number of placements in specific jobs, retention rates, etc.?

Once a relationship is established with one agency, other agencies with similar services will probably contact the employer. One successful placement will open other avenues of opportunity.

Meeting and Evaluating Candidates

An employer has a job to fill and a person with a disability applies. This person is like any other applicant except for a physical, mental, or learning disability. If the person did not believe that he or she was qualified, no application would have been filed. It is the employer's responsibility to determine if the disabled person is qualified. This assessment of qualifications must be done in the same manner as for any other applicant.

Set forth below are some suggestions for dealing with disabled applicants.

Greeting the Applicant

When in doubt as to whether to help an individual around the limitations caused by his or her disability, the following questions should allow the applicant to tell what, if anything, is needed:

1. May I be of assistance?
2. Is there anything I can do to make your visit more pleasant?

The following should be considered when dealing with certain applicant limitations:

1. If the applicant has a visual limitation or is blind, identify yourself, shake hands, and offer the applicant the option of taking your arm for direction if you need to go to another location. Let the applicant feel the back of the chair where he or she is to sit. If a guide dog accompanies the applicant, let it do its job.
2. If the applicant has a hearing limitation and you have no experience in sign language, look at the individual, speak in your regular tone of voice, and be prepared to exchange information in writing. Have a couple of note pads and pencils handy.
3. If the applicant is accompanied by an interpreter, speak to the applicant. The interpreter will ask to sit next to you to better handle the interview.
4. If the applicant has mental limitations, there is no need to "talk down." Greet him or her as you would any other applicant and use the vocabulary common to the job. In a few minutes, you will have a good understanding of the level at which the individual can communicate.

Remember the following:

1. *Wrong perspective.* "If I were in your shoes, I don't know how I could possibly do this job."
2. *Right perspective.* "This person is applying for the job of (*name of job*). He or she does have a disability. If I became disabled, but was capable of performing this job, would I not wish to be treated like any other applicant without a disability? Let's see about the applicant's experience, training, and education; then we'll deal with the possibility that the disability might require an accommodation for the individual to do the job's functions."

Handling the Application

Follow the employer's regular procedures. If the applicant's disability prevents him or her from filling out an application, offer assistance or allow it to be taken home, stating a specific time for its return. This action is a reasonable accommodation to the employer's application procedures.

Testing the Applicant

If the employer requires any type of test and the applicant's disability does not interfere, the test should be administered in the same manner as for any other applicant. Blindness, motor impairment affecting the use of hands or eye/hand coordination, and learning disabilities can prevent an applicant from passing some tests even though he or she might have the ability to do the job. Rely instead on the applicant's work experience, training, and education. Remember, when the applicant's impairment makes it impractical to complete a test, particularly one which is timed, the results may reflect the testing of the individual's impairment-related limitations instead of predicting the applicant's abilities and potential job success. The following should be considered in dealing with certain disabilities and how they might affect test performance:

1. Under some circumstances, a test should be read to an applicant who has a visual impairment. For example, many individuals with visual impairments successfully hold typing positions. To test a person with a visual impairment, typing tests are put on a dictating machine and then scored in the same way as for any other applicant. If an applicant has a hearing impairment, ask some questions that will indicate whether or not the applicant understands the instructions.
2. If the applicant has a learning disability, success or failure on the test could depend solely on its instructions. Try to modify the instructions to accommodate the applicant's disability.
3. Persons who have recovered from mental illness might not be able to sustain test pressure. Honest and open discussion regarding this will help in deciding if the test is really needed.

Discussing Reasonable Accommodation

The issue of accommodation should be raised only after the individual is determined to be qualified as a potential job candidate. If the applicant is not qualified, tell him or her why; i.e., explain the training and experience that other persons who perform the job possess, which he or she lacks or must obtain to become a successful applicant. In this way, the applicant will understand that his or her rejection was truly based on a lack of qualification rather than on a disability.

The interview of a potentially successful candidate should end with a visit to the worksite. At that time, a better understanding of the tasks to be performed can be obtained. If a reasonable accommodation is needed, the degree of accommodation can be discussed.

Working with Agencies

If the applicant has been referred by or trained by a rehabilitation agency, the employer will have access to additional information. While it is always preferable to interview an applicant alone, the nature of the disability might require the presence of the agency counselor. This will help open the door.

Closing the Interview

If the applicant is qualified and the employer is not prepared to make a hiring offer, the usual reasons given to applicants who are not hired immediately apply, such as, "Thank you for applying, we will notify you in the future regarding any openings."

Deciding What the Job Is

Job analysis is the process of breaking down a particular job into its component parts. This is a useful tool in interviewing, selecting, training, and promoting employees as well as for determining compensation. It is especially helpful when dealing with disabled applicants or employees.

The first step in a job analysis is to prepare a list of the required tasks. Next, the following questions should be asked about each task:

1. How is the task performed; i.e., what methods, techniques, and tools are used?
2. How often is the task performed; i.e., are the tasks performed less frequently as important to success as those done more frequently?
3. How much time is allotted to perform the task? Is the pace consistent?
4. Why is the task performed?
5. Where is the task performed?

6. How is success measured?
7. What happens if the task is done incorrectly?
8. What aptitudes are necessary; i.e., what is the potential to learn and accomplish a skill?
9. What knowledge is necessary; i.e., the level of general or technical information?
10. What skills are necessary?
11. How much physical exertion is required, such as lifting, standing, bending, reaching, twisting, crawling, etc.?

Supplement the above with knowledge from other sources, including:

1. Interviewing employees and supervisors
2. Observing the job
3. Using employee task logs and questionnaires

Job analysis is particularly useful when hiring the disabled. A careful match of the individual's aptitudes and abilities with the particular job enhances the success probability. The job analysis also helps in determining if a job accommodation is necessary. Accommodation can include:

1. Additional assistance to the individual with a disability
2. A physical change to the worksite
3. A restructuring of tasks

Restructuring of tasks is particularly helpful with employees who have mental or emotional disabilities. For example, employees who are recovering from a mental illness may initially need task assignments that are routine. Eventually, these assignments become boring as the employee's health improves. As a means of preparing the employee for more significant assignments, tasks can be gradually added or redesigned so that they become more interesting. A job analysis will help in defining or redefining the necessary skill level for the position. Finally, a job analysis helps reassure supervisors about the real capability of a person with a disability.

Accommodating Employees with Disabilities

Employers have many resources available to assist in modifying, adapting, and providing accessibility to their buildings and facilities for the newly disabled employee. Some of these are provided at no cost. State vocational rehabilitation agencies are a good source for this assistance. Another resource is the Job Accommodation Network (JAN), which offers toll-free telephone consultation (1-800-526-7234).

In addition to job modification, structural changes may need to be made. Structural changes may be minimal, involving only ramping, doorway widening, and making restrooms accessible. In most cases, the cost of increasing accessibility may be relatively small. Tax incentives to employers that make their facilities and vehicles accessible to disabled or elderly persons should be reviewed under federal and state tax statutes. [See, e.g., 26 U.S.C. § 190 (1994) (tax incentive under the Internal Revenue Code).]

Often accommodation involves no more than taking a common-sense approach that need not be expensive to be effective. Many situations can be handled with little or no expense. The person with the disability is usually the best person with whom to start. He or she may have already solved the problem or be able to offer constructive advice on what needs to be done.

Wheelchair Users

Wheelchair users need space for their chairs when entering and leaving as well as in work areas. Local building codes state the amount of space required. Often, simply raising an ordinary desk or worktable on blocks will allow the user to draw his or her chair up to the work area and work comfortably. Specially designed workstations, as well as those that can be raised and lowered mechanically, are available. The employer should also consider limitations in the range of reach for wheelchair users and others with upper body strength and extension problems. Moving equipment and/or devices from one side of a workstation to the other may be all that is needed to allow an individual to function productively. When necessary items are out of reach and cannot be moved, a variety of devices are available to extend an individual's reach and grasp.

Hearing-Impaired Individuals

Helping accommodate hearing-impaired individuals may be no more complicated than turning a receptionist's desk to face the door. A variety of devices are available for telephones to amplify hearing and speech. Devices that flash lights instead of ringing bells can be provided for emergency alarms as well as telephones. Some hearing-impaired persons cannot use regular telephones even if the phones are adapted with amplifying devices. Instead, individuals with severe hearing loss use telecommunication devices for the hearing-impaired (TDDs). TDDs make the telephone accessible and productive to people who would otherwise not be able to use it. For greatest efficiency, the "sender" and "receiver" should each have a TDD.

Vision-Impaired Individuals

Individuals with limited or no vision can be accommodated in various ways. Examples include raised lettering or Braille symbols on signs and elevator buttons. A variety of magnification devices exist. Devices that produce Braille symbols or synthesized speech can assist those with severely limited or no vision to read printed material and access computers. While these devices may be expensive initially, they often pay for themselves in increased productivity.

Severe Strength and Motion Limitations

Individuals with severe strength and motion limitations, such as that caused by quadriplegia, can also be accommodated. Switches that can be operated with the mouth or a head stick can be connected to telephones, computers, and manufacturing equipment, as can floor strips that are triggered when a wheelchair rolls across.

Mental Disabilities

Special equipment to accommodate individuals who are mentally disabled or those who have recovered from some form of mental disability may not be required. Speak with the individual about it. Providing extra training and guidance to the individual, or breaking a complex task down into simpler components, may be all that is needed to ensure understanding and productivity. Working closely with the person's rehabilitation counselor should also be considered. Avoid giving too many instructions at once. Try to limit the number of individuals giving instructions. Multiple instructors often can confuse a situation as much as multiple instructions.

Obtaining Supervisor Support

Gaining supervisor support and commitment requires planning, education, support, and feedback. The supervisor is the key to the success of the employee with a disability.

Supervisors can be prepared for the specific limitations and needs of individual employees by providing them with written information, contacts with community resources, and coaching from those who have successfully supervised employees with disabilities. Depending upon the employer's size, it might be best to develop a training program for all supervisors, using knowledgeable individuals who can lead discussions about the supervisor's role. This will create an internal network and increase awareness throughout the organization. Use accurate facts and data to help the supervisor enter the relationship with a realistic, positive attitude.

Knowledge of an individual's performance expectations, reliability, and special needs is essential. For example, knowing that most employees with disabilities are extremely dependable and responsible will aid the supervisor to view an individual as an asset. However, apprehension may not totally disappear until the supervisor has experienced some degree of success in dealing with employees who have disabilities.

Ongoing support from others in the employer's organization is required, particularly from top-level management. Management must be clear about its commitment, providing consistent goals to the supervisor and the employee. This may include bonuses for supervisors who successfully manage employees with disabilities. The employer should also listen to the supervisor's concerns, provide feedback, praise his or her successes, and encourage efforts that will make the supervisor a role model for others.

Begin by involving the supervisor in the employment process, including recruitment, interviewing, and job modification. The supervisor will know what is expected of him or her, and will become aware of the independence that most employees with disabilities attempt to attain. The supervisor's goal should be to treat the employee with a disability the same as other employees. Being overly cautious or protective will have a negative effect on the employee's career mobility, self-esteem, and relationships with co-employees.

The supervisor may be unsure of his or her own abilities and require extra assistance and support. Increasing understanding and ability to supervise employees with disabilities needs to become an integral part of the supervisor's responsibilities. Success of the supervisor can be ensured by:

1. Carefully planning the employment process for gaining support
2. Involving the supervisor in the employment process
3. Providing education and resources
4. Providing assistance and feedback
5. Rewarding results
6. Publicizing the employer's commitment and actions so that everyone becomes part of the process

Integrating Employees with Disabilities

Integrating employees with disabilities into the employer's organization can be achieved through the STEP process:

S   Safety
T   Training
E   Efficiency
P   Privacy

Safety

Because physical examinations tend to screen out qualified individuals with disabilities, they must be used in a manner consistent with business necessity and safe job performance, and be administered only after an employment offer is made. Co-employees do not need to know detailed medical history, but may, for example, be informed of any medical alert or emergency situations involving diabetic shock reaction, the possibility of seizures, inability to hear fire alarms, etc. General rules of safety should be explained to all employees. Adaptations to safety procedures for individuals with disabilities should be outlined. Establishing a "buddy" system may help, especially during emergency situations. Emergency preparation should be planned, communicated, and conducted.

Training

Any employee's success depends on orientation and training. This is especially true when an employee has a disability. In some cases, a veteran employee should take charge of the new employee and teach work rules and procedures, under the supervisor's direction. Review job duties along with testing accommodations and adaptations. Rework the duties if necessary, but remember it is important that co-employees recognize that the individual who has a disability can perform the essential tasks. Do not forget the basics. The most detailed job training and orientation can be undermined if more fundamental needs of getting around or finding the restrooms are not addressed adequately. Co-employees should be encouraged to be part of assisting new employees to adapt.

Efficiency

Introduce the new employee to the organization and the job by outlining the duties and procedures. When accommodations are made, the supervisor should explain to co-employees what alterations and/or adaptations will be made to duties or procedures. It is important and essential that the supervisor dispel any myths or unspoken concerns that co-employees may have about an employee with a disability.

After a reasonable orientation period, the supervisor must treat employees with disabilities consistently with their nondisabled counterparts. If job performance problems occur, they should be addressed immediately. Early identification of the employee with a behavioral or medical problem should be based entirely on evidence of unsatisfactory work performance and related factors.

Supervisors should not be diagnosticians, psychologists, or medical experts, but must notice changes in behavior and recognize when people are not working safely and effectively. Inform the employee immediately of performance deficiencies. Outline specific actions for improvement, preferably in writing. Allow the employee to help identify corrective action, involving medical and rehabilitation specialists as necessary.

Remember to praise and recognize good performance. Avoid patronizing employees with disabilities. Encourage team spirit whenever possible. All members of the team have unique talents and skills which contribute.

Privacy

Only that information necessary for safe job performance should be shared in the workplace. The supervisor must have the necessary medical information to evaluate job assignments, risks, and functional characteristics of the employee. However, the employee's privacy of medical records and history must be preserved to the maximum extent possible.

The detailed history and exact medical diagnosis are generally not shared in the workplace with those who do not have a need to know this information in a job-related performance situation. Information necessary for emergency procedures, health, and safety reasons should be secured and maintained by the supervisor with the proper confidentiality and job-related considerations.

Career Accessibility

Individuals with disabilities are just like other employees. They want to do a good job, they appreciate constructive supervision, and they want to get ahead.

The myth that individuals with disabilities are grateful just to work and are happy to stay in entry-level positions is precisely that: a myth! Some individuals need or want a steady routine, but most enjoy new challenges. Individuals with disabilities are no exception. The following can be helpful in providing career accessibility to individuals with disabilities:

1. *Goal setting.* Recognize that individuals with disabilities have career goals. Sit down with these employees and discuss these goals. If the goals seem unreasonable, ask the employees what they think it would take for them to achieve the goals. See if a consensus can be reached. If the goals are unreasonable for business reasons, indicate that they are. Do not automatically assume that the employee's disability will be a barrier. The biggest barrier may be the employer's lack of understanding.
2. *Team building.* It is easy to isolate employees with disabilities from others. Make sure these employees have opportunities not only to work with others on group projects but, when appropriate, to assume leadership roles.
3. *Networking.* Bring employees with disabilities not only into formal work groups but also into informal employee gatherings. Do not assume that just because an employee uses a wheelchair, he or she would not be interested in joining the ski club, or that an employee who is deaf would not like to attend the company dance. People with disabilities enjoy all sorts of social and athletic activities. Very often, important business is discussed at these

events. All employees should be given the opportunity to participate. Events should be scheduled at facilities accessible to individuals with disabilities.

4. *The mentor system.* Anyone can benefit from the guidance of a more experienced employee. Encourage employees with disabilities to find mentors, disabled or not. When these employees become more experienced, encourage them to be mentors to other new employees, who may or may not be disabled.

5. *Performance evaluations.* Every employer differs in how it evaluates employees. Some procedures are formal, written documents. Others are less formal and oral. Whatever procedure is followed, treat employees with disabilities like all other employees. If jobs have been restructured to accommodate disabilities, employees should only be evaluated on those tasks that they are expected to perform. Apply the same performance criteria to those employees that would be applied to all other employees. Trying to "give a break" does not encourage employees with disabilities to perform up to standards, and may cause resentment among other employees.

6. *Training.* Give employees with disabilities similar opportunities for training. If there are formal classes, make sure that they are held in accessible facilities. Materials may have to be made available in large print for individuals who are visually impaired. Interpreters should be considered for participants who are hearing impaired. If one of the employees with a disability happens to be an expert in a skill or topic to be taught, consider having that person be the trainer for the course. [Adapted from the President's Committee on Employment of People With Disabilities, *Ready, Willing and Available: A Business Guide for Hiring People With Disabilities,* Appendix B (1989).]

MINIMIZING LITIGATION RISKS DURING THE HIRING PROCESS

Due to litigation's high cost, employers should attempt to structure their hiring procedures and policies to minimize their litigation risk by:

1. Ensuring that interviewers do not make improper or exaggerated promises

2. Examining the employer's personnel policies, handbooks, and manuals to make certain that they contain no promises the employer is unable or unwilling to keep by removing any language that might imply that employment is other than at-will; i.e., that the employment relationship can be discontinued by either the employee or the employer at any time, for any or no reason, with or without notice by:

a. Avoiding terms like "permanent employee"

    b. Changing "probationary period" to "initial review period"

    c. Considering including in each employee handbook a statement:

       (i) That "These policies are subject to unilateral change without notice"

      (ii) Preserving the at-will nature of the employment relationship by disclaiming the creation of any employment contract by emphasizing that the employment relationship can be ended by either the employee or the employer at any time, for any or no reason, with or without notice

    d. If the publication contains work rules or a list of termination reasons, it should state that the rules/list is not all inclusive and that they are only guidelines

3. Having every applicant sign a written acknowledgment that any employment with the employer is at-will and that the employment relationship can be discontinued by either the employee or the employer at any time, for any or no reason, with or without notice. This acknowledgment should be included as part of the actual application. A statement should also exist that the application has been read in its entirety.

CHECKLIST BEFORE EMPLOYMENT

This form should be used as a record to ensure that the employer's procedures and policies are adequately explained to employees to obtain a consistent understanding and use during the hiring process:

CHECKLIST BEFORE EMPLOYMENT FORM

The Company asks that you complete the following checklist before beginning employment. It is important that the Company orient you to its procedures and policies. By signing in the appropriate place, you are acknowledging that the corresponding topic has been fully explained and that any questions you may have have been answered to your satisfaction.

TOPIC	EMPLOYEE SIGNATURE
1. Employment date.	_____
2. Rate of pay/compensation.	_____
3. I understand I may be requested to perform various unrelated tasks from time to time.	_____
4. I understand that my supervisor will introduce me to my fellow employees and personnel in other departments I may have contact with at various times.	_____

5. I have answered all questions accurately and completely on my Employee's State Withholding (W4) Allowance Certificate. _____

6. I have answered all questions accurately and completely on my IRS Employee's Withholding (Federal W-4) Allowance Certificate. _____

7. I have answered all questions accurately and completely on my Employment Eligibility Verification (Form 1-9). _____

8. I have completed my Employee Information Sheet. _____

9. I have received and read a copy of the Employee Handbook-Book number ____. _____

10. I have received and read a copy of the Group Insurance Benefits Booklet. I also received and completed an enrollment card for these benefits. _____

11. I have received and read a copy of the Company-paid, weekly income insurance plan. _____

12. I have received and read a copy of the plan summary for the profit-sharing program and understand when I am eligible to participate and the benefits I can derive through participation in the plan. _____

13. I have been informed that my employment is at-will and that I or the Company can end the employment relationship at any time, for any or no reason, with or without notice. _____

_____
Date

_____
Employee Signature

_____
Supervisor's Signature

HIRING POLICIES

The following sets forth examples of employer hiring policies:

HIRING POLICY GOALS

The following goals are to be applied in all employment decisions and actions:

1. Select, retain, and promote employees based on individual ability, performance, and experience, avoiding actions influenced by personal relationships and discriminatory practices.
2. Recognize employees as individuals with different abilities, needs, and motivations, and encourage individual initiative, creativity, and thought in accomplishing job assignments.
3. Maintain a working environment that provides opportunities for personal growth and advancement and that permits maximum individual progress consistent with ability and performance.
4. Promote from within whenever there is a current employee whose ability, experience, motivation, education, and performance demonstrate position qualification.
5. Use internal and external developmental activities, including normal and special job assignments, to assist employees in preparing themselves for advancement.
6. Evaluate employee performance on a regular basis and provide the evaluation's results to employees on a timely basis to assist them in their development.
7. Provide communication systems that encourage self-expression and open dialogue throughout the Company to help ensure constructive, prompt, and fair work-related problem resolution.
8. Recognize the value of a stable work force and give consideration to length of satisfactory service as well as performance in employee reduction and restoration.
9. Maintain a structure of employee benefits that provides reasonable protection against economic hazards caused by illness, disability, or death, and for income after retirement that is applied equitably to all employees in accordance with overall Company guidelines.
10. Establish compensation programs that attract and retain quality employees, motivate employee initiative, and reward superior performance.
11. Comply with all laws and regulations affecting employee relations, including collective bargaining agreements.

HIRING POLICY

Section 1. Purpose. It is the Company's policy to hire a qualified employee. This selection will be based on qualifications, skill, training, personality, and ambition displayed by the applicant.

Section 2. Applicability. Anyone being hired as an employee is subject to this hiring procedure. Employees hired on a temporary, part-time, or other basis through an outside temporary service agency are also subject to this hiring policy.

Section 3. General Procedures. Job openings not filled from within will be filled by referrals, walk-ins, or advertisement respondents. Active files for applicants are maintained by the Human Resources Department for six (6) months. These may be used and should be reviewed when seeking new employees. The Plant Manager or Manager requesting additional employees should submit in writing a request identifying the job, position, and need to the Human Resources Department.

Prior to employing an individual, certain preliminary steps must be taken to ensure uniformity of personnel practices and compliance with federal and state employment statutes. The following procedures are to be used:

(a) Reception. The applicant will be met in the Human Resources Department's lobby where literature and information concerning the Company will be made available. All referred applicants, walk-ins, or advertisement respondents report to this area first. Each of these applicants will be treated with the same consideration as a customer. All applicants, whether hired or not, can spread good will for the Company or give it a bad name, based on the treatment they receive. The Company's policy is to maintain a good image for attracting qualified applicants.

(b) Preliminary Interview and Screening by the Human Resources Department. A short preliminary interview by the Human Resources Department's staff will be held with the applicant to identify the most promising applicants and those who are not qualified.

(c) Application. After the preliminary interview, all applicants are given an application to complete. The questions used on this application are in compliance with federal and state fair employment practice (FEP) statutes and regulations. The application also includes clauses covering falsification of records and an agreement to submit to job-related medical testing after an employment offer is made. The applicant is also asked at this time for information under the Immigration Reform and Control Act (IRCA) of 1986. If the applicant cannot comply with this Act, he or she will not be considered for employment. Once obtained, IRCA information will be kept separate from the application.

(d) Testing. All applicants who are approved as possible candidates whether they are referred by employees, walk-ins, or advertisement respondents, will not be tested until job requests are given to the Human Resources Department. An outside agency will do the testing to ensure that the Company adheres to federal and state fair employment practice (FEP) statutes which require that the overall selection process show no evidence of adverse impact on minority groups.

(e) Interview with Prospective Supervisor. If the applicant's testing proves positive, an interview with the prospective supervisor takes place. The times for the interviews are set up to be mutually convenient for the supervisor and the applicant. This interview is set up to: (a) assess the applicant; (b) describe the job and working conditions to the applicant by touring the area in which he or she would work; and (c) create goodwill for the Company, whether or not the applicant is hired. To accomplish these objectives, the supervisor must be alert, perceptive, able to keep accurate records, free from prejudice, and even-tempered. Supervisors must also avoid any questioning or conduct that violates federal and state fair employment practice (FEP) statutes. After the interview, the applicant will be told that he or she will be contacted by the Human Resources Department. The supervisor cannot offer the job to the employee. A checklist will be given to the supervisor to make sure that certain points are covered during the interview. The supervisor will return the application with the completed interview checklist to the Human Resources Department for determination as to whether to continue the hiring procedure.

(f) **Reference Checking.** If the interview proves positive, the Human Resources Department will check references with former employers, schools attended, etc. The applicant must sign a consent form to be sent to certain employers who might not be willing to forward information regarding the applicant.

(g) **Preliminary Selection by the Human Resources Department after Consultation with the Prospective Supervisor.** A preliminary selection will be made by the Human Resources Department and the supervisor after they are satisfied that qualified applicants are available. If no qualified applicants are available, other applicants will be sought.

(h) **Final Selection by the Plant Manager, Prospective Supervisor, and the Human Resources Department.** A final selection will be made by the Plant Manager, the prospective supervisor, and the Human Resources Department after all are satisfied that a qualified applicant is available. All must agree on wages, terms, and conditions of employment for the new employee. A checklist will be used to cover these points.

(i) **Placement-Hiring of the Applicant.** The Human Resources Department will contact the selected applicant and offer employment subject to the satisfactory completion of a job-related medical examination. Details of the wages, terms, and employment conditions will be discussed. If the applicant accepts, the Human Resources Department will set up a time for the employee to sign in and begin the Company's orientation program after the results of the medical examination are received.

Section 4. Rejected Applicants. In most circumstances, a number of applicants will be interviewed for a particular position. It is conceivable that at times more than one applicant will progress through the interview procedure, but only one will be chosen. If other applicants would have been eligible for the position, these approved applicants will be retained in a special referral file for up to six (6) months to be considered for additional openings that might occur either in the same department or in other departments or shifts. As openings develop, these applicants will be referred to supervisors for consideration, along with additional new applicants.

Chapter 2

Pre-Employment Screening Fundamentals

Hiring is the human resource function that identifies qualified applicants for employment. During this process, considerable personal information must be obtained by the employer and disclosed by individuals seeking employment.

All information disclosed by applicants may be subject to employer verification. In verifying this information, other data may be revealed that may or may not be employment related. The additional data may be obtained with or without the applicant's consent or knowledge. After the applicant is hired, the information may again be expanded through attendance records, compensation data, medical reviews, benefit reports, performance evaluations, disciplinary notices, etc.

The employer's objective is to collect as much information as is legally permissible to properly evaluate the individual for the job to be filled. Unfortunately, however, the employer may collect information that is not legally permissible. The applicant's concern is that only job-related information is collected by the employer.

The human resource principles, procedures, and policies applicable to pre-employment screening along with the major federal and state statutes affecting this area are reviewed in this Chapter. Areas discussed include advertisements, applications, and interviews.

ADVERTISEMENTS

Newspaper advertisements in the help-wanted section are a common employer recruitment method. Many individuals make their first employer contact through newspaper advertisements. Depending upon the advertisement's content, the individual may inquire further or may refrain from making an inquiry.

Advertisements must be prepared to comply with federal and state fair employment practice (FEP) statutes. They should also avoid making binding employer contractual commitments. [See, e.g., *Willis v. Allied Insulation Co.*, 174 So.2d 858 (La. 1965) (advertisement's terms created binding employer contractual commitments).]

Drafting

Several preliminary considerations can ensure an advertisement's success by:

1. Checking the job description and job specifications to be sure they are correct for the advertisement
2. Conducting a job analysis if there is doubt about a job description's or job specification's content or accuracy. Incorrect job descriptions or job specifications may inadvertently result in an adverse impact by improperly eliminating minority applicants who do not meet the advertised specifications but nevertheless could perform the job tasks. [See *Pearson v. Furnco Constr. Corp.*, 563 F.2d 815 (7th Cir. 1977) (permitting plaintiffs the opportunity to demonstrate entitlement to jobs for which employer concealed opportunities).]
3. Writing the advertisement so that it can be easily read, omitting technical language
4. Selling the job to prospective applicants by writing advertisements to be appealing in structure and content, considering:
   a. Printing style
   b. Borders
   c. Layout
   d. Factual statements that highlight the job's major features
5. Not specifying sex, race, religion, age, national origin, disability, or anything relating to these areas to avoid applicant challenges under federal and state fair employment practice (FEP) statutes
6. Not using help-wanted advertisements under "male" and "female" headings unless sex is a bona fide occupational qualification. [See, e.g., *Pittsburgh Press Co. v. Pittsburgh Comm'n on Human Relations*, 413 U.S. 376 1973) (sex-based and sex-designated help wanted columns illegal).]
7. Wording advertisements to avoid creating contractual commitments by not suggesting:
   a. Long-term employment
   b. Permanent employment
   c. Guaranteed job security
   d. Guaranteed wages or salary
   e. Career security. [See, e.g., *Willis v. Allied Insulation Co.*, 174 So. 2d 858 (La. 1965) (advertisement's terms created binding employer contractual commitments).]
8. Ensuring consistency. The employer should centralize responsibility for advertisement development, writing, and placement with one group, namely the human resources staff, to minimize problems
9. Using inclusive language. Advertisements should not refer to the assumed gender of applicants but should use neutral terms such as "applicants," "candidates," and "employees." Terms which describe the job in ways that indicate a gender preference should be avoided. For example, instead of "waitress," use "waitress/waiter" or "server"

Advertisement Forms

The following employment advertisements should be considered as a guide:

ADVERTISEMENT

KING'S INN

• Porter

• Secretary

• Host/Hostess

Apply in person at [address]

Equal Opportunity Employer

ADVERTISEMENT

RADIOLOGY TECHS

REGISTERED AND NEW GRADS
Opportunity to work at General Hospital. The working
environment is caring, dynamic, and team-oriented.

Competitive salary and comprehensive benefits.

Interested applicants should call or write:

HUMAN RESOURCE DEPARTMENT
GENERAL HOSPITAL
[address]
[telephone]

Equal Opportunity Employer

ADVERTISEMENT

MAINTENANCE MECHANIC

PIPEFITTER & PLUMBER

1st shift. $18.49/hr. Applicant must have journeyperson's license.

Minimum 3-4 yrs. industrial experience

Contact [name] at [telephone]
NAME
Address

Equal Opportunity Employer

ADVERTISEMENT

PERSONNEL SECRETARY

An international based company seeks individual to assist in
Human Resources Dept. Responsibilities will include processing
medical insurance, maintenance of employee files, workers'
compensation claims, reports, typing, and clerical work
plus other independent projects.

For consideration, send your resume to:
[Address]

Equal Opportunity Employer

APPLICATIONS

The application's purpose is to solicit job-related information from an applicant to enable the employer to begin making an informed hiring decision. It is not the final selection tool. The application is but one part of the overall hiring process that is supplemented by interviews, data verification, testing, etc.

At one time, employers could inquire into almost any area. Today, constraints through federal and state fair employment practice (FEP) statutory protections apply to many traditional areas of employer inquiry involving age, race, color, national origin, marital status, pregnancy, disability, etc.

Employer inquiries that should be avoided begin with the application and extend throughout, and even beyond, the employment relationship. These information collection concerns do not merely limit the employment information that can be permissibly solicited, but require that, once this information is collected, the employer use it properly and protect it from unwarranted disclosures. The employer has a responsibility to make certain that employee personal matters in its records remain confidential and protected. Unauthorized employment information disclosure may impose employer responsibility. [See *Board of Trustees v. Leach*, 258 Cal. App.2d 281, 65 Cal. Rptr. 588 (1968) (unauthorized reading of an employee's personnel file imposed employer responsibility).]

By inquiring into non-job-related areas, the employer may obtain information that is not job-related and eliminate certain applicants from consideration based on this information. In subsequent litigation, the employer may be required to defend the use of the non-job-related information requested or to explain why the non-job-related information was collected but not used. This may be very difficult for the employer, especially where the information discloses matters unrelated to the job's duties.

Advantages

An application is an important document because:

1. It can assist the employer in limiting wrongful termination liability [See, e.g., *Novosel v. Sears, Roebuck & Co.*, 495 F. Supp. 344 (E.D. Mich. 1980) (application disclaimer enforceable to preserve at-will employment relationship)]
2. It provides an initial means of consenting to employer procedures and policies, for example, if the employer desires to conduct applicant alcohol and drug screening, the application could include consent language to minimize litigation exposure [See, e.g., *Green v. Halliburton Co.*, 674 F.Supp. 1447 (D. Wyo. 1987) (private sector employer's alcohol and drug testing program upheld where all employees were required to read and sign its policy, evidencing employee consent and understanding)]
3. It may provide a basis for terminating an employee who has falsified or omitted information requested on the application [See, e.g., *Dart Indus., Inc.*, 56 Lab. Arb. (BNA) 799 (1971) (Greene, Arb.) (termination for application falsification).]

Preparation

Initially, the employer must determine what information is needed to evaluate which applicant is best suited for a position. This may involve inquiries into education, professional licenses or certifications, previous work experience, special skills, talents, fluency in a foreign language, etc. Special needs for a position may warrant that certain additional information be requested.

After determining what job-related and general background information should be collected from the applicant, the remainder of the application should be drafted to preserve applicant privacy and limit employer liability by:

1. Informing the applicant that the employment is at-will and can be discontinued by either the employee or the employer at any time, for any or no reason, with or without notice
2. Providing an applicant's acknowledgment that any information falsification or omission may result in termination
3. Requiring the applicant's representation that the information provided is complete and accurate
4. Including a release protecting the employer and those persons the employer contacts regarding references
5. Inquiring only whether the applicant has any physical condition or limitations that would disqualify him or her from performing the particular job for which the application is submitted
6. Not inquiring regarding the applicant's filing for and/or receiving of benefits related to workers' compensation, work-related illnesses or injuries, because this may be considered retaliation or disqualification for employment consideration for these benefits' receipt [See, e.g., *Darnell v. Impact Indus.*, 105 Ill.2d 158, 473 N.E.2d 935 (1984) (termination for filing workers' compensation claim prohibited)]
7. Collecting only information that is relevant to specific employment decisions
8. Telling applicants, employees, and former employees what use will be made of the collected information
9. Letting applicants know what kinds of information will be maintained
10. Adopting reasonable procedures to ensure that application information is accurate, timely, and complete
11. Limiting application disclosure internally and externally

Inquiries That Should Be Avoided

Applicants are typically requested to furnish basic information involving name, address, job being applied for, experience, and education. The application form can yield information needed to compare adequately an applicant's qualifications to the job specifications to begin narrowing the selection process.

Improperly structured applications can cause an employer problems. Employers should consider using this standard in determining whether an inquiry should be made: "How does this inquiry ensure a job-related selection?" Inquiries should not be made where they are not job-related.

Application inquiries that may be difficult for employers to justify, and could result in federal or state fair employment practice (FEP) complaints, include those relating to:

1. Age
2. Birth date
3. Arrests
4. Availability for Saturday and Sunday work
5. Bonding refusal
6. Children under 18
7. Citizenship of a country other than the United States
8. Credit record
9. Eye color
10. Garnishment record
11. Hair color
12. Height
13. Marital status
14. Number of children
15. Personal financial information
16. Sex
17. Spouse's employment status
18. Spouse's name
19. Weight
20. Religious preference

Application Forms

The employer should prepare its application with the objectives of gathering the information necessary to make job-related hiring decisions and providing a foundation for defending against employment litigation that may arise if hiring does not result or if termination subsequently occurs. Carefully drafting applications will minimize employer litigation exposure. The following application was designed with federal and state fair employment practice (FEP) considerations in mind:

APPLICATION

PLEASE PRINT

Date:_____

Name: _____

Street: _____

City: _____

State: _____ Zip Code:_____

Business telephone: (   ) _____

Home telephone: (   ) _____

How were you referred?   ___ Newspaper   ___ School
                          ___ On my own   ___ Company employee
                          ___ Agency   ___ Other

Name of referral source: _____

TYPE OF WORK DESIRED

Indicate the position for which you are applying:_____

_____

What is your minimum weekly salary requirement?_____

Date available for work: _____

Do you have any commitments to another employer that might affect your employment with us? _____

_____

_____

EDUCATIONAL DATA

School	Print Name, Number, and Street, City, State, and Zip Code for Each School Listing	Type of Course or Major	Graduated?
High school:	_____	_____	_____
College:	_____	_____	_____
Graduate school:	_____	_____	_____
Trade, Business, Night, or Correspondence:	_____	_____	_____
Other:	_____	_____	_____

MILITARY EXPERIENCE

Were you in U.S. Armed Forces?   ___ Yes   ___ No

If yes, what branch? _____

Rank at separation: _____

Briefly describe your duties:_____

EMPLOYMENT HISTORY

List present employer or most recent employer first (use other side of this application, if necessary). May we contact these employers? ____ Yes ____ No

Employer: Length of time employed: Supervisor's name:

_____   _____   _____

Address:

_____

Telephone: _____   Your job title: _____

Salary:_____

Duties:_____

_____

Reason for leaving:_____

Employer: Length of time employed: Supervisor's name:

_____   _____   _____

Address:

_____

Telephone: _____   Your job title: _____

Salary:_____

Duties:_____

_____

Reason for leaving:_____

Employer: Length of time employed: Supervisor's name:

_____   _____   _____

Address:

_____

Telephone: _____   Your job title: _____

Salary:_____

Duties:_____

_____

Reason for leaving:_____

Employer: Length of time employed: Supervisor's name:

_____   _____   _____

Address:

_____

Telephone: _____   Your job title: _____

Salary:_____

Duties:_____

_____

Reason for leaving:_____

GENERAL INFORMATION

Have you previously applied for employment at this Company?
_____ Yes _____ No

If yes, when?_____

Have you previously been employed at the Company or its subsidiaries?
_____ Yes _____ No

If yes, when?_____

Are any of your relatives employed by the Company? (Note: In accordance with Company policy this may affect your assignment, if hired)
_____ Yes _____ No

If yes, please list relative's name and department:_____

Relationship: _____

Please include any other information you think would be helpful in considering you for employment, including additional work experience, articles/books published, activities, accomplishments, etc. **Exclude all information indicative of age, sex, race, religion, color, national origin, and disability.**

_____

_____

_____

APPLICANT'S REPRESENTATIONS FOR EMPLOYMENT

Should I be employed by the Company, I agree to conform to the Company's rules and regulations, and agree that as an at-will employee my employment and compensation can be terminated, at any time, for any or no reason, with or without notice, at the option of either the Company or me.

I certify that the information provided on this application is true, correct, and complete to the best of my knowledge and agree that falsified information or significant omissions may disqualify me from further consideration for employment and may be considered justification for termination if discovered at a later date.

I authorize persons, schools, current employer and previous employers, and organizations named in this application to provide the Company with any relevant job-related information that may be required. I further release all parties providing job-related information from any and all liability or claims for damages whatsoever that may result from this job-related information's release, disclosure, maintenance, or use.

This application has been read by me in its entirety.

_____   _____
Signature   Date

The following application was designed to solicit as little information as possible by the employer, but to place the information disclosure burden entirely on the applicant to make the choices regarding what information to reveal:

APPLICATION

   Please send one copy of this form along with a resume outlining your qualifications to:

Employer's name and address:_____

_____

_____

Name: _____   Date: _____

Street: _____

City: _____   State: _____   Zip code:_____

Current position: _____

Currently employed at: _____

How long? _____

Ultimate employment goal? _____

_____

Next employment step? _____

_____

Why? _____

_____

_____

Are you willing to relocate? _____

Where? _____

Why? _____

_____
Signature

Application: Affirmative Action Information

An employer may seek and obtain information regarding an applicant's race, sex, or ethnicity as needed for implementation of affirmative action programs, voluntary or court-ordered, or other government reporting or record-keeping requirements and for studies to identify and resolve possible problems in the recruitment and testing of members of minority groups and/or females to ensure equal employment for all persons. The employer should indicate to prospective employees that providing the information is voluntary, unless the employer is under a specific court order to obtain it.

The employer must be able to demonstrate that this data was collected for legitimate business purposes. This information should be kept separate from regular permanent employee records to ensure that it is not used to discriminate in making personnel decisions.

To protect against the improper use of this information by their selecting officials, employers should consider collecting this information by the use of a "tear-off sheet." After completing the application and the tear-off sheet, the latter is separated from the application and used only for purposes unrelated to the selection decision. The tear-off sheet should state the purpose for which the information is being collected, and that the information will not be available or used for making employee selections to satisfy any applicant fears that the information might be used to discriminate.

APPLICATION:
AFFIRMATIVE ACTION INFORMATION

To aid in the Company's commitment to equal employment opportunity, applicants are asked to voluntarily provide the following information. This section will be separated from the application immediately upon filing and will not be the basis for any employment decisions now or in the future.

_____ Male
_____ Female

Your Age Group

1. Under 21 _____   5. 50-59 _____
2. 21-29 _____   6. 60-69 _____
3. 30-39 _____   7. 70 and over _____
4. 40-49 _____

Please check the one which best describes your race/ethnicity:

A. Mexican, Mexican-American   C. Cuban _____
   Chicano _____   D. Any other Spanish/Hispanic _____
B. Puerto Rican _____

If not Hispanic, check:

E. White _____   L. Aleut _____
F. Black _____   M. Hawaiian _____
G. Filipino _____   N. Samoan _____
H. American Indian _____   O. Japanese _____
   (Specify tribe)   P. Chinese _____
   _____   Q. Korean _____
I. Vietnamese _____   R. Guamanian/Chamorro _____
J. Asian Indian _____   X. Other, not listed _____
K. Eskimo _____

Check any major disability you have a record of which may have impeded your securing, retaining, or advancing in employment:

1. Hearing _____   5. Developmental _____
2. Sight _____   6. Other disability
3. Speech _____   Specify: _____
4. Physical Orthopedic/   7. No disability _____
   amputations _____

Are you a veteran, spouse of a 100% disabled veteran, or a widow or widower of a veteran? _____ Yes _____ No

Only applicants who check "Yes" will be verified for veterans preference points in examinations which allow the addition of these points.

Application Employment Contract Disclaimer Forms

To preserve the at-will employment relationship to permit either the employee or the employer to end the employment relationship at any time, for any or no reason, with or without notice, an employer should consider placing a disclaimer within the application that covers the following: [See, e.g., *Novosel v. Sears, Roebuck & Co.*, 495 F. Supp. 344 (E.D. Mich. 1980) (application disclaimer enforceable to preserve at-will employment relationship); see also Decker, *Handbooks and Employment Policies as Express or Implied Guarantees of Employment—Employer Beware!*, 5 U. Pitt. J.L. & Com. 207 (1984).]

APPLICATION EMPLOYMENT CONTRACT DISCLAIMER

In consideration of my employment, I agree to conform to the Company's rules and regulations, and agree that as an at-will employee my employment and compensation can be terminated, at any time, for any or no reason, with or without notice, at the option of either the Company or me. I understand that no manager or representative, other than the Chief Executive Officer or (*Name*), has any authority to enter into any agreement for employment for any specified time period, or to make any agreement contrary to this disclaimer. Any agreement for employment for any specified time period must be in writing and signed.

APPLICATION EMPLOYMENT CONTRACT DISCLAIMER

I certify that the information contained in this application is true and correct to the best of my knowledge and understanding and that information falsification is grounds for not hiring or termination. I authorize the references listed above to provide any and all job-related information concerning my previous employment and any pertinent job-related information they may have, and release all parties from liability for any damage that may result from furnishing this job-related information. **In consideration of my employment, I agree to conform to the Company's rules and regulations, and as an at-will employee my employment and compensation can be terminated at any time, for any or no reason, with or without notice by either the Company or me.** I understand that no Company manager or representative, other than the Company's President or Vice-President, has any authority to enter into any agreement for employment for any specified time period, or to make any agreement contrary to the foregoing.

Application Information Release Form

To protect the employer in securing applicant references or other applicant information, the following form should be considered as part of the application:

APPLICATION INFORMATION RELEASE FORM

I authorize schools, references, prior employers, and physicians or other medical practitioners to provide my record, reason for leaving employment, and all other job-related information they may have concerning me to the Company and I release and hold harmless all parties providing this job-related information from any and all liability or claims for damages whatsoever that may result from this job-related information's release, disclosure, and use.

INTERVIEWS

Unlike the application's written inquiry, the interview is primarily oral although a written record may be created. After the initial interview, others may be conducted prior to the final hiring decision.

Because of federal and state fair employment practice (FEP) statutes, employers must take special care in applicant interviews. The employer cannot use an applicant's race, color, sex, age, national origin, religion, marital status, or disability as a basis for an employment decision, unless the employer is hiring pursuant to goals and timetables contained in its affirmative action plan. [See Executive Order No. 11246 (Affirmative Action), 3 C.F.R. § 339 (1964-1965 Compilation), reprinted in 42 U.S.C. § 2000e note, issued on Sept. 24, 1965, as amended.] Similarly, an interviewer should not ask an applicant questions related to these areas, nor should a former employer be asked these questions during a written or telephone reference check.

Interview Process

Employer success depends upon applicant quality. Quality recruitment is based upon the employer's reputation with its employees, the general public, customers, and the competition. The interview process should:

1. Be used to:
   a. Gather additional job-related information about an applicant not disclosed in the application
   b. Judge demeanor and presence

2. Permit the employer to:
   a. Expand on topics concerning educational background, the reasons for leaving prior employers, prior experience, training, etc
   b. Question unaccounted-for time periods between schools or previous jobs, as these time gaps may indicate relevant information which the applicant might not disclose
   c. Resolve any conflicting information obtained through a reference check

Minimizing Litigation Risks During Interviews

To maximize the benefits that can be derived from interviews, and to prevent statements during an interview that may lead to liability, the employer should use:

1. Well-informed and well-prepared interviewers who:
   a. Prior to the interview study:
      (i) Applications
      (ii) Resumes
      (iii) Other pertinent information
   b. Know what further job-related information should be obtained from the applicant during the interview
   c. Know what information to convey about the employer
   d. Know what information to convey about the particular job for which the applicant has applied
2. Interviewers who do not "sell" applicants on the employer with statements involving:
   a. Overemphasizing the employer's virtues to avoid creating enforceable employee rights against the employer if the employee is later terminated
   b. Becoming specific and promising definite employment terms and conditions greater than or different from the employer's oral or written policies, to avoid binding commitments [See, e.g., *Toussaint v. Blue Cross & Blue Shield of Mich.*, 408 Mich. 579, 292 N.W.2d 880 (1980) (employer liability for interviewer's statement that the employee would be employed as long as he did his job)]
   c. Asking questions that could be considered discriminatory; i.e., only job-related inquiries should be used

Interview Methods

The following types of interview methods should be considered:

1. Nondirective interview:
   a. Interviewer structures questions in response to the applicant's unique needs and qualifications
   b. Applicant is permitted to talk freely

      c. The interview topics are determined by the interviewer but the applicant is allowed to develop his or her individual responses

      d. Uses a set of specific questions prepared in advance of the interview

2. Patterned interview:

      a. Uses a set of specific questions prepared in advance of the interview

      b. Attempts to limit applicant responses to specific information

      c. Provides information to the applicant that is planned beforehand

      d. Interviewer summarizes both applicant responses and the progress of the interview

3. Structured interview:

      a. In structured interviewing, the responsibility shifts almost entirely to the interviewer

      b. It is the interviewer's role to understand the position's scope, including the job specifications, duties, pay, benefits, and tasks by:

         (i) Structuring questions and information items to adequately inform applicants about the position and to elicit information about their qualifications for it

         (ii) Comparing the applicant's responses to the position's needs and determining if the person matches the position

4. Group interview:

      a. Involves two or more interviewers

      b. A simultaneous interview of an applicant occurs in the same setting where each interviewer asks the applicant at least one question

5. Stress interview: Involves the purposeful introduction of stress into an interview, to gauge an applicant's ability to function under stress

6. Depth interview:

      a. This is a structured interview

      b. Questions thoroughly measure an applicant's qualifications within a specific area

Interview Evaluation

The following form is intended to be used by the interviewer in evaluating the applicant for a position opening:

INTERVIEWER'S EVALUATION

Applicant's Name: _____ Interview Date: _____

Interviewer's Name: _____

Position Applied For: _____

Job-Related Tasks: *Applicant's Knowledge:*

_____   _____

_____   _____

_____   _____

_____   _____

_____   _____

Job Knowledge Strengths: _____

_____

_____

_____

_____

Job Knowledge Weaknesses: _____

_____

_____

_____

_____

Overall appraisal of the applicant: Match the applicant's qualifications with the job position's requirements and circle the overall applicant rating.

Excellent   Above Average   Average   Below Average   Poor

_____
Signature

Interview Policies

The following interview policy is intended to acquaint interviewers with what questions should be asked and which should be avoided to minimize employer liability for improper information collection, maintenance, use, or disclosure and these guidelines are also applicable to applications:

INTERVIEW INQUIRY POLICY

Instructions to Interviewers: The following are examples of interview inquiries that should be avoided and their acceptable counterparts, if any:

Age

Inquiries regarding the applicant's date of birth or age should not be asked. [See, e.g., *Goodyear Tire and Rubber Co.*, 22 Fair Empl. Prac. Cas. (BNA) 755 (W.D. Tenn. 1979) (age discrimination in that maximum applicant age of 40 for tire builders not a valid BFOQ).] Dates of elementary, high school, college, or other school attendance should also be avoided. They may reveal the applicant's age. The question should be posed as, "Do you have a high school education? If not, how many years have you completed?" This question includes attainment of a General Education Diploma (G.E.D.), but does not differentiate between it and a high school diploma.

Unacceptable

1. What is your age?

2. When were you born?

3. Dates of attendance or completion of elementary, high school, college, or other school. This may reveal age.

Acceptable

1. Statement that hire is subject to verification that the applicant meets legal age requirements

2. If hired, can you show proof of age?

3. Are you over eighteen years of age?

4. If under eighteen, can you, after employment, submit a work permit?

Arrest, Criminal Record

Without proof of business necessity, an employer's use of arrest records to disqualify applicants is not permitted. [See, e.g., *Gregory v. Litton Sys., Inc.*, 316 F. Supp. 401 (C.D. Cal. 1970), *aff'd with modification not here relevant*, 472 F.2d 631 (9th Cir. 1972) (race discrimination against black employee for employer inquiring into arrest record).] Regarding a conviction, an employer must be able to show that the inquiry is substantially related to an applicant's suitability to perform major job duties. Conviction records should be cause of rejection **only** if their number, nature, or recentness would cause the applicant to be unsuitable for the position. If the question is asked, it is recommended that this clarifier be added, "A conviction will not necessarily disqualify you from the job for which you have applied."

Unacceptable	*Acceptable*
1. Arrest record	1. Have you ever been convicted of a felony, or, within two years, a misdemeanor which resulted in imprisonment? This question should be accompanied by a statement that a conviction will not necessarily disqualify the applicant from the job requested
2. Have you ever been arrested?	

Birthplace, Citizenship

The Immigration Reform and Control Act of 1986 (IRCA) requires employers to verify the legal status and right to work of all new hires. Employers should not ask applicants to state their national origin, but should ask if they have the legal right to work in the United States, and explain that verification of that right must be submitted **after** the decision to hire has been made. [See, e.g., *Smith v. Union Oil Co.*, 17 Fair Empl. Prac. Cas. (BNA) 960 (N.E. Cal. 1977) (national original discrimination).]

Unacceptable	*Acceptable*
1. Birthplace of the applicant, applicant's spouse, or relatives	1. Can you, prior to employment, submit verification of your legal right to work in the United States?
2. Are you a U.S. citizen?	2. Statement that this proof is required after employment
	3. Requirements that the applicant produce naturalization, first papers, or alien card prior to beginning employment

Bonding/Credit

Answers to bonding and credit questions are almost always irrelevant to job performance. [See, e.g., *United States v. Chicago*, 549 F.2d 415 (7th Cir. 1977) (disqualifying applicants based on credit checks).] Because census figures indicate that minorities, on the average, are poorer than whites, consideration of these factors by employers can have an adverse impact on minorities. Requests of this nature could probably be shown to be improper unless clearly required by business necessity and direct job-relatedness.

Unacceptable	*Acceptable*
1. Questions regarding refusal or cancellation of bonding	1. Statement that bonding is a condition of hire based on the position's requirements

Military Service

Questions relevant to experience or training that was received while in the military or to determine eligibility for any veteran's preference required by law are acceptable. Employers should not reject applicants with less than an honorable discharge from military service. Minority service members have had a higher proportion of general and undesirable discharges than non-minority members of similar aptitude and education. [See, e.g., EEOC Dec. No. 74-25, 10 Fair Empl. Prac. Cas. (BNA) 260 (1973) (4.2% of whites and 7.5% of blacks receive general discharges; 2.6% of whites and 5.2% of blacks receive undesirable discharges).] If there is a job-related reason for asking information about military service and discharge type, the question should be accompanied by a statement that a dishonorable or general discharge is not an absolute bar to employment.

Unacceptable	*Acceptable*
1. General questions regarding military service that pertain to date, type of discharge, etc. This may reveal the applicant's age	1. Questions regarding relevant skills acquired during the applicant's United States military service
2. Questions regarding service in a foreign military. This may reveal the applicant's nationality	

Name

Name other than the applicant's current name could be used for a discriminatory purpose. For example, a female's maiden name might be used as an indication of her religion or national origin. [See, e.g., *Allen v. Lovejoy*, 553 F.2d 522

(6th Cir. 1977) (sex discrimination in requiring married females, but not married males, to change their surnames to that of their spouses on personnel forms).] This item also constitutes an inquiry into marital status, which is information that may be legitimately requested **after** the decision to hire is made for the purposes of employment benefit eligibility. If, however, an employer needs to verify education and employment history, the question could be asked, "If any of your employment or education was under a different name, please indicate and provide the name."

Unacceptable	*Acceptable*
1. Maiden name	1. Have you ever used another name?
	2. Is any additional information regarding a name change, assumed name use, or nickname necessary to check on your work or education record? If yes, please explain.

National Origin

Some English skill is probably required for most jobs. Fluency or absence of an accent may not be relevant to the job. If English language skill is not a requirement of the work to be performed, it could be a criterion that would unfairly eliminate certain minority groups. Additionally, some jobs may prefer bi-lingual individuals. [See, e.g., *Rogers v. EEOC*, 454 F.2d 234 (5th Cir. 1971), *cert. denied*, 406 U.S. 957 (1972) (denying employee services to minorities based on language).] Ultimately, however, care must be taken regarding an English language proficiency requirement, and the requirement **should not exceed** the level of proficiency necessary for the job in question.

Unacceptable	*Acceptable*
1. Questions regarding nationality, lineage, ancestry, national origin, descent, or parentage of the applicant, applicant's parents, or spouse	1. Language the applicant reads, speaks, or writes for job-related purposes
2. What is your mother tongue?	
3. Language commonly used by the applicant	
4. How the applicant acquired the ability to read, write, or speak a foreign language	

Notice in Case of Emergency

Prior to hiring, this information may constitute sex discrimination by revealing marital status or national origin discrimination by revealing an ethnic name where the person is unmarried and parents must be notified. This information can be obtained after hiring.

Unacceptable	Acceptable
1. Name and address of relative to be notified in case of accident or emergency	1. After hiring, name and address of person to be notified in case of accident or emergency can be obtained

Organizations/Activities

This inquiry may reveal race, religious creed, color, national origin, ancestry, and sex information unrelated to the job's requirements.

Unacceptable	Acceptable
1. List all organizations, clubs, societies, and lodges to which you belong	1. List job-related organizations, clubs, professional societies, or other associations to which you belong. Omit those indicating or referring to your race, religious creed, color, national origin, ancestry, sex, or age

Physical Condition/Disability

An employer may not ask about the existence, nature, or severity of a disability and may not conduct medical examinations until **after** it makes a conditional job offer to the applicant. [See *Griffin v. Steeltek, Inc.,* 160 F.3d 591 (10th Cir. 1998) (under the Americans with Disabilities Act (ADA) nondisabled job seeker can sue for improper interview question as to the nature or severity of a disability); but see *Armstrong v. Turner Industries, Inc.,* 141 F.3d 554 (5th Cir. 1998) (a single isolated violation of the Americans with Disabilities Act's (ADA's) hiring provision without proof that the hiring decision was itself discriminatory does not give rise to a claim).] **[See Appendices A and B.]** This prohibition ensures that the applicant's hidden disability is not considered prior to the assessment of the applicant's non-medical qualifications. At this pre-offer stage, employers **may** ask about an applicant's ability to perform specific job-related functions. An employer also may ask other questions that are not disability-related and may require examinations that are not medical, provided that all applicants are asked these questions or are given these examinations.

After a conditional offer is made, an employer may require medical examinations and may make disability-related inquiries if it does so for all entering employees in the job category. If an examination or inquiry screens out an individual because of disability, the exclusionary criterion must be job-related and consistent with business necessity. The employer must also show that the criterion cannot be satisfied and the essential job functions cannot be performed with reasonable accommodation.

Any medical information obtained **must** be kept **confidential** by the employer. This means that the employer must collect and maintain the information on separate forms and in separate medical files not part of the employee's personnel file.

If the individual is screened out for safety concerns because they are deemed to pose a "direct threat," the employer must demonstrate that the decision was based on objective, factual evidence that these individuals pose a significant risk of substantial harm to themselves or others, and that the risk cannot be reduced below the direct threat level through reasonable accommodation.

An employer may inform applicants on an application form or job advertisement that the hiring process includes a specific selection procedure; i.e., an interview, written test, or job demonstration. Applicants may be asked to inform the employer of any reasonable accommodation needed to take a pre-offer examination, interview, or job demonstration within a reasonable time period prior to the examination, interview, or job demonstration.

An employer may ask an applicant whether they can perform specified job-related functions with or without reasonable accommodation. An employer may also ask an applicant to describe or demonstrate how they would perform job-related functions, with or without a reasonable accommodation, because these inquiries elicit information about an applicant's ability, not information about an applicant's **disability**.

An employer may not ask whether the applicant needs reasonable accommodation for the job. For example, an employer may not ask: "Would you need a reasonable accommodation in this job or to perform this specific function?"

Unacceptable	*Acceptable*
1. Questions regarding the applicant's general condition, state of health, or illness	1. Statement by the employer that the offer may be made contingent on the applicant passing a job-related physical examination
2. Questions regarding receipt of workers' compensation	2. Do you have any physical condition or disability that may limit your ability to perform the job requested? If yes, what can be done to accommodate your limitation?

3. Do you have any physical disabilities or handicaps?

3. Can you perform the functions of this job with or without reasonable accommodation? (Examples: Can you carry a 20-pound bag? or Can you distinguish color for color-coded wires?) If the applicant needs a reasonable accommodation to demonstrate his or her ability, that accommodation should be provided or the person should be permitted to explain how they could do the job with accommodation

4. Height and weight

4. Please describe/demonstrate how you would perform these functions?

5. Do you have AIDS?

5. How well can you handle stress?

6. Do you have asthma?

6. Can you meet this job's attendance requirements?

7. Do you have a disability which would interfere with your ability to perform the job?

7. Do you illegally use drugs?

8. Do you ever get ill from stress?

8. Do you have the required licenses or certifications to perform this job?

9. How many sick days did you take last year?

10. Why do you need a wheelchair?

11. Have you ever been injured on the job?

12. Have you ever been treated for drug or alcohol problems?

13. What prescription drugs are you currently taking?

14. Do you have any medical condition that we should know about?

Race, Color

Eye and hair color are not related to job performance and may serve to indicate an employee's race, religion, or national origin. The name and location of colleges attended have been used by employers to determine the applicant's race. If this question is asked, it must be used to help determine the applicant's fitness for the job.

Unacceptable

1. Questions regarding the applicant's race or color

2. Questions regarding the applicant's complexion or color of skin, eyes, or hair

3. Requirement that the applicant affix a photograph to the application

4. Requesting the applicant, at his or her option, to submit a photograph

5. Requiring a photograph after interview but before employment

Acceptable

1. Statement that a photograph may be required after employment

References

The employer cannot ask an applicant's references for information that is not job-related. Likewise, the applicant's references cannot submit to the employer non-job-related information.

Unacceptable

1. Questions of the applicant's former employers or acquaintances which elicit information specifying the applicant's race, color, religious creed, national origin, ancestry, physical handicap, disability, medical condition, marital status, age, or sex

Acceptable

1. By whom were you referred for a position?

2. Names of persons willing to provide professional and/or character references for the applicant

Religion

Inquiries related to religion are not job-related unless the employer is a religious institution. In all other cases, they should be avoided.

Unacceptable	*Acceptable*
1. Questions regarding the applicant's religion	1. Statement by the employer of regular days, hours, or shifts to be worked
2. Religious days observed	
3. Does your religion prevent you from working weekends or holidays?	

Sex, Marital Status, Family

Questions regarding marital status should not be asked. It is doubtful that this information could be job-related and has been used discriminatorily in the past. Inquiring as to Mr., Miss, Mrs., or Ms. is simply another way of asking the applicant's sex or for marital status. Information regarding family needed for tax, insurance, social security, or for other similar legitimate business purpose may be obtained **after** employment.

The number of persons dependent upon the applicant for support is not relevant to a determination of whether or not the applicant can perform the job. [See, e.g., Phillips v. Martin Marietta Corp., 400 U.S. 542 (1971) (sex discrimination regarding preschool children).] This information can be requested **after** hire.

Pre-employment information about child care arrangements should be avoided. An employer may not have different hiring policies for males and females with preschool age children. Even if asked of both males and females, the question may still be suspect. This information has been used discriminatorily because of society's general presumption that the female is the primary caregiver. If the employer's concern is whether or not the employee will be able to attend work regularly, the question that could be asked is, "Is there anything which would interfere with your attending work regularly?"

Information about friends or relatives working for the employer is not relevant to an applicant's competence, unless it affects the employee's assignment in not being supervised or managed by relatives. Requesting this information may indicate a preference for friends and relatives of present employees. The composition of the present work force may indicate that this preference would reduce or eliminate employment opportunities for minorities, or restrict employment opportunities for females.

Lowest acceptable salary has been used by some employers in a discriminatory manner. Females, for example, generally have held poorer paying jobs than males, and have been paid less than males for the same work. As a result of these past practices, a female might be willing to work for less pay than a male would find acceptable. It is unlawful to pay a female less than a male employee who is or was performing the same or similar work. A legitimate inquiry would be whether applicants will accept a pre-determined salary or a salary within a pre-determined range, based on the value of the job, with variations depending on each applicant's job-related experience, qualifications, and seniority, if relevant.

Employers should only ask for information on licenses and certifications relevant to the job rather than information on any type of trade or professional license or certification. Similarly, information regarding a current driver's license should only be requested if a driver's license is needed to perform the job's essential functions.

Inquiries should not be made into an applicant's previous address or length of residence since it is not related to the applicant's ability to perform the job. The crucial factor is the employer's ability to justify this request and ability to prove that it is not used in a discriminatory manner by possibly disclosing minority status, sex, or national origin.

Unacceptable	*Acceptable*
1. Questions indicating the applicant's sex	1. Name and address of parent or guardian if the applicant is a minor
2. Questions indicating the applicant's marital status	2. Statement of the employer's policy regarding work assignment of related employees
3. Number and/or ages of children or dependents	
4. Questions regarding pregnancy, childbearing, or birth control	
5. Name(s) of spouse or children of the applicant	
6. Questions regarding child care	

Union Affiliation and Membership

Questions relating to an applicant's union affiliation or membership should be avoided. This may indicate an anti-union animus violating the National Labor

Relations Act (NLRA). [See, e.g., *Phelps Dodge Corp. v. NLRB*, 313 U.S. 177 (1941) (refusing to hire job applicants who were union members).]

Unacceptable	*Acceptable*
1. Have you ever been affiliated with or a member of a union?	1. The Company's collective bargaining agreement with its union requires that once you are employed that you either become a union member or pay a fair share fee for the union's services. Will you accept employment upon this condition?
2. What do you think about unions?	
3. If the Company had a union, would you join it?	
4. Are your relatives or close friends members of unions?	

Chapter 3

Data Verification

After an application is submitted and interviews are conducted, employers use various procedures to verify applicant information. Data verification may occur with or without the applicant's consent or knowledge.

Verification is the selection method that checks applicant information accuracy. Almost every qualification an applicant offers for employment consideration can be verified. Verification sources include previous employers, schools, colleges, military records, certifying or licensing bodies, public records, etc. Public records include those from courts, law enforcement agencies, licensing bureaus, tax assessors, and financial departments.

Some verification sources are more accurate than others. Verifying a college degree can be accomplished by contacting the college registrar, while a driver's license can be checked with the state driver's license department. However, it is sometimes more difficult to obtain accurate information from previous employers. Employers may be more cooperative when the information request is accompanied by an applicant-signed release to disclose this information.

Information accuracy can be substantially increased by informing applicants that the information they furnish will have a direct bearing upon their hiring. Applicants should be instructed that the information they furnish will be carefully verified. These procedures greatly decrease the inconsistency between information furnished by applicants and that obtained through verification.

Some companies provide employers with services that include verifying job experience, work performance, attendance, training, education, criminal convictions, motor vehicle driving, records, military records, etc. These companies also conduct applicant background searches and provide comprehensive reports by reviewing credit bureau records and interviewing coworkers and neighbors to determine an applicant's reputation regarding honesty, alcohol, drug abuse, etc. Employers using these companies for information verification should ensure that only job-related information is procured. If other than job- related information is furnished, the employer may be liable for this information's use if it adversely affects the employee.

Verification information may be irrelevant and not job-related. To safeguard employee interests and minimize employer litigation exposure, procedures and policies must be developed to counteract these problems. This Chapter reviews policies relevant to employment data verification that are inherent in arrest records, credit checks, criminal convictions, fingerprints, immigration requirements, photographs, physical examinations, reference checks, and skill testing.

ARREST RECORDS

Many employers believe that arrest history is critical, or at least relevant, to employment. Arrest information raises employee concerns because it indicates only that a law enforcement agency believed that probable cause to arrest existed for some offense. It does not reflect guilt, nor that the person actually committed the offense.

Refusing employment or terminating employees because of arrest records is not permitted absent evidence that it is job-related to the employer's business. [See *Gregory v. Litton Sys.*, Inc., 316 F. Supp. 401 (C.D. Cal. 1970), *aff'd with modifications not here relevant*, 472 F.2d 631 (9th Cir. 1972) (arrest record inquiries prohibited as unnecessarily disqualifying minority applicants).] Even when a legitimate pre-employment inquiry is made regarding arrest records, an applicant's rejection based solely on an arrest record may violate federal and state statutes.

Drafting

In drafting arrest record policies, the following should be considered:

1. Applicable federal and state statutes
2. That a differentiation be made between arrest and conviction
3. That a careful evaluation be made of the frequency and severity of arrests
4. Age at time of the arrest
5. The elapsed time since an arrest
6. The whole individual; i.e., his or her aptitudes, abilities, interests, and educational level, rather than one aspect of personal history
7. The job's nature and its relation to the employability of those with arrest records
8. Geographic location of the incidents involved

Sample Policies

The following example should be considered in drafting arrest record policies:

ARREST RECORD POLICY

Section 1. Conviction. A "conviction" shall include a plea, verdict, or finding of guilt, regardless of whether sentence is imposed by a court. It shall not include an arrest.

Section 2. Collection. The Company shall not ask an applicant or employee to disclose, through any written form or verbally, information concerning an arrest or detention that did not result in conviction or information concerning a referral to and participation in any pretrial or post-trial diversion program.

Section 3. Use. The Company shall not seek from any source or utilize as a factor in determining any employment condition including hiring, promotion, termination, apprenticeship, or any other training program leading to employment, any record of arrest or detention that did not result in conviction or any record regarding a referral to and participation in any pretrial or post-trial diversion program.

Section 4. Exception. The Company may ask an applicant or employee about an arrest for which the applicant or employee is out on bail or on his or her own recognizance pending trial.

CREDIT CHECKS

Credit information collection, maintenance, use, and disclosure present significant applicant concerns by potentially revealing non-job-related data. This information may be used by employers in evaluating applicants and/or employees for hiring, promotion, reassignment, or retention. Sometimes credit information is obtained for non-job-related purposes. Personal finances are generally not relevant to the job applied for or held.

Federal statute places certain restrictions on credit information used for employment purposes. [See, e.g., 15 U.S.C. §§ 1681-1681(t) (1994) (Fair Credit Reporting Act).] Non-job-related credit reports may violate federal and state fair employment practice (FEP) statutes. A requirement that applicants and employees have a good credit record may have to be justified by a legitimate job-related business necessity. [See, e.g., *United States v. Chicago*, 549 F.2d 415 (7th Cir. 1977) (credit check for police officer not job-related).] This requirement, however, should have a direct relationship to the job's duties.

Drafting

In drafting credit check policies, the following should be considered:

1. Review applicable federal and state statutes
2. Select a reputable credit agency and periodically review the choice
3. Notify the applicant and/or employee that a credit check will be performed and indicate:

    a. The types of information expected to be collected that are not collected on the application, and, as to information regarding character, general reputation, and mode of living, each area of inquiry

    b. The techniques that may be used to collect the information

    c. The sources that are expected to provide the information

    d. The parties to whom and circumstances under which information about the individual may be disclosed without authorization and the information that may be disclosed

    e. The statutory procedure by which the individual may gain access to any resulting record

    f. The procedures the individual may use to correct, amend, or dispute any collected record

    g. That information in any report prepared by a consumer reporting agency may be retained by that organization and subsequently disclosed by it to others

4. Obtain the applicant's and/or employee's written consent for undertaking a credit check

5. Do not share the information received regarding an applicant and/or employee with potential creditors

6. Limit credit checks to job-related information and purposes

7. Consider credit information highly confidential and sensitive

8. Certify that credit information will only be used for a job-related purpose

Sample Policies

The following should be considered in drafting credit check policies:

CREDIT CHECK POLICY

Section 1. Definitions. For the purposes of this policy, the following terms shall mean:

    a. *Consumer report.* Any report containing information relating to an individual's credit record or manner of obtaining credit directly from a creditor of the individual or from a consumer reporting agency; and also shall include information pertaining to an individual's character, general reputation, personal characteristics, or mode of living obtained through personal interviews with neighbors, friends, or associates of the individual reported on, or others with whom he or she is acquainted or may have knowledge concerning any of these information items.

    b. *Consumer reporting agency.* Any person who, for monetary fees or dues, regularly engages in assembling or evaluating employment information to be used regarding individuals.

    c. *Employment purposes.* A report used by the Company for evaluating an individual for employment, promotion, reassignment, retention, etc.

    d. *Individual.* A person who has applied for employment or who is currently employed by the Company.

Section 2. Procurement. The Company shall request a consumer report only for legitimate employment purposes, which must be job-related.

Section 3. Written Permission. The Company shall procure a consumer report only after written permission from the individual has been received.

Section 4. Information Inspection. The Company shall, upon request and proper identification of any individual, allow the inspection of any and all consumer reports maintained regarding that individual.

Section 5. Confidentiality. The Company shall maintain all consumer report information in strict confidence and shall not disclose it absent the individual's written permission.

Credit Check Consent Form

The following should be used to safeguard the employer's interest in requesting credit-related information from an applicant or employee:

CREDIT CHECK CONSENT FORM

Based on the requirements of the job for which I am applying, I authorize (Company's Name) to conduct a job-related credit check.

_____   _____

Date   Applicant's/Employee's Name

CRIMINAL CONVICTIONS

Criminal convictions present different employee concerns than do arrests. A conviction is a final societal judgment made by a court, another judicial body, or by an individual before a court regarding an individual's criminal actions. Unlike arrests, a conviction record is complete. Guilt and accountability have been finalized.

Employees should be uneasy about conviction information collection, maintenance, use, and disclosure. Even though an employer may take employment actions based on criminal convictions when it correlates the offense's nature, gravity, and time elapsed since the conviction to job-relatedness, concerns remain over subsequent use and disclosure. [See, e.g., *Richardson v. Hotel Corp. of Am.,*

332 F. Supp. 519 (E.D. La. 1971), *aff'd mem.*, 468 F.2d 951 (5th Cir. 1972) (legitimate employee termination for conviction).] Improper conviction record use may violate federal and state fair employment practice (FEP) statutes.

Drafting

In drafting criminal conviction policies, the following should be considered:

1. Applicable federal and state statutes
2. The job and its responsibilities
3. The time, nature, and number of convictions
4. Each conviction's facts
5. Each conviction's job-relatedness
6. The length of time between a conviction and the employment decision
7. Employment history before and after the conviction
8. Rehabilitation efforts
9. Whether the particular conviction would prevent job performance in an acceptance businesslike manner
10. Age at the time of the conviction
11. The conviction's geographic location

Sample Policies

The following example should be considered in drafting conviction record policies:

CONVICTION RECORD POLICY

Section 1. Conviction. A "conviction" shall include a plea, verdict, or finding of guilt, regardless of whether sentence is imposed by a court.

Section 2. Conviction's Use. The Company may consider any conviction as a possible justification for the refusal, suspension, revocation, or termination of employment when it directly relates:

    a. To the applicant's possible performance in the job applied for; or

    b. To the employee's possible performance in the job which the employee holds.

Section 3. Conviction's Job-Relatedness. In determining whether a conviction is job-related, the Company will consider, among other things:

    a. The job and its responsibilities;

    b. The time, nature, and number of convictions;

    c. Each conviction's facts;

    d. Each conviction's job-relatedness;

e. The length of time between a conviction and the employment decision;

f. Employment history before and after the conviction;

g. Rehabilitation efforts;

h. Whether the particular conviction would prevent job performance in an acceptable businesslike manner;

i. Age at the time of the conviction; and

j. The conviction's geographic location.

Section 4. Excluded Convictions. The Company will not consider:

a. Convictions which have been annulled or expunged;

b. Convictions of a penal offense for which no jail sentence may be imposed; or

c. Conviction of a misdemeanor in which the period of twenty years has elapsed since the conviction's date and during which there has been no subsequent arrest or conviction.

FINGERPRINTS

Fingerprinting has generally been considered a valid employer collection method related more to verifying information than to compulsory incriminating fact extraction. Despite its primary use in verifying information, some states regulate fingerprinting to limit employer abuses. [See, e.g., Cal. Labor Code § 1051 (West 1971) (California's statute regulating fingerprinting).] Statutes may prohibit an employer from requiring that an applicant or employee be fingerprinted for the purpose of furnishing information to a third party, as a condition precedent to securing or retaining employment, where this information could be used to the applicant's or employee's detriment. [See, e.g., Cal. Labor Code § 1051 (West 1971) (California's statute regulating fingerprinting).]

Drafting

In drafting fingerprint policies, the following should be considered:

1. Review applicable statutes

2. To verify employee identity, where this is in doubt, or for receipt of an employee benefit

Sample Policies

The following example should be considered in drafting fingerprint policies:

FINGERPRINT POLICY

The Company shall not require, as a condition to securing or retaining employment, that an applicant or employee be fingerprinted where fingerprints could be used to the applicant's or employee's detriment in a non-job-related situation. However, fingerprinting may be required for job-related purposes.

IMMIGRATION

The Immigration Reform and Control Act of 1986 (IRCA) creates an additional recordkeeping requirement for employers in an attempt to curtail illegal immigration into the United States. It requires every employer to ask applicants for specific written verification establishing that they can be employed. Civil and criminal penalties may be imposed on employers who knowingly hire or recruit an alien. [Immigration Reform and Control Act of 1986. Pub. L. No. 99-603, 100 Stat. 3359 (codified in scattered sections of 7 U.S.C. § 2025; 8 U.S.C. §§ 1101, 1152-1153, 1160-61, 1184, 1186-87, 1252, 1254-55a, 1258-59, 1321, 1324-24b, 1357, 1364-65; 18 U.S.C. § 1546; 20 U.S.C. §§ 1091, 1096; 29 U.S.C. §§ 1802, 1813, 1816, 1851; 42 U.S.C. §§ 303, 502, 602-03, 672-73, 1203, 1320b-7, 1353. 1396b, 1436a, 1437r).]

IRCA prohibits employers from discriminating against applicants based on their national origin. It is an unfair immigration-related employment practice to discriminate against any individual in hiring, recruitment, or termination because of that individual's national origin or citizenship status.

The potential for employer problems exists in the collection of age, national origin, or other potentially discriminatory data-required by IRCA. To minimize employer intrusions by not obtaining sensitive applicant data, the required IRCA information should not be collected until immediately after hiring. Once collected, it should be maintained separate from the employee's personnel file, to prevent disclosures that could have a discriminatory impact. This will minimize employee challenges arising out of federal and state fair employment practice (FEP) statutes.

Guidelines for Completing the Employment Eligibility Verification Form (Form I-9)

The following are guidelines for completing Form I-9 (Employment Eligibility Verification Form):

Verifying Employment Eligibility. The Immigration Reform and Control Act of 1986 (IRCA) requires employers to hire only citizens and aliens who are authorized to work in the United States. The Employment Eligibility Verification Form (Form I-9) has been developed for verifying that persons are eligible to work. IRCA requires an employer to:

1. Have all employees complete Form I-9 when they begin working
2. Check documents establishing employee identity and eligibility to work
3. Properly complete Form I-9
4. Retain Form I-9 for at least three years
5. Retain Form I-9 until one year after the person leaves employment, if the person is employed for more than three years
6. Present Form I-9 for inspection to an Immigration and Naturalization Service (INS) or Department of Labor (DOL) officer upon request

Unlawful Discrimination. If the employer has four or more employees, the employer may not discriminate against any individual other than an unauthorized alien in hiring, terminating, recruiting, or referring for a fee because of that individual's national origin or, in the case of a citizen or intending citizen, because of his or her citizenship status.

The Civil Rights Act of 1964 (Title VII) and the remedies against discrimination it provides are applicable. Title VII prohibits discrimination against any individual on the basis of national origin in hiring, termination, assignment, compensation, and other employment terms and conditions. National origin discrimination claims against employers with fifteen or more employees should be filed with the Equal Employment Opportunity Commission (EEOC).

Under IRCA, national origin discrimination charges against employers with four through fourteen employees, and citizenship discrimination charges against employers with four or more employees, should be filed with the Office of Special Counsel in the Department of Justice. Discrimination charges may be filed either by the person who believes that he or she was discriminated against in employment on the basis of national origin or citizenship status, by a person on their behalf, or by INS officers who have reason to believe that discrimination has occurred. Discrimination charges must be filed within 180 days of the discriminatory act. The Office of Special Counsel will notify the employer by certified mail within ten days upon receipt of a discrimination charge. After investigating the charge, the Special Counsel may file a complaint with an administrative law judge. If the Special Counsel does not file a complaint within 120 days of receiving the charge, the person making the charge (other than an INS officer) may initiate the filing of a complaint with an administrative law judge. The administrative law judge will conduct a hearing, and issue a decision.

Employers found to have engaged in discriminatory practices will be ordered to cease the prohibited practices. They may also be ordered to:

1. Hire, with or without back pay, individuals directly injured by the discrimination
2. Pay a fine of up to $ 1,000 for each individual discriminated against, or up to $2,000 for each individual in cases of employers previously fined
3. Keep certain records regarding applicant and employee hiring

Should a court decide that the losing party's claim has no reasonable basis in fact or law, the court may award attorneys' fees to prevailing parties other than the United States.

Penalties for Prohibited Practices. If an investigation reveals that an employer has violated IRCA regarding employees hired after November 6, 1986, INS may take action. Violations of IRCA include civil penalties for:

1. *Hiring or continuing to employ unauthorized employees.* Employers determined to have knowingly hired unauthorized employees or to be continuing to employ persons knowing that they are or have become unauthorized may be fined as follows:
   a. First violation of not less than $250 and not more than $2,000 for each unauthorized employee
   b. Second violation of not less than $2,000 and not more than $5,000 for each unauthorized employee
   c. Subsequent violations of not less than $3,000 and not more than $10,000 for each unauthorized employee
2. *Failing to comply with recordkeeping requirements.* Employers who fail to properly complete, retain, and present for inspection the Form I-9 as required by law may be fined as follows:
   a. Civil fines of not less than $100 and no more than $1,000 for each employee for whom the form was not completed, retained, or presented
   b. In determining penalties, consideration shall be given to the business's size, good faith efforts to comply, the seriousness of the violation, and whether the violation involved unauthorized employees
3. *Requiring indemnification.* Employers found to have required a bond or indemnity from an individual against liability may be fined $1,000 and ordered to make restitution, either to the person who was required to pay the indemnity, or, if that person cannot be located, to the United States Treasury
4. *Recruiting unauthorized seasonal agricultural workers outside the United States.* Employers who knowingly recruit unauthorized workers outside the United States to perform seasonal agricultural labor may face the same penalties as for hiring unauthorized workers, unless the workers recruited have been granted Special Agricultural Worker (SAW) status

Criminal penalties for violation of IRCA include:

1. *Engaging in a pattern or practice of knowingly hiring or continuing to employ unauthorized employees.* Employers convicted for having engaged in a pattern or practice of knowingly hiring unauthorized aliens after November 6, 1986, may be fined as follows:
   a. Fines of up to $3,000 per employee and/or six months imprisonment

     b. The same penalties apply to engaging in a pattern or practice of recruiting unauthorized seasonal agricultural workers outside the United States

     c. Criminal sanctions will be reserved for serious or repeated violations

2. *Engaging in fraud, false statements, or otherwise misusing visas, immigration permits, and identity documents.* Persons who use fraudulent identification or employment eligibility documents or documents that were lawfully issued to another, or who make a false statement or attestation for purposes of satisfying the employment eligibility requirements may be imprisoned for up to five years, or fined, or both

Persons for Whom Form I-9 Must Be Completed

1. For persons hired after May 31, 1987, a Form I-9 must be completed:
     a. Within three business days of the date of the hire
     b. If the person is employed for less than three days, the employer must complete Form I-9 before the end of the employee's first working day
2. Employers need not complete Form I-9 for:
     a. Persons hired before November 7, 1986
     b. Persons hired after November 6, 1986, who left employment before June 1, 1987
     c. Persons employed for domestic work in a private home on an intermittent or sporadic basis
     d. Persons who provide labor and are employed by a contractor providing contract services such as employee leasing
     e. Persons who are independent contractors

How to Complete Form I-9. Form I-9 contains two sections. The employee completes the first section containing Steps 1, 2, and 3. If a preparer or translator assists the employee, the preparer or translator completes Step 4. The second section, containing Steps 5 and 6, should be completed by the employer.

When completing Form I-9, the employee will need to provide a document or documents that establish identity and employment eligibility. Some documents establish both identity and employment eligibility. These documents appear in List A on the bottom half of Form I-9. Other documents establish identity alone (List B) or employment eligibility alone (List C). If the person does not provide a document from List A, he or she must produce one from List B and one from List C.

The employer should review the document or documents provided by the person. Documents should appear to be genuine and relate to the individual.

If employees cannot complete Section 1 by themselves or need the form translated, someone may assist them. The preparer or translator should read the form to the employee, help with Step 1 and Step 2 as needed, have the employee sign or mark the form, and follow Step 4.

If a minor under age 16 cannot produce a List A document or one of the identity documents on List B, he or she is exempt from producing one if:

1. A parent or legal guardian completes Section 1 and writes in the space for the minor's signature the words, "minor under age 16"
2. The parent or legal guardian completes the "Preparer/Translator Certification"
3. The employer writes in Section 2 the words, "minor under age 16" under List B in the space after the words, "Document Identification #"

If this procedure is followed, the minor must still procure a List C document showing employment eligibility.

Instructions for Recruiters and Referrers for a Fee. IRCA's provisions also apply to those who recruit persons and refer them to potential employers in return for a fee, and to those who refer or provide documents or information about persons to employers in return for a fee. The provisions do not apply to persons who recruit for their own company or business. Union hiring halls that refer union members or nonunion individuals who pay membership dues are not considered to be recruiters or referrers for a fee.

Starting June 1, 1987, they should complete Form I-9 when a person they refer to an employer is hired by that employer. The form should be completed within three business days of the hire.

Recruiters and referrers may designate agents to complete the verification procedures on their behalf, including national associations or employers. If the employer who hires the referred individual is designated as the agent, the employer need only provide the recruiter or referrer with a Form I-9 photocopy. Recruiters or referrers who designate someone to complete the verification procedures on their behalf are still responsible for compliance with IRCA, and may be found liable for violations.

Recruiters and referrers must retain the Form I-9 for three years after the date the referred individual was hired by the employer. They must also present forms for inspection to an INS or DOL officer after three days' advance notice. The penalties also apply to recruiting and referring unauthorized employees for a fee which occurs on or after June 1, 1987.

Applicable Documents for Verifying Employment Eligibility. Certain documents have been designated for determining IRCA employment eligibility. The employee must provide a document or documents that establish identity and employment eligibility.

Some documents establish both identity and employment eligibility. These are listed on the Form I-9 under List A, "Documents That Establish Identity and Employment Eligibility." If a person does not provide a document from List A, he or she must provide one document that establishes identity and one document that establishes employment eligibility.

To establish identity, the person must provide a document in List B. To establish employment eligibility, one of the immigration documents in List C must be furnished.

If an employee is unable to provide the required document or documents within three days, he or she must at least produce, within three days, a receipt showing that he or she has applied for the document. The employee must produce the document itself within 21 days of hiring.

LIST A
Documents That Establish Identity and Employment Eligibility

1. United States Passport
2. Certificate of United States Citizenship (INS Form N-560 or N-561)
3. Certificate of Naturalization (INS Form N-550 or N-570)
4. Unexpired foreign passport which:
   a. Contains an unexpired stamp reading "Processed for I-551. Temporary Evidence of Lawful Admission for permanent residence. Valid until _____. Employment authorized;" or
   b. Has attached thereto a Form I-94 bearing the same name as the passport and containing an employment authorization stamp, so long as the period of endorsement has not yet expired and the proposed employment is not in conflict with any restrictions or limitations identified on the Form I-94
5. Alien Registration Receipt Card (INS Form I-151) or Resident Alien Card (INS Form I-551), provided that it contains a photograph of the bearer
6. Temporary Resident Card (INS Form I-688)
7. Employment Authorization Card (INS Form I-688A)

LIST B
Documents That Establish Identity

For individuals 16 years of age or older:

1. State-issued driver's license or state-issued identification card containing a photograph or, if the driver's license or identification card does not contain a photograph, identifying information should be included listing name, date of birth, sex, height, color of eyes, and address
2. School identification card with a photograph
3. Voter's registration card
4. United States military card or draft record
5. Identification card issued by federal, state, or local government agencies
6. Military dependent's identification card
7. Native American tribal documents

8. United States Coast Guard Merchant Mariner Card
9. Driver's license issued by a Canadian government authority

For individuals under age 16 who are unable to produce one of the documents listed above:

1. School record or report card
2. Clinic, doctor, or hospital record
3. Daycare or nursery school record

LIST C
Documents That Establish Employment Eligibility

1. Social Security number card, other than one which has printed on its face "not valid for employment purposes," that must be an original card issued by the Social Security Administration; a facsimile such as a metal or plastic reproduction that people can purchase is not acceptable
2. An original or certified copy of a birth certificate issued by a state, county, or municipal authority bearing an official seal
3. Unexpired INS employment authorization
4. Unexpired reentry permit (INS Form I-327)
5. Unexpired Refugee Travel Document (INS Form I-571)
6. Certification of Birth issued by the Department of State (Form FS-545)
7. Certification of Birth Abroad issued by the Department of State (Form DS-1350)
8. United States Citizen Identification Card (INS Form I-197)
9. Native American tribal document
10. Identification Card for use of Resident Citizen in the United States (INS Form I-179)

Temporary United States Visas Suitable for Employment

In administering requirements under the Immigration Reform and Control Act of 1986 (IRCA), the following should be considered regarding visas:

1. B-1 (Business Visitor)
   a. Uses
      Permits entry by an alien:
      (i) To participate in commercial transactions, to negotiate contracts, to consult with business associates, to litigate, to participate in scientific, educational, professional or business conventions or conferences, or to undertake independent research
      (ii) Who is otherwise classifiable as an H-1, coming to perform services for which no salary will be paid by a United States source

(iii) Already employed abroad coming to undertake training in the United States who would otherwise be classifiable as an H-3 and who will continue to receive salary from the foreign employer alone

(iv) To furnish technical information and assistance under the Foreign Assistance Act

(v) Who is a personal or domestic servant of an employer in the United States who holds temporary status as a B, E, F, H, I, J, or L under certain specified circumstances

b. Duration of Stay

(i) Issued for one year or more depending upon Governmental reciprocity, subject to unlimited revalidation

(ii) Permits United States entry for six months, stay subject to renewal in six-month increments through an INS district office

c. Method of Procurement

Alien applies at a United States consular post abroad

d. Documentation

(i) Nonimmigrant visa application

(ii) Proof of foreign employer's sponsorship and/or reasonably permanent employment or business connections and/or family, social, cultural, or other associations abroad are sometimes required

e. Comments

(i) United States employer may pay living expenses for B-1 business visitor

(ii) Honorarium or other fees may also constitute allowable expenses

2. E-I/E-2 (Treaty Traders & Investors)

a. Uses

Entry by managers, executives, and specialized knowledge employees pursuant to a treaty of trade or commerce between the United States and the same country of which the employer and the visa applicant are nationals

b. Duration of Stay

(i) Issued for four-year periods by United States consulate posts abroad, subject to unlimited revalidation so long as the visa holder remains in treaty employment in the United States

(ii) Issued by INS stateside for two-year periods in connection with a status change request

c. Methods of Procurement

Alien either applies at a United States consular post abroad or, if already in the United States, at the INS district office with jurisdiction in the United States

d. Documentation

Proof of the following is required:

(i) That the alien will be employed as a manager, executive, or specialized-knowledge employee

(ii) That his or her nationality is the same as that of the treaty employer

(iii) That 51 percent of the trade of the United States treaty entity is with the treaty country

(iv) That the treaty employer is owned or incorporated in the treaty country

(v) That the United States entity is well established and is a growing concern

(vi) In the case of treaty investment visas, that the United States investment is substantial and appropriate to the scope of the enterprise

  e. Comments

Spouses of treaty traders and investors are permitted to work but are not permitted to adjust to permanent resident status in the United States if this work was performed

3. F-1 (Academic Students)

  a. Uses

F-1 visa holders or academic students may receive work permission from the INS for off-campus employment:

(i) After completion of one full year of study in the United States, provided the student can demonstrate economic necessity, due to unforeseen circumstances arising subsequent to entry or change to student status

(ii) For practical training purposes in connection with completion of an academic program

  b. Duration of Stay

(i) F-1 students may remain in the United States for the duration of their academic program and any approved period(s) of practical training, plus 60 days

(ii) No more than 12 months of practical training may be approved, regardless of the number of academic programs engaged in

  c. Method of Procurement

(i) F-1 students must receive approval from the INS prior to engaging in off-campus employment which is other than practical training

(ii) F-1 students must apply for practical training approval, whether to be obtained during vacation periods or following completion of studies, from the INS

  d. Documentation

Proof that comparable training is unavailable in the student's home country, but that employment opportunities in the field are now or will be available at home upon training completion in the United States

4. H-1 (Temporary Workers of Distinguished Merit and Ability)

  a. Uses

Employment in the United States by professionals or other persons of distinguished merit and ability

b. Duration of Stay
   (i) May be issued initially for three years
   (ii) Renewable for additional two years, provided no change in circumstances occurs
   (iii) Approval of sixth year subject to extraordinary documentation requirements
   (iv) New petition will not be entertained until the alien has spent one year abroad
c. Method of Procurement
   (i) Employer files I-129B petition in duplicate with the INS regional adjudication center with jurisdiction over the place of employment
   (ii) Alien obtains visa at designated United States consular post abroad or applies for a status change with the INS in the United States if maintaining status
d. Documentation
   (i) Employer must show that:
      a. The alien's position is professional in nature
      b. The alien possesses the requisite education and/or experience requirement
      c. The alien's intended stay is temporary in nature
      d. The H-1 classification is not being sought principally to enable the employee to enter the United States permanently in advance of the availability of a visa number
   (ii) The alien must show that:
      a. He or she has not abandoned his or her foreign residence
      b. He or she will return abroad before his or her authorized stay terminates

5. J-1 (Exchange Visitors)
   a. Uses
      Persons in training for employment in United States companies or affiliates abroad
   b. Duration of Stay
      (i) Business and industrial trainees—eighteen months
      (ii) Teachers and instructors—two years
      (iii) Research scholars—three years
   c. Method of Procurement
      (i) The authorized employer or agency issues an eligibility certificate for exchange visitor status
      (ii) The alien is interviewed for eligibility at a United States consular post abroad
   d. Documentation
      The alien must show:
      (i) That the intended activities in the Untied States conform to the program description

(ii) That the skills to be acquired in the United States will be useful in the home country

(iii) That the alien will maintain a residence abroad, while residing in the United States, which he or she has no intention of abandoning

e. Comments

(i) In many cases, J visa holders cannot change status to the H or L category or adjust to permanent resident status

(ii) In most cases, J visa holders must return to the home country for a period of two years at the expiration of their approved program; the INS does not view waivers of this requirement favorably

(iii) Participation in more than one exchange visitor program requires special State Department approval

(iv) Spouses of J-1 visa holders (J-2s) are permitted to work only upon a showing that it is necessary for the support of the spouse and children of the J-1

(v) Exchange visitor program skills are limited by country according to United States Information Agency bulletin

6. L-1 (Intracompany Transferees)

a. Uses

Employment in the United States by managers, executives, and specialized-knowledge personnel (professional and nonprofessional) employed abroad by the sponsor employer or an affiliate, for at least one year prior to application for intracompany transfer

b. Duration of Stay

(i) Issued initially for a period up to three years pursuant to an approved employer petition

(ii) A two-year extension is available to accomplish the original purpose for admission

(iii) Maximum approved stay—six years; sixth year subject to extraordinary documentation requirements

(iv) If the United States employer is newly opened, the initial term is limited to one year; the petition will be reexamined thereafter to determine bona fides

c. Method of Procurement

(i) Employer files I-129B petition in duplicate with the INS regional adjudication center with jurisdiction over the place of employment

(ii) Alien obtains visa at a designated United States consular post abroad, or applies for a status change through the INS

d. Documentation Employer must show:

(i) That the alien's position is managerial or executive, or that it involves specialized knowledge

(ii) That the alien was employed in the qualifying capacity for one year abroad prior to the petition (United States employment does not count)

(iii) That it is a parent, branch, affiliate, subsidiary, or joint venture partner of the transferring firm abroad

(iv) That it will continue to do business in at least one country abroad after the transfer; regular, systematic, and continuous provision of goods and/or services, not the mere presence of an agent or an office abroad

(v) If the alien is being transferred to a new United States office, lease or purchase agreement and proof of financial liability to pay the alien

(vi) If the alien is an owner or major shareholder, that there is an assignment abroad available post-transfer

(vii) That the L-1 is not being sought principally to enable the alien to enter the United States permanently in advance of the availability of a visa number

(viii) The alien may have to show prospects of work abroad post-temporary United States assignment; prior employment history in the United States and abroad will be relevant

Counterfeit Document Detection

In determining the legitimacy of documents presented for Immigration Reform and Control Act of 1986 (IRCA) verification, employers should:

1. Be aware of the document's information
2. Determine whether the information pertains to the individual presenting the document; etc, if the person appears to be 18 and the identification says 45, there is a problem; if a male presents an identification with a female's picture, there is also a problem
3. Look for alterations of an official document through erasures, photograph substitutions, etc.; official documents are never altered but are replaced
4. Check to be sure the document is squarely cut
5. Ascertain that printing and engraving is parallel with the document's edges, along with being sharp, clear, and unbroken
6. View documents as suspect where printing and engraving is dull, unclear, broken, or blurred
7. Not deny employment to someone based on a suspect document, but contact the local INS office for verification of the document's number
8. Check with the state employment agency to determine if it has a certification process to verify an applicant's documents through the INS and issue a letter of certification to potential employers, with the certification letter serving as eligibility proof

Sample Policies

The following example should be considered in drafting Immigration Reform and Control Act of 1986 (IRCA) policies:

UNLAWFUL IMMIGRATION DISCRIMINATION

The Company will not discriminate against any individual other than an unauthorized alien in hiring, disciplining, terminating, recruiting, etc. because of that individual's national origin or, in the case of a citizen or intending citizen, because of his or her citizenship status.

PHOTOGRAPHS

Photographing applicants during the initial hiring process raises objections. Race, color, national origin, sex, age, and disability may be unnecessarily revealed for non-job-related use. These applicant interests have been protected primarily under federal and state fair employment practice (FEP) statutes. However, employers have been permitted to photograph employees at the workplace, when a legitimate job-related business purpose existed. [See, e.g., *Thomas v. General Elec. Co.,* 207 F. Supp. 792 (W.D. Ky. 1962) (permissible to take motion pictures to study plant layout and evaluate employee jobs).] Legitimate employee photographs may be used to improve safety, for example, or to identify employees who are violating employer rules.

Drafting

In drafting photograph policies, the following should be considered:

1. Review applicable federal and state statutes
2. Not require photographs on applications or at interviews
3. Use photographs only for legitimate business purposes; i.e., for job performance monitoring
4. Obtain employee consent when photographs are used in employer literature or advertisements

Sample Policies

The following example should be considered in drafting photograph policies:

PHOTOGRAPH POLICY

The Company shall not require, as a condition to securing or retaining employment, that an applicant or employee be photographed where photographs could be used to the applicant's or employee's detriment in a non-job-related manner.

Photograph Consent Form

A consent to use employee photographs should be executed at hiring, and may take the following form:

PHOTOGRAPH CONSENT

The Company may use my name, picture, or likeness for any advertising, publicity, or other legitimate business purpose, regardless of whether I am employed by the Company when my name, picture, or likeness is used. This consent is given in consideration of my employment. The legitimate use of my name, picture, or likeness will not result in an invasion of privacy, defamation, intentional infliction of emotional distress, or a violation of any other property right that I may have. I understand that I will receive no additional consideration, compensation, or benefit if my name, picture, or likeness is used. Any negatives, prints, or other material for printing or reproduction in connection with the use of my name, picture, or likeness shall be the Company's property.

_____   _____

Date   Employee

_____

Witness

PHYSICAL EXAMINATIONS

The employer's right to require applicants to undergo a physical examination is considered basic to the hiring process. [See *Conveyor Co.*, 38 Lab. Arb. (BNA) 1141 (1962) (Roberts, Arb.) (employer's good faith right to require physical examination).] Physical examinations may be administered at the final hiring process step after an employment offer has been made that is contingent upon satisfactory completion of a job-related physical examination. Situations also arise that necessitate requiring job-related physical examinations during the employment relationship. [See, e.g., *Pittsburgh Plate Glass Co.*, 52 Lab. Arb. (BNA) 985 (1969) (Duff, Arb.) (employer's right to require physical examination after sick leave).]

Employers may require employees to have physical examinations under legitimate job-related circumstances. This need may arise where an employee desires to return to work following an accident, sick leave, or extended layoff, has exercised a bid on a job requiring greater physical effort, etc. [See, e.g., *Chris-Craft Corp.*, 27 Lab. Arb. (BNA) 404 (1956) (Bothwell, Arb.) (employer could require physical examination in recall).] It has also been acknowledged that this right is not an absolute one exercisable at the employer's whim that cannot be arbitrarily insisted upon without reasonable grounds. [*Conchemco, Inc.*, 55 Lab. Arb. (BNA) 54 (1970) (Ray, Arb.).] Unreasonable requests for physical examinations could expose employers to liability under federal and state fair employment practice (FEP) statutes.

Drafting

In drafting physical examination policies, the following should be considered:

1. Conditions for administering
   a. After an employment offer has been made
   b. After hiring
      (i)   Accidents
      (ii) Sick leave
      (iii) Layoff
      (iv) Job bids
2. Partial or full payment by
   a. Applicant
   b. Employee or
   c. Employer
3. Establishing relationships with one or more physicians because the physician
   a. Understands the job's physical requirements
   b. Is able to provide a faster conclusion regarding employment eligibility
   c. Is familiar with required paperwork
   d. Provides a more convenient means for dialogue with the human resources staff
4. Dispute resolution

Sample Policies

The following examples should be considered in drafting physical examination policies:

PHYSICAL EXAMINATION-HEALTH CARE EMPLOYER

As an employment condition, employees will be required at the Company's cost to have a job-related physical examination completed by a physician currently licensed to practice in [state's name] after an employment offer has been made. A written statement from the examining physician shall verify that the individual is free from communicable diseases that may disqualify him or her for the position for which he or she is seeking employment. A written report of a chest x-ray completed within the past 60 calendar days or a tuberculin skin test (Mantoux) done within 72 hours after the employee reports to work will also be required. All employees with a positive reaction from the skin test will be required to have a chest x-ray at their expense. During employment, the Company at its cost, reserves the right to require employees as a condition to continuing or maintaining employment to undergo periodic job-related physical examinations.

PHYSICAL EXAMINATION REQUIRED

To determine medical fitness for employment after an employment offer has been made, the Company may require job-related physical examinations by a Company-employed physician at the Company's expense. Should an employee be found medically unfit to work at his or her assigned job, the Company will furnish the employee a copy of the physician's report or a physician's statement. Any employee may also be examined at his or her own expense by a physician selected by him or her and the physician's report may be submitted to the Company for consideration.

PHYSICAL EXAMINATION REQUIRED FOR CONTAGIOUS DISEASES OR FOR SANITARY MEASURES

Section 1. Contagious Diseases. The Company may require physical examinations for contagious diseases. To protect the lives and well-being of all, employees with untreated or incurable contagious diseases may be given an unpaid medical leave, laid off, or terminated, depending upon the medical evaluation.

Section 2. Sanitary Measures. The Company may require a physical examination of any employee should it appear necessary as a sanitary or safety measure. The physical examination shall be made by the Company's physician at the Company's expense.

PHYSICAL EXAMINATION AFTER ACCIDENT
OR SICKNESS

Section 1. Physical Examination Required. If an employee has been absent because of accident or sickness, the Company may require a job-related physical examination by a physician of the employee's choice.

Section 2. Result Disputes. Should the Company disagree with the employee's physician's decision, he or she may be examined by a physician of the Company's choosing, provided that notification of this intent is given to the employee. Any costs incurred by this physician will be paid by the Company.

If the Company's physician indicates that the employee can return to work, the employee will be notified in writing by the physician making the determination.

If the matter cannot be resolved, the Company and the employee will select a third physician. The third physician will examine the employee and make a determination concerning the employee's status. Any expense incurred by the third physician will be paid by the Company. The third physician's finding will be final and binding on the employee and the Company.

PHYSICAL EXAMINATIONS FOR EMPLOYEES
IN HAZARDOUS JOBS

To protect employees while working on jobs that may constitute health hazards, employees may, upon the Company's request or the employee's, be given a Company-paid physical examination. If the examination is made by a Company physician, the physical examination report, upon the employee's written request, will be sent to the employee's physician.

PHYSICAL EXAMINATION EMPLOYEE
COMPENSATION

The Company may require employee job-related physical examinations or tests made by its physician at its expense. Where possible, the physical examination will be scheduled during the employee's normal working hours. The Company will compensate the employee for the time involved at the employee's applicable pay rate for a Company-required physical examination that occurs during the employee's normal working hours or outside the employee's normal working hours.

PHYSICAL EXAMINATION INFORMATION AVAILABLE TO EMPLOYEE'S PHYSICIAN

Employee physical examinations may be arranged by the Company only when job-related and only after notifying the employee with an explanation of the specific reasons for the examination. Report copies of these physical examinations and medical treatments will be maintained by the Company in its Medical Department and will be available to the employee's physician if authorized in writing by the employee.

PHYSICAL EXAMINATION CONFIDENTIALITY

The Company will maintain physical examination result confidentiality. These results shall be furnished only to the employee's designated physician upon the employee's written authorization; provided that the Company may use or supply physical examination results in response to subpoenas, requests to the Company by any governmental agency authorized by law to obtain these reports, and in arbitration or litigation of any claim or action involving the Company.

PHYSICAL EXAMINATION RESULTS DISPUTE: MEDICAL ARBITRATOR

Section 1. Physical Examinations Required. An employee must meet certain job-related health and physical fitness standards as determined by a physical examination given by a Company-designated physician after an employment offer has been made. After employment, periodic job-related physical examinations may be offered or required to aid an employee in improving health or to enable the Company to ensure its employees' health.

Section 2. Results. An employee, upon request, shall have the opportunity to discuss his or her physical examination's results with the Company's physician. Upon the employee's request, the information will be made available to his or her personal physician.

Section 3. Result Disputes. Should the Company's physician determine that an applicant/employee cannot perform the job hired for or currently held because of an existing medical condition, and should a dispute arise between the Company's physician and the employee's personal physician regarding the determination, a complaint may be filed with the Human Resources Department.

If the complaint is not resolved by the Human Resources Department, the applicant/employee, the Company's physician, and the applicant's/employee's personal physician shall exchange x-rays and medical reports within ten (10) calendar days of the date the complaint was filed with the Human Resources Department.

If, after exchanging of x-rays and medical reports, final agreement cannot be reached regarding the medical findings and conclusions, the applicant/employee may, within fourteen (14) calendar days after the exchange, refer the dispute to the Company's President, who shall attempt to resolve the problem by examining all available medical evidence.

If a dispute still exists regarding the applicant's/employee's medical condition after the Company President's review, the dispute may be presented to an impartial medical arbitrator selected by mutual agreement of the parties in accordance with the following:

a. Within fourteen (14) calendar days following the dispute's referral to the Company's President, all x-rays and medical reports shall be forwarded to the medical arbitrator.

b. With fourteen (14) calendar days thereafter, the medical arbitrator shall conduct whatever employee examination is deemed necessary and appropriate, and shall meet with the two physicians, along with any medical experts, to discuss the findings.

c. Within fourteen (14) calendar days thereafter, the medical arbitrator shall submit to the Company and the applicant/employee a written determination.

d. Any of the time limits provided herein may be extended by the parties' mutual written agreement.

e. The charges and expenses of the medical arbitrator shall be paid by the Company.

f. The determination of the medical arbitrator shall be final and binding on the Company and the applicant/employee.

REFERENCE CHECKS

Reference checks represent another employer effort to compile and verify the most complete and accurate information regarding applicants. From the former employer's perspective, detailed reference requests present a litigation risk against the former employer by the former employee. Many employers limit their reference request response to verifying the former employee's employment dates, job title, and salary. However, requesting detailed references from former employers is one precaution an employer can take during the hiring process to limit its vulnerability to employment litigation.

Some states statutorily regulate employee references. [See, e.g., Cal. Labor Code §§ 1050, 1052 (West 1971) (California's statute regulating employee references).] Federal and state fair employment practice (FEP) statutes along with claims for invasion of privacy and defamation may also offer employee protection. [See, e.g., *Cummings v. Walsh Constr. Co.*, 561 F. Supp. 872 (S.D. Ga. 1983) (invasion of privacy without broad public disclosure); *Lewis v. Equitable Life*

Assurance Soc'y, 361 N.W.2d 875 (Minn. Ct. App. 1985), *aff'd in pertinent part,* 389 N.W.2d 876 (Minn. 1986) (defamation where false termination reason given to employees).]

As long as only job-related information is requested, references should not place the prospective employer or a former employer in jeopardy for employee claims. A defense to an invasion of privacy or defamation claim is that a former employer has a qualified privilege to communicate in good faith when responding to an inquiry by a prospective employer with a legitimate job-related information interest.

By failing to request references, the employer may risk negligent hiring liability. [See, e.g., *Welch Mfg., Div. of Textron, Inc. v. Pinkerton's, Inc.*, 474 A.2d 436 (R.I. 1984) (prior company theft by a security guard); *Burch v. A & G Assocs., Inc.*, 122 Mich. App. 798, 333 N.W.2d 140 (1983) (assault committed by a driver).] Negligent hiring arises out of employee acts committed while in the employer's service but outside the employee's employment scope. While an employer generally is not liable for employee acts outside of the employment's scope, employer liability for negligent hiring has been found where an employee was responsible for others' safety or security.

General Considerations

In the narrowest sense, references are those individuals listed by an applicant who can furnish pertinent information about the applicant's qualifications. Normally, references are requested as part of the application. References are sometimes considered valueless, because applicants may only use persons whom they feel will provide favorable information, and because the information furnished is usually subjective and/or not job-related. Reference problems can be minimized by placing the following constraints on applicants:

1. Applicants should be instructed to list only those references who have known the applicant for a given time period and have direct knowledge of the applicant's qualifications as they relate to the job's specifications
2. Request the applicant briefly to justify why the reference is qualified to provide this information
3. Applicants should be requested to sign releases waiving their rights to review job-related information furnished by a reference
4. References should be sent a copy of the waiver, indicating that the applicant has waived review rights
5. References should be sent a copy of the job specifications and requested to use their knowledge to compare the applicant's qualifications with the job's specifications
6. References should be contacted in person or by telephone to discuss an applicant's qualifications or to verify information

Reference Check Methods

Proper reference checking is time-consuming. It demands personal involvement and extends beyond having someone make telephone calls to references listed on an application. Possible approaches to reference-checking include:

1. Meeting with the applicant's references because:
   a. People are much more willing to be open in person
   b. It provides the opportunity to interpret facial expressions and body language which may, in addition to words, indicate how the reference actually feels about the applicant's prior work performance
2. Using the telephone
3. Checking references by mail

Providing References

In providing references, the following should be considered:

1. Review the legal aspects concerning what job-related information can be disclosed
2. Check that the human resources staff has distributed procedures and policies regarding job-related information disclosure:
   a. Content
   b. Circumstances
   c. Eligible persons
3. Ensure that the job-related information's accuracy is substantiated by factual records
4. Communicate the procedure and policy regarding references
5. Instruct all personnel that they are not to discuss another employee's performance with those outside the company
6. Maintain a policy of truthfulness and accuracy in making employee evaluations, especially in cases involving termination decisions
7. Ensure that communications, whether oral or written, internal or external, concern job-related matters only
8. Use a written release, where possible, to obtain the employee's consent to provide job-related information to prospective employers and to release the employer from all claims that might arise from providing references
9. Centralize the process of providing references
10. Provide job-related information on a need-to-know basis only

Reference Checking Cautions

In checking references, the following should be considered:

1. Obtain the employee's written permission to check references

2. Check references before making the final job offer
3. If a discrepancy exists between facts or recommendations, a more extensive investigation should be undertaken
4. Be skeptical of all subjective evaluations, especially those that do not include verifiable acts or behavior
5. View silence as an indication for further investigation; an employer may attempt to avoid wrongful termination litigation by negotiating a settlement with an employee that includes no unfavorable references
6. Obtain as many references as possible, and investigate all of them before the applicant is hired
7. Interview the applicant thoroughly and make complete notes of the interview
8. Ask the applicant to explain any gaps in employment history
9. Ask the applicant to state what his or her previous supervisor or manager would say if asked about the applicant's job qualifications
10. Encourage the applicant to sign a form releasing job-related information from former employers
11. Although expensive, the use of a commercial service to investigate the applicant may be desirable, especially for higher-level positions or positions of a sensitive nature.

Sample Policies

The following example should be considered in drafting reference policies:

REFERENCE CHECKING POLICY

Absent an employee or a former employee's written consent, the Company will not provide job-related or other information, except name, job title, and employment dates, regarding its current or former employees unless required by federal or state law or court order. All employee information requests must be referred to the Human Resources Department. Supervisors or other employees are not permitted to respond to a reference request. Telephone inquiries will not be answered. Only written inquiries from the person seeking the information on that person's letterhead with name and title will be considered.

Information Release Form

The following forms should be used by employers when requesting references on behalf of applicants or employees:

INFORMATION RELEASE FORM

I, __(Name)__ , hereby authorize the Company to release the following job-related information regarding my employment with the Company to (Company's Name, Person, etc.) and release you from any and all liability arising out of the disclosure of this job-related information:

Job-Related Information List:

_____

_____

_____

_____

_____

Date:_____   _____
                                              Signed

INFORMATION RELEASE FORM

Employment reference for:

_____

Job Title: _____

I have stated to the ____(Company's Name)____ that I was employed by you as a ___(Position Title)___ . I request that the following job-related information be furnished by you for reference purposes to this employer and I consent to you providing this job-related information regarding my past employment, work performance, attendance record, abilities, and reason for my employment separation. I further release you from any and all liability that may arise out of your release of this job-related information.

_____
                              (Name)

_____
           (Date)

Employed as: _____

From:_____   To:_____

Reason for leaving:_____

_____

_____

_____

Would you re-employ this individual:_____

Please check below the rating that most accurately describes this individual:

	Satisfactory	Unsatisfactory
Work Quality	_____	_____
Work Quantity	_____	_____
Cooperation	_____	_____
Supervision	_____	_____
Attendance	_____	_____

Other remarks regarding job-related performance that may be relevant to the position requested: _____

_____

_____

_____

_____
(Name)

_____
(Position)

_____
(Company)

_____
(Address)

_____
(Telephone)

_____
(Date)

Telephone Reference Check

The following form should be used by employers when requesting references on behalf of applicants or employees through a telephone reference check:

TELEPHONE REFERENCE CHECK

Applicant's name: _____

Person contacted:_____ Title:_____

Company: _____

Business type: _____

Address: _____

Telephone: _____

Dates of employment: _____

_____

_____

Position : _____

Job functions: _____

Work quantity: _____

_____

_____

Work quality: _____

_____

_____

Initiative: _____

_____

_____

Work habits:_____

_____

_____

Cooperation with others: _____

_____

_____

Attendance: _____

_____

_____

Limitations: _____

_____

_____

Reason for separation: _____

_____

_____

Would you re-employ? _____ Why/Why not? _____

_____

_____

_____

Would you recommend the applicant for this position (describe position)? _____

_____

Why/Why not? _____

_____

Completed by: _____

Position title: _____

Date: _____

SKILL TESTING

Employers desire to fill jobs with applicants qualified for the work assigned. Skill testing offers an objective standard by which to predict job performance. Some tests, however, eliminate minorities from certain positions. [See *United States v. South Carolina*, 434 U.S. 1026 (1978); *Dothard v. Rawlinson*, 433 U.S. 321 (1977); *Washington v. Davis*, 426 U.S. 229 (1976); *Albemarle Paper Co. v. Moody*, 422 U.S. 405 (1975); *Griggs v. Duke Power Co.*, 401 U.S. 424 (1971); *United States v. Georgia Power Co.*, 474 F.2d 906 (5th Cir. 1972); *Hicks v. Crown Zellerbach Corp.*, 319 F. Supp. 314 (E.D. La. 1970); *Hobson v. Hansen*, 269 F. Supp. 401 (D.D.C. 1967).]

Educational and industrial psychologists have played a major role in developing tests that attempt to predict job performance. These tests remove some of the subjectivity used in employee selection. Employment testing has developed into a highly sophisticated and technical field with its own language, its own standards, and its own complex methodology. Testing is:

> not primarily a legal subject; it is part of the general field of educational and industrial psychology, and possesses its own methodology, its own body of research, its own experts, and its own terminology. The transition of a technical study such as this into a set of legal principles requires a clear awareness of the limits of both testing and law. It would be entirely inappropriate for the law to ignore what has been learned about employment testing in assessing the validity of these tests. At the same time, the science of testing is not as precise as physics or chemistry, nor its conclusions as provable. While courts should draw upon the findings of experts in the field of testing, they should not hesitate to subject these findings to both the scrutiny of reason and the

guidance of Congressional intent. [See *Guardians Ass'n of N.Y. City Police Dep't v. Civil Serv. Comm'n*, 630 F.2d 79, 89 (2d Cir. 1980).]

Test is a generic word encompassing a systematic method of measuring applicant qualifications through pencil and paper instruments, oral questions, the performance of exercises, or the manipulation of objects. Tests may be commercially prepared or custom-constructed by an employer or consultant. Tests can be grouped into the following categories:

1. *Achievement test,* which measures the extent of a person's knowledge or competence within a field
2. *Aptitude test,* which measures innate or acquired capacities to learn an occupation
3. *Interest inventory,* which, while nominally a test, is more a self-assessment of interests that either correlate to those individuals who are successfully employed in a particular occupation or can otherwise be used to determine an individual's suitability for a particular job
4. *Manual dexterity or motor test,* which measures a number of motor functions, including reaction time, quickness of arm movements, multilimb coordination, and finger dexterity
5. *Mental ability test,* which measures the ability to reason, perceive relationships, understand numerical properties, and solve quantitative problems
6. *Performance test,* which measures demonstrated performance, usually on a piece of equipment
7. *Sensory test,* which measures hearing and vision, including color vision
8. *Situational test,* which is a generic term for a variety of exercises that measure an applicant's responses to workplace situations
9. *Competitive group exercise,* which assigns roles to applicants who receive various instructions concerning how the role should be played
10. *In-basket test,* which evaluates applicants' abilities to handle a work basket of events representative of those encountered on the job they are seeking
11. *Computer game,* which measures the ability of applicants to evaluate information, usually quantitative data, plan responses, and make decisions
12. *Work sample,* which measures an applicant's performance on an important job task representative of what could actually occur on the job
13. *Role playing,* which is typically two persons playing assigned roles; however, role playing differs from group exercises with assigned roles because only two people are involved. It is used to test for applicant knowledge, training skills, and abilities in handling employee performance appraisal interviews, evaluating employee ideas, assisting employees in receiving help for personal problems, and resolving disciplinary problems

14. *Assessment center,* a selection method in which participants engage in multiple exercises, some of which are simulations, and their performance is appraised by pooled assessments of trained assessors

Federal fair employment practice (FEP) statutes generally require that a protected classification not be a factor in employment selection. [See *Melanson v. Rantoul,* 536 F. Supp. 271 (D.R.I. 1982).] If a selection procedure has a disproportionate impact that excludes protected persons, its use is unlawful unless the procedure is demonstrably a reasonable job performance measure; i.e., unless it is job-related or justified by business necessity. [See *Griggs v. Duke Power Co.,* 401 U.S. 424 (1971).]

Under the Civil Rights Act of 1964 (Title VII), [42 U.S.C. §§ 2000e-1 to 2002-17 (1994) (Civil Rights Act of 1964)] the Uniform Guidelines on Employee Selection Procedures have been developed. [43 Fed. Reg. 38290, 29 C.F.R. § 1607.1 *et seq.* (1999). The Uniform Guidelines, as published by the Office of Federal Contract Compliance and Procedures (OFCCP), are found at 41 C.F.R. pt. 60-3.] [See **Appendix C.**] The Guidelines define a *selection procedure* broadly as any measure, combination of measures, or procedure used as a basis for an employment decision, including hiring, promotion, membership, referral, retention, selection, training, or transfer. Selection procedures include traditional paper and pencil tests, performance tests, training programs, probationary periods, informal or casual interviews, unscored application forms, and physical, educational, and work experience requirements.

Title VII does not prohibit employers from giving or acting on the results of a professionally developed ability test where the test, its administration, and action on it are not designed, intended, or used to discriminate. However, a professionally developed test must be job-related. [See *Griggs v. Duke Power Co.,* 401 U.S. 424 (1971).]

Skill Testing Effectiveness and Propriety

The following should be considered regarding skill testing effectiveness and propriety:

1. Objectivity, by identifying characteristics of mind and skill necessary for a particular job while disregarding race, religion, politics, sex, residence, age, etc.
2. Validity, in that the test actually measures what it purports to measure by evaluating applicants in exactly the same relationship to one another as they would stand after on-the-job performance
3. Reliability as a consistent measuring instrument, in that a person taking the same test on different occasions should receive substantially the same score each time

Skill Testing Use Determinations

In determining whether testing should be used, the following should be considered:

1. A determination of the selection objective: a given position, occupation, program, career, etc
2. A determination of basic selection standards: what skills and knowledge are necessary
3. Labor market: whether qualified applicants are available for testing
4. Cost utility: whether the testing can be done economically without becoming extremely costly

Drafting

In drafting skill testing policies, the following should be considered:

1. Review applicable federal and state statutes
2. Do not over-rely on tests
3. Use other screening methods, including interviews, background verifications, and reference checks, along with tests
4. Use test results as added information
5. Contact the test's developer to recheck the test if someone receives an extremely poor score but has good recommendations, job performance, etc.
6. Use tests at the end of the hiring process when applicants have been narrowed to the best choices
7. Maintain test score confidentiality
8. Ensure that the test is job-related and does not measure extraneous non-job-related factors

Sample Policies

The following example should be considered in drafting skill testing policies:

TESTING POLICY

Section 1. Testing Procedures. In addition to written, oral, and performance tests, the Company may authorize an evaluation of education and experience, and other types of tests, singly or in combination as job-related circumstances warrant. For promotional tests, the Company may authorize other performance criteria involving seniority and performance evaluations developed under a uniform system.

Section 2. Test Scheduling. The Company shall give due consideration to the convenience of the applicants, consistent with its needs, in determining dates, times, and locations of tests.

Section 3. Security.

    a. The Company will establish appropriate procedures to ensure that all applicants for a test are given equal opportunity to demonstrate their qualifications in that:

        (i) The Company will establish proper precautions to prevent an unauthorized person from securing in advance questions or other materials to be used in a test, unless the questions or materials are available to all applicants; and

        (ii) When the conditions under which a test is held have materially impaired its competitive nature or worth in assessing qualifications, the Company will order that the tests or appropriate sections thereof, if severable, be cancelled. New tests or parts of tests may be substituted, if possible.

    b. The Company will establish appropriate procedures to ensure that the identity of the applicants in all tests does not adversely affect the objective rating or scoring of test papers.

    c. The Company will disqualify an applicant who impersonates another or has another person impersonate himself or herself in connection with a test, or who uses or attempts to use unauthorized aids or assistance, including copying, or attempting to copy from or helping or attempting to help another applicant in any part of a test, or who otherwise seeks to attain undue advantage in connection with the test.

    d. No applicant in a test shall copy, record, or transcribe any test question or answer, or remove from the testing room any question sheet, answer sheet, booklet, scrap papers, notes, or other papers or materials related to the test's content. Applicants shall be notified of this action and no examiner, proctor, monitor, or other person charged with the supervision of an applicant or group of applicants shall have authority to waive it. The Company may disqualify a candidate or refuse to certify an eligible person who violates this Section.

Section 4. Preservation of Test Records. The Company shall ensure that the following documents are maintained as official records:

    a. The test's original copy;

    b. The test's description;

    c. The test's instructions;

    d. The scoring keys or other scoring standards used;

    e. The examiners' reports; and

    f. The resulting eligible list.

Section 5. Test Paper Inspection.

a. The Company will, upon request of an applicant, authorize the applicant to inspect his or her test documents in the presence of an authorized Company official. The inspection shall not include authorization to copy test instructions, questions, or answers, and will be conducted to maintain security of the testing program.

b. The Company may authorize review of the application and test papers of an applicant, upon request and for official purposes, by law enforcement or other public officials where there are legitimate inspection reasons. Copies of test materials will not be made available except as provided by applicable statutes or regulations.

c. The Company will authorize the disclosure of applications and test papers to a private individual only where the individual seeking access can demonstrate a clear necessity to pursue a legitimate legal right. The Company will take necessary precautions to avoid disclosure of the identities of the persons whose applications and test papers are being examined. Where it is evident that the information release would operate to prejudice or impair a person's reputation or personal security, access to the information shall be denied.

Section 6. Information Regarding Unsuccessful Applicants. Except as provided in Section 5 (Test Paper Inspection), the test papers of applicants who failed all or part of a test or who voluntarily withdrew from the test shall not be exhibited or disclosed nor shall information be released concerning their test participation.

Chapter 4

Federal and State Statutes Affecting the Hiring Process

MAJOR FEDERAL STATUTORY PROVISIONS

Age Discrimination In Employment Act of 1967 (ADEA)

The Age Discrimination in Employment Act (ADEA) prohibits discrimination in employment, including termination, on account of age, provided that the employee is over the age of 40. [29 U.S.C. §§ 621-634 (1994) (Age Discrimination in Employment Act).] The ADEA applies to public and private sector employers employing 20 or more workers for at least 20 weeks per year.

There are several exceptions to the general prohibition against an employer's use of an employee's age in making an employment decision. An employer is free to observe the terms of a bona fide seniority system or any bona fide employee benefits plan such as retirement, pension or insurance plans, so long as observance of the terms of the plan is not used as a subterfuge to evade the ADEA's purposes. Traditionally, it is not a violation of the ADEA where age is a bona fide occupational qualification reasonably necessary to the normal operation of a particular business. The termination or discipline of employees for good cause is another exception under the ADEA.

The involuntary retirement of employees in the protected age bracket on account of age pursuant to a seniority system or employee benefit plan is generally not permissible. However, compulsory retirement for bona fide executives aged 65 and over entitled to receive income in excess of $44,000 per year is permissible.

Filing procedures under the ADEA are patterned after the Civil Rights Act of 1964 (Title VII). The complaining individual must file a charge of unlawful discrimination with the Equal Employment Opportunities Commission (EEOC) within 180 days of the alleged unlawful act or within 300 days if a state agency is involved. The EEOC will investigate the complaint and attempt conciliation before bringing a court action. It will not issue a "right-to-sue" letter to the complaining individual, however, as it would under Title VII. The ADEA only requires that the discrimination charge be filed with the EEOC at least 60 days before suit is brought in court. Also unlike Title VII, the ADEA expressly provides for a jury trial.

Americans with Disabilities Act (ADA)

The Americans with Disabilities Act (ADA) was created by Congress to eliminate discrimination in employment against those with physical or mental disabilities. [29 U.S.C. §§ 12101-12213 (Supp. 1992) (Americans with Disabilities Act).] The Equal Employment Opportunities Commission (EEOC) administers the ADA and enforcement procedures under the ADA are the same as for the Civil Rights Act of 1964 (Title VII).

The ADA applies to the same employers covered by Title VII; i.e., employers in interstate commerce who employ 15 or more employees each working day during 20 weeks of the current or preceding calendar year. Indian tribes and bona fide private clubs are specifically excluded from coverage.

Under the ADA, an employer may not discriminate against a qualified individual with a disability. A "qualified individual" is an individual who, with or without reasonable accommodation, can perform the essential functions of his or her job.

Civil Rights Act of 1964 (Title VII)

The United States Equal Employment Opportunity Commission (EEOC) was created by Congress in 1964 to administer Title VII of the Civil Rights Act of 1964. [42 U.S.C. §§ 2000e-1 to 2002-17 (1994) (Civil Rights Act of 1964).] Title VII prohibits discrimination in employment on the basis of race, color, religion, sex, or national origin. The EEOC was given the authority to investigate and conciliate complaints of alleged employment discrimination.

Title VII applies to those employers in interstate commerce who employ 15 or more employees each working day during 20 weeks of the current or preceding calendar year. Indian tribes, bona fide private clubs, and religious institutions are specifically excluded from coverage. Employment agencies, labor organizations, and joint labor-management apprenticeship committees also are governed by Title VII.

An individual who believes he or she is the victim of employment discrimination must file a complaint with the EEOC within 180 days of the alleged discriminatory act or within 300 days of the act where a state fair employment agency is present. The EEOC is required to first allow the state's fair employment agency 60 days in which to investigate and resolve a complaint. However, while the EEOC is required to give substantial weight to the findings and orders issued by the state agency, the EEOC is not bound by them. The EEOC will conduct its own investigation of the charge. Following its investigation, the EEOC may:

1. Recommend dismissal of the charge
2. Issue a finding of "probable cause"
3. Institute a lawsuit on behalf of the individual complainant or
4. File a class action lawsuit

Upon finding "probable cause," the EEOC will attempt conciliation. If conciliation fails or the EEOC recommends dismissal, the EEOC will issue a "right-to-sue" letter to the complaining individual. The individual then has 90 days within which to file a private lawsuit in federal district court. The EEOC may intervene in a private lawsuit, but may not file its own action after a private lawsuit has been filed.

Equal Pay Act

Under the Equal Pay Act, paying workers of one sex at a rate different from that paid the other sex, where the jobs in question involve equal skill, effort, and responsibility and are performed under similar working conditions in the same establishment is unlawful. [29 U.S.C. § 206(d) (1994) (Equal Pay Act).] The Equal Pay Act is enforced by the Equal Employment Opportunities Commission (EEOC).

Unless a specific exemption applies, the sex-bias ban on the payment of wage differentials applies to employees of any enterprise that has two or more employees engaged in interstate commerce, or in the production of goods for interstate commerce, or in handling or otherwise working on goods or materials that have moved in or were produced for interstate commerce.

When a violation of the Equal Pay Act occurs, an equalizing of wages may be accomplished only by increasing those of the lower paid sex to those of the higher paid sex. The standard used in comparing the work performed by different sex groups is substantial equality. The jobs need not be identical.

National Labor Relations Act (NLRA)

The National Labor Relations Act (NLRA) was enacted to provide a method in the private sector of establishing employee representation for collective bargaining purposes by eliminating coercion, restraint, or interference with employee rights. [29 U.S.C. §§ 151-168 (1994).] To implement the NLRA's policies, the National Labor Relations Board (NLRB) was created to regulate private sector employment relations. The NLRB has judicial and rule-making powers.

The NLRA applies to private sector employers and employees involved in interstate commerce. Enterprises covered by the Railway Labor Act are excluded along with public sector employers and those engaged in agriculture.

Employees have the right to self-organization, to engage in concerted activities such as strikes, to bargain collectively through representatives of their own choosing, and to refrain from these activities. The NLRA regulates employer illegal conduct through unfair labor practices. An employer cannot interfere with, restrain, or coerce employees in the exercise of their NLRA rights. It cannot dominate, support, or interfere with the formation or administration of a labor organization. Likewise, an employer cannot discriminate in hiring, tenure of employment, or any term or condition of employment to encourage or discourage labor organization. [*Id.* 29 U.S.C. § 158(a)(3) (1992); see, e.g., *Republic Aviation Corp. v. NLRB*, 324 U.S. 793 (1945) (termination of a union steward by an employer for wearing union insignia constituted a violation).] Employees are protected in filing unfair labor practice charges and participating in their investigation. The employer cannot refuse to bargain collectively with its employees' representative. [29 U.S.C. § 158(a)(4) (1992); see *Stop-N-Go Foods*, 279 N.L.R.B. 344 (1986) (refusal to hire illegal where based on applicant's prior unfair labor practice charge filing and testifying against prior employer).]

The NLRA's representation procedures empower the NLRB to determine the appropriate bargaining unit and the extent of employee interest. NLRB procedures are available to certify a union elected by a majority of employees who vote in an appropriate bargaining unit, to decertify an incumbent union, and to certify or modify a bargaining unit's structure.

The NLRA outlines the procedure for enforcement and review of NLRB orders in unfair labor practice cases. Decisions in representation cases generally are reviewable only in the context of a related unfair labor practice case, when the representation proceedings become part of the "entire record." An aggrieved party may file a petition to enforce or deny any NLRB order in the federal court of appeals for the circuit within which the alleged unfair labor practice occurred, or the District of Columbia. Injunctive relief is available while an unfair labor practice complaint is pending.

STATE STATUTES

Fair Employment Practice (FEP) Statutes

Fair employment practice (FEP) statutes prohibiting employment discrimination are found in various states. Because these FEP statutes were enacted in response to different state needs and political pressures they are not exactly alike. The typical FEP statute contains a list of employer actions involving hiring and termination that must be exercised in a nondiscriminatory manner. They prohibit employers from making inquiries that express any limitation because of race, creed, color, national origin, sex, age, or disability. [See, e.g., Alaska Stat. § 18.80.220 (1986); Ariz. Rev. Stat. Ann. § 41-1463(B) (1985); Cal. Gov't Code

§§ 11135, 12900 (West 1980); Colo. Rev. Stat. § 24-34-402 (1980); Conn. Gen. Stat. § 46a-60 (1986); Del. Code Ann. tit. 19. § 711 (1985); D.C. Code Ann. § 1-2512 (1981); Ga. Code § 34-1-2 (age) § 34-6A-4 (disability) (1982); Hawaii Rev. Stat. § 378-2 (1985); Idaho Code §§ 56-701, 67-5909 (1980); Ill. Rev. Stat. ch. 68. § 2-102 (West Supp. 1999); Ind. Code § 22-9-1-2 (1986); Iowa Code § 601A.6 (1975); Kan. Stat. Ann. § 44-1009 (1986); Ky. Rev. Stat. § 344.040 (1986); La. Rev. Stat. Ann. § 46:1721 (West 1982) (disability only); Me. Rev. Stat. Ann. tit. 5, § 4572 (Supp. 1999); Mass. Gen. Laws Ann. ch. 151B. § 4 (West 1982); Minn. Stat. § 363.03 (Supp. 1999); Mo. Rev. Stat. § 213.010 (Supp. 1999); Mont. Code Ann. § 49-2-303 (1985); Neb. Rev. Stat. § 48-1104 (1984); Nev. Rev. Stat. § 613.330 (1986); N.H. Rev. Stat. Ann. §§ 275:40, 354-A:1 (1977); N.M. Stat. Ann. § 28-1-17 (1978); N.Y. Exec. Law § 296 (Compil. 1983); N.C. Gen. Stat. §143-422.2 (1985); N.D. Cent. Code § 34-01-19 (1980); Okla. Stat. tit. 25 § 1302 (1986); Or. Rev. Stat. § 659.030 (1983); Pa. Stat. Ann. tit. 43. §§ 951-963 (Purdon 1991); R.I. Gen. Law § 28-5-7 (1986); S.C. Code Ann. § 1-13-10 (Law. Co-op. 1986); S.D. Codified Laws Ann. § 20-13-10 (1979); Tenn. Code Ann. § 4-21-105 (1985); Utah Code Ann. § 34-35-6 (Supp. 1999); Vt. Stat. Ann. tit. 21 § 495 (Supp. 1999); Wash. Rev. Code §§ 49.60.030.49.60.180 (1982); Wis. Stat. §§ 111.31, 111.321, 111.322, 111.325 (Supp. 1999); Wyo. Stat. § 27-9-105 (1985).]

Labor Relations Statutes

States have adopted private and public sector labor relations acts similar to the provisions of the National Labor Relations Act (NLRA) that regulate collective bargaining. [Private Sector. See, e.g. Ala. Code § 25-7-35 (1986); Ariz. Rev. Stat. Ann. §§ 23-1305, 23-1242 (West 1983); Ark. Stat. Ann. § 81-202 (1976); Cal. Lab. Code § 922 (West 1972); Colo. Rev. Stat. § 8-2-104 (1974 & Supp. 1999); Conn Gen. Stat. § 31-105 (West 1987); Ga. Code Ann. §§ 34-6-6, 34-6-21, 34-6-22 (1982); Hawaii Rev. Stat. § 377-6 (1985); Iowa Code Ann. § 731.1 (West 1979); Kan. Stat. Ann. § 44-808 (1986); La. Rev. Stat. Ann. § 23:983 (West 1985); Mass. Gen. Laws Ann. tit. 149, § 20 (West 1982); Minn. Stat. §§ 179.12, 179.18, 179.60 (1966); Miss. Code Ann. § 71-1-47 (1973); Nev. Rev. Stat. §§ 163.340, 614.080 (1986); N.H. Rev. Stat. Ann. § 275.1 (1978); N.C. Gen. Stat. §§ 95-80, 95-81 (1985); N.D. Cent. Code § 34-01 (1980); Or. Rev. Stat. § 663.125 (1983); Pa. Stat. Ann. tit. 43, §§ 211.1-.13 (Purdon 1992); R.I. Gen. Law § 28-7-13 (1986); S.C. Code Ann. § 41-1-20, 41-7-70 (Law. Co-op. 1986); S.D. Codified Laws Ann. § 60-8-6 (1978); Tenn. Code Ann. § 50-1-210 (1983); Tex. Code Ann. art. 5207(a) (Vernon 1987); Utah Code Ann. §§ 34-34-8, 34-34-9, 34-34-13, 34-20-8 (1974); Va. Code §§ 40.1-60, 40.1-61 (1986); Wyo. Stat. §§ 27-7-109, 27-7-110 (1985). Public Sector. See, e.g., Conn Gen. Stat. §7-470(c) (1984) (municipal employees); Conn. Gen. Stat. § 10-153e(d) (1984) (teachers); Del. Code Ann. tit. 14, § 4002(e) (Supp. 1999) (public school employees); Del. Code

Ann. tit. 19, § 1301(5) (1985) (public employees); Hawaii Rev. Stat. § 89-2(5) (Supp. 1999) (public employees); Ill. Pub. Labor Relations Act § 7.111. Rev. Stat. ch. 48 § 1607 (1984) (Municipal employees); Illinois Educational Labor Relations Act § 10(a), Ill. Rev. Stat. ch. 48 § 1710(a) (1984) (public school employees); Ind. Code § 20-7.5-1-2(n) (1968) (educational employees); Me. Rev. Stat. Ann. tit. 26, § 965(l)(C) (Supp. 1999) (municipal public employees); Me. Rev. Stat. Ann. tit. 26, § 979-D(l)(E)(l) (Supp. 1999) (state employees); Me. Rev. Stat. Ann. tit. 26. § 1026(1)(C) (Supp. 1999) (university employees); Me. Rev. Stat. Ann. tit. 26, § 1285(1)(E) (Supp. 1999) (judicial employees); Mass. Gen. Laws Ann. ch. 150E. § 6 (West 1984) (public Employees); Mich. Comp. Laws § 423.215 (1978) (public employees); Minn. Stat. Ann. §§ 179A.06(5), 179A.07(2) (West Supp. 1999) (public employees); Minn. Stat. Ann. §§ 179A.06(5), 179A.07(2) (West Supp. 1998) (public employees); Mont. Code Ann. § 39-31-305(2),(3) (1983) (public employees); N.H. Rev. Stat. Ann. § 273-A:5(I) (1978) (public employees); N.M. State Personnel Board Regulations for Labor Management Relations §§ 2d. 7a (1983) (state employees); N.Y. Civ. Serv. Law § 204(3) (McKinney 1983) (public employees); N.D. Cent. Code § 15-38.1-12(4) (1981) (teachers); Ohio Rev. Code Ann. § 4117.01(G) (Page Supp. 1999) (public employees); Or. Rev. Stat. § 243.650(4) (1985) (public employees); Pa. Stat. Ann. tit. 43, §§ 217.1-217.10 (Purdon 1992) (police officers and firefighters); Pa. Stat. Ann. tit. 43, §§ 1101.101-1101.2301 (Purdon 1991) (all other public employees); Tex. Rev. Civ. Stat. Ann. art 5154c-1(7)(b) (Vernon Supp. 1999) (police officers and firefighters); Vt. Stat. Ann. tit. 21, § 1725(a) (1978) (municipal employees); Wash. Rev. Code Ann. § 41.59.030(4) (Supp. 1999) (public employees, except educational); Wash. Rev. Code Ann. § 41.59.020(2) (Supp. 1999) (educational employees); Wis. Stat. Ann. § 111.70(1)(a) (West Supp. 1999) (municipal employees); Wis. Stat. Ann. § 111.81(1) (West Supp. 1999) (state employees).]

Where a state act is patterned after the NLRA's language, decisions under the NLRA may offer guidance in interpreting the state statute. [See, e.g., *Ronnie's Bar, Inc. v. Pennsylvania Labor Relations Bd.*, 411 Pa. 459, 192 A.2d 664 (1963); *Southeast Furniture Co. v. Indus. Comm'n.*, 100 Utah 154, 111 P.2d 153 (1941).] While NLRA decisions may be helpful, they are not binding on the state in interpreting its statute. [*Cooper v. Nutley Sun Printing Co.*, 36 N.J. 189, 175 A.2d 639 (1961).]

Appendix A

Pre-Employment Disability-Related and Medical Examination Equal Employment Opportunities Commission (EEOC) Guidance

		Number
		915.002
EEOC	NOTICE	
		Date
		5/19/94

1. <u>SUBJECT</u>: Enforcement Guidance: Pre-employment Disability-Related Inquiries and Medical Examinations Under the Americans with Disabilities Act of 1990.
2. <u>PURPOSE</u>: This enforcement guidance sets forth the Commission's position under the Americans with Disabilities Act of 1990, on pre-employment disability-related inquiries and medical examinations.
3. <u>EFFECTIVE DATE</u>: Upon receipt.
4. <u>EXPIRATION DATE</u>: As an exception to EEOC Order 205.001, Appendix B, Attachment 4, § a(5), this Notice will remain in effect until rescinded or superseded.
5. <u>ORIGINATOR</u>: ADA Division, Office of Legal Counsel.
6. <u>INSTRUCTIONS</u>: File after [_____] of Volume II of the Compliance Manual.
7. <u>SUBJECT MATTER</u>:

EMPLOYMENT POLICIES

Executive Summary: Enforcement Guidance on Pre-employment Disability-Related Inquiries and Medical Examinations Under the Americans with Disabilities Act of 1990

Introduction

The EEOC's "Enforcement Guidance on Pre-employment Disability-Related Inquiries and Medical Examinations Under the Americans with Disabilities Act" concerns the ADA's restrictions on an employer's use of disability-related inquiries and medical examinations. The Guidance has been issued for interim use by EEOC investigators, pending coordination with other federal agencies under Executive Order 12067.

As discussed in the Guidance, the ADA is unique among federal civil rights laws in that it flatly prohibits certain inquiries and examinations at the pre-offer stage of the hiring process. The Guidance provides detailed information and instructions for investigators to use in determining whether an inquiry is disability-related and whether an examination is medical. The document also provides guidance concerning the use of such inquiries and examinations at the post-offer stage.

Rationale and Legal Framework

The ADA's provisions concerning medical examinations and disability-related inquiries reflect the intent of Congress to prevent discrimination against individuals with hidden disabilities. In the past, applicants were often asked about their medical conditions at the time that they submitted their applications. If an applicant who disclosed a disability was then rejected, s/he would not know whether the rejection was because of the disclosure of disability, or because of a non-medical criterion.

Under the ADA, an employer may not ask about the existence, nature, or severity of a disability and may not conduct medical examinations until after it makes a conditional job offer to the applicant. This prohibition ensures that the applicant's hidden disability is not considered prior to the assessment of the applicant's non-medical qualifications. At this preoffer stage, employers may ask about an applicant's ability to perform specific job-related functions. An employer also may ask other questions that are not disability-related and may require examinations that are not medical.

After a conditional offer is made, an employer may require medical examinations and may make disability-related inquiries if it does so for all entering employees in the job category. If an examination or inquiry screens out an individual because of disability, the exclusionary criterion must be job-related and consistent with business necessity. The employer also must show that the criterion cannot be satisfied and the essential functions cannot be performed with reasonable accommodation.

Any medical information obtained must be kept confidential by the employer. This means that the employer must collect and maintain the information on separate forms and in separate medical files. The employer may disclose the information only to persons and entities specified in the ADA.

Application of ADA Provisions

Below is a list of some common acceptable and unacceptable pre-offer inquiries and examinations. However, investigators are instructed to consult the Enforcement Guidance for more information on any inquiry/examination.

A. **Disability-Related Inquiries** are inquiries/series of inquiries that are likely to elicit information about a disability. Inquiries about the ability to perform job functions are not disability-related inquiries. See § IV(A) of the Enforcement Guidance.

The following examples are inquiries which are not disability-related:

- Can you perform the functions of this job (essential and/or marginal), with or without reasonable accommodation?
- Please describe/demonstrate how you would perform these functions (essential and/or marginal).
- Do you have a cold? Have you ever tried Tylenol for fever? How did you break your leg?
- Can you meet the attendance requirements of this job? How many days did you take leave last year?
- Do you illegally use drugs? Have you used illegal drugs in the last two years?
- Do you have the required licenses to perform this job?
- How much do you weigh? How tall are you? Do you regularly eat three meals per day?

The following examples are disability-related inquiries:

- Do you have AIDS? Do you have asthma?
- Do you have a disability which would interfere with your ability to perform the job?
- How many days were you sick last year?

EMPLOYMENT POLICES

- Have you ever filed for workers' compensation? Have you ever been injured on the job?

- How much alcohol do you drink each week? Have you ever been treated for alcohol problems?
- Have you ever been treated for mental health problems? What prescription drugs are you currently taking?

A. **Medical Examinations** are procedures/tests that seek information about an individual's physical or mental impairment, or physical or psychological health. See § V(A) of the Enforcement Guidance.

The following factors are used in determining whether any particular test is medical:

- whether the test is administered by a health care professional or trainee;
- whether the results of the test are interpreted by a health care professional or trainee;
- whether the test is designed to reveal an impairment or the state of an individual's physical or psychological health;
- whether the test is invasive (e.g., requires drawing of blood, urine, breath, etc.);
- whether the test measures physiological/psychological responses (as opposed to performance of a task);
- whether the test is normally done in a medical setting; and
- whether medical equipment/devices are used for the test.

The above factors should be used to analyze any challenged test. However, the following are tests which generally are not medical:

- physical agility/physical fitness tests which do not include medical monitoring;
- certain psychological tests, such as tests which simply concern an individual's skills or tastes; and
- tests for illegal use of drugs.

It is important to note, however, that disability-related inquiries may not be asked as part of a pre-offer test, even if that test is not otherwise medical.

The following examples are tests which, depending on the test and application of the above-factors, might be medical:

- certain psychological tests;
- certain vision tests; and
- certain alcohol tests.

Table of Contents

I Introduction

This enforcement guidance concerns the provisions of Title I and portions of Title V of the Americans with Disabilities Act of 1990 (ADA) (codified as amended at 42 U.S.C. §§ 12101-17, 12201-13 (Supp. IV 1992)), regarding pre-employment disability-related inquiries and medical examinations. For purposes of ADA enforcement, "pre-employment" refers to the time period before an individual actually starts work for an employer. It includes (1) the period before an applicant has been given a conditional job offer ("pre-offer stage"), and (2) the period after a conditional job offer has been extended, but before the individual starts work ("post-offer stage").[1]

Under the ADA and the Commission's implementing regulations and interpretive guidance, the permissibility of pre-employment disability-related inquiries and medical examinations depends on whether a conditional offer of employment has been extended to an applicant.[2] As discussed below, disability-related inquiries and medical examinations are prohibited at the pre-offer stage. However, such inquiries and examinations are permissible after a conditional offer has been extended to an applicant, but before the individual has started work.

In this document, the Commission provides enforcement guidance concerning the following:

- the rationale for the ADA's provisions regarding disability-related inquiries and medical examinations (Section II);
- the statutory and regulatory framework (Section III);
- the definition of the term **inquiries concerning the existence, nature, or severity of a disability** and guidance concerning specific, commonly used pre-offer inquiries (Section IV);

---

[1] A number of terms are used by employers and ADA commentators to refer to preemployment medical examinations (e.g., pre-placement examinations, entrance examinations). This policy guidance covers all such examinations which are medical in nature, as defined herein.

[2] The ADA is unique among most civil rights laws in that it flatly prohibits certain inquiries and examinations at the pre-offer stage. Under most other civil rights laws, pre-offer questions about protected status are not unlawful in and of themselves. See, eg., Policy Guidance No. N-915-043 (9/7/90) ("Job Advertising and Pre-Employment Inquiries Under The Age Discrimination in Employment Act (ADEA)") at 9-11, Fair Empl. Prac. Man. (BNA) 405:4027, 4032-33.

- the definition of the term **medical examinations** and guidance concerning specific, commonly used pre-offer examinations (Section V); and
- guidance regarding post-offer, pre-employment inquiries and examinations (Section VI).

II Rationale

The ADA's provisions concerning medical examinations and disability-related inquiries reflect the intent of Congress to prevent discrimination against individuals with "hidden" disabilities such as epilepsy, diabetes, mental illnesses, heart disease, HIV infection/AIDS, and cancer. The guiding principle of these provisions is that while employers may ask applicants about the ability to perform job functions, employers may not ask about disability at the pre-offer stage.

As indicated in the ADA's legislative history, employment applications and interviews historically have requested information concerning an applicant's physical and/or mental condition.[3] This information "was often used to exclude applicants with disabilities—particularly those with so called hidden disabilities . . . before their ability to perform the job was even evaluated."[4]

For example, applicants have in the past been asked about their medical conditions at the same time that they were completing other parts of the application process, such as submission of a written application or resume. If an applicant who disclosed a disability was then rejected, s/he would not necessarily have known whether the rejection was due to the disability, or due to some other criterion (*e.g.*, insufficient skills or experience). Accordingly, Congress established a process within the ADA to isolate an employer's consideration of an applicant's non-medical qualifications from any consideration of the applicant's medical condition.

III The Statutory and Regulatory Framework

Under the law, an employer may not ask about the existence, nature, or severity of a disability and may not conduct medical examinations until <u>after</u> the employer determines that the applicant is qualified for the job and makes a conditional employment offer to the applicant.[5] This prohibition is to ensure that an applicant's possible hidden disability (including a prior history of a disability)

---

[3] H.R. Rep. No. 485 pt. 2, 101st Cong., 2d Sess. 72 (1990) [hereinafter House Education and Labor Report].

[4] <u>Id.</u>

[5] 42 U.S.C. § 12112(d)(2); 29 C.F.R. § 1630.13(a), 1630.14(a), (b). The ADA does <u>not</u> prohibit pre-offer inquiries that are unrelated to disability, even if those inquiries have no relationship to the job. However, as a practical matter, employers may find it desirable to avoid making inquiries that are not job-related.

is not considered by the employer prior to the assessment of the applicant's non-medical qualifications, An employer may not make disability-related inquiries or require a medical examination, even if the employer intends to shield itself from the answers to the inquiries or results of the examination until the post-offer stage.

Employers may ask, at the pre-offer stage, about an applicant's ability to perform specific job-related functions. For example, an employer may state the physical requirements of a job (such as the ability to lift a certain amount of weight, or the ability to climb ladders), and ask if an applicant can satisfy these requirements, with or without reasonable accommodation.[6]

An employer also may ask an applicant to describe or demonstrate how s/he would perform job-related tasks with or without reasonable accommodation. As described below in § IV.B.5, an applicant with a disability may be asked to describe or demonstrate performance of job tasks if all applicants for the job category are asked to do so. Employers also may ask a particular applicant to describe or demonstrate performance if the applicant has a known disability which may interfere with or prevent the performance of job-related functions.[7]

Once a conditional job offer is made, the employer may require medical examinations and make disability-related inquiries. If the employer rejects the applicant after a medical examination or disability-related inquiry, investigators will closely scrutinize whether the rejection was based on the results of that examination or inquiry.[8]

If the examination or inquiry screens out an individual with a disability as a result of the disability, the employer must demonstrate to the investigator that the exclusionary criterion is job-related and consistent with business necessity. Furthermore, the employer must show that the criterion cannot be satisfied and the essential job functions cannot be performed with reasonable accommodation.[9]

In addition, if the individual is screened out for safety concerns (i.e., because s/he is deemed to pose a "direct threat"), the employer must demonstrate to the investigator that the decision was based on objective, factual evidence that this individual poses a significant risk of substantial harm to him/herself or others, and

---

[6] See 29 C.F.R. pt. 1630 app. § 1630.14(a). Consistent with the statute, if an employer asks whether an applicant can perform certain functions, the employer is advised to state that the performance may be with or without reasonable accommodation.

[7] 29 C.F.R. pt. 1630 app. § 1630-14(a). In either case, if an applicant with a disability is asked to demonstrate how s/he would perform a job-related function, the employer must either provide any reasonable accommodation needed to allow the applicant to explain how, with the accommodation, s/he would perform the function.

[8] See § VI.A for a discussion of withdrawal of an offer after a post-offer medical examination or disability-related inquiry.

[9] 42 U.S.C. § 12112(b); 29 C.F.R. § 1630.10.

that the risk cannot be reduced below the direct threat level through reasonable accommodation.[10]

IV Inquiries Concerning the Existence, Nature, or Severity of a Disability

A. What Is an Inquiry Concerning the Existence, Nature, or Severity of a Disability?

An inquiry concerning the existence, nature, or severity of a disability is an inquiry (or series of inquiries) that is likely to elicit information about a disability. This means that an employer could reasonably expect that an applicant's response to the inquiry (e.g., either a positive or negative response) would likely indicate whether the individual has a disability. Thus, for example, an employer cannot ask whether an individual has a particular disability. Similarly, an employer cannot make inquiries that are so closely related to disability that the individual's response is likely to elicit information about a disability. Investigators should evaluate inquiries on a case-by-case basis to determine whether they are disability-related.

Example 1: R asks applicants: "Do you have 20/20 corrected vision?" This inquiry is not likely to elicit information about whether an applicant has a disability because many persons who do not have 20/20 corrected vision do not have a disability. R may make this inquiry at the pre-offer stage. However, if an applicant answers, "No," R may not follow up this permissible question with impermissible questions, such as, "What is your corrected vision?" and/or "What is your uncorrected vision?" Either of these inquiries is likely to elicit information about whether an applicant has a disability because it will disclose whether an individual has a severe vision impairment. R may not make either inquiry at the pre-offer stage.

Example 2: R asks applicants: "How well can you handle stress?" and "Do you work better or worse under pressure?" These inquiries are not likely to elicit information about whether an applicant has a disability because many persons who do not handle stress/pressure well do not have a disability. R may make these inquiries at the pre-offer stage. However, R may not follow up these permissible inquiries with impermissible inquiries, such as, "Have you sought treatment for your inability to handle stress?" This inquiry is likely to elicit information about whether the applicant has a mental disability.

---

[10]See 29 C.F.R. pt. 1630 app. § 1630.2(r).

Example 3: R asks applicants the following series of questions: "Do you ever get ill from stress?" "Does stress affect your ability to be productive?" and "Have you ever been unable to 'cope' with work-related stress?" This series of inquiries, taken together, is likely to elicit information as to whether an applicant has a substantially limiting psychological impairment. R may not make these inquiries at the pre-offer stage.

Example 4: R, an airline, asks applicants for customer service positions the following questions on R's employment application: "Do you have open skin sores?"; "Do you have boils?"; "Do you have fever?"; "Do you have dark urine?"; and "Do you have jaundice?" This series of inquiries, taken together, is likely to elicit information about whether an applicant may have a number of disabilities, such as AIDS. R may not make these inquiries at the pre-offer stage.

Information volunteered by an individual in response to a non-disability related inquiry would not be a basis for an investigator to conclude that the inquiry was disability-related.[11]

Example 5: R asks an applicant whether he can perform a particular job function, and in answering the inquiry, the applicant states that he has multiple sclerosis. R has not made a prohibited pre-offer inquiry. Rather, the applicant has volunteered information about a disability, unsolicited by R.

However, where an individual voluntarily discloses a disability, an employer may not make follow-up inquiries concerning the disability at the pre-offer stage. Such follow-up inquiries would be prohibited disability-related inquiries.

Example 6: R asks an applicant whether he can perform a particular job function, and in answering the inquiry, the applicant states that he has multiple sclerosis. As noted in the previous example, R has not made a prohibited pre-offer inquiry. However, R may not then ask the applicant questions about his multiple sclerosis at the pre-offer stage, such as, "How debilitating is your multiple sclerosis?"; "Does it limit your ability to work?"; or "Do you expect your condition to get worse?"

B. Specific Inquiries
   1. Direct Inquiries About Disabilities
   Direct inquiries about a disability are specifically prohibited.

---

[11]However, the applicant's having volunteered disability-related information may be evidence that the employer had knowledge of a disability if the employer later allegedly engages in an adverse action on account of disability.

Example 1: R may not make inquiries such as, "Are you an alcoholic?" or "Do you have AIDS?"

An employer may not make such inquiries about a disability at the preoffer
stage even if the employer legitimately would be able to exclude the applicant
because of the disability.

Example 2: A federal law prohibits someone with epilepsy from
working as an interstate truck driver. R, a trucking company, still
may not ask (at the pre-offer stage) whether CP, a truck driver
applicant, has epilepsy.

Example 3: R asks applicants, "Do you have a disability that would
prevent you from performing the essential functions of the job with
or without reasonable accommodation?" This inquiry is about disability and is prohibited at the pre-offer stage, even though R may in
fact refuse to hire an applicant who cannot perform essential functions with or without reasonable accommodation.

2. Inquiries Concerning Performance of job Functions: As discussed
above, an employer may inquire about an applicant's ability to
perform job-related functions, with or without reasonable accommodation. These inquiries are not prohibited preoffer inquiries
because Congress intended to allow inquiries about an applicant's
ability to perform job functions.[12]

Example 1: R may state to an applicant, "This job requires an
employee to transport twenty pound bags of frozen frog legs from a
loading dock, down two flights of steps, to a processing machine.
Can you perform this function with or without reasonable accommodation?"

Example 2: R may state to an applicant, "This job requires an
employee to maneuver through four-foot diameter underground
sewer tunnels for four hours per day. Can you perform this function
with or without reasonable accommodation?"

Example 3: R may state to an applicant, "This job requires an
employee to prepare written reports containing detailed factual
summaries and analyses. These reports must frequently be prepared
within tight time frames. Can you perform this function with or
without reasonable accommodation?"

---

[12]See House Education and Labor Report at 72 (the statute "makes it clear that an employer may
make pre-employment inquiries into the ability of an applicant to perform job-related functions").

An employer may inquire about an applicant's ability to perform both essential and marginal functions.[13]

> Example 4: If a secretarial job involves typing as an essential function, and driving as a marginal function, R may ask about an applicant's ability (with or without reasonable accommodation) to both type and drive.

3. Inquiries About Impairments: Inquiries about impairments are treated differently than inquiries about disabilities because an impairment may, or may not, be a disability.[14] Investigators should bear in mind that an impairment is a disability only if it substantially limits one or more major life activities.[15] Thus, inquiries about impairments are unlawful at the pre-offer stage only if they are likely to elicit information about the applicant's disability.

Although an impairment is not always a disability, inquiries about impairments often reveal disability-related information. Investigators, therefore, should closely scrutinize such inquiries to determine whether they are likely to elicit disability-related information.

> Example 1: R asks an applicant with a broken leg, how she broke her leg. Asking "how" the applicant broke her leg focuses only on the manner in which she broke her leg (e.g., skiing, rollerblading), and is not likely to disclose whether the applicant has a disability (i.e., the inquiry does not concern the extent of the break, or the duration of the healing period).[16] Under these facts, R has not made a prohibited pre-offer inquiry about disability.

> Example 2: R is hiring a word processor to type information into a computer. R asks an applicant with a broken arm how he broke his arm. For the reasons stated in the previous example, this is not a prohibited pre-offer inquiry. However, R then goes on to ask how extensive the break was, when the arm is expected to heal, and whether the applicant will have full use of his arm in the future. This series of inquiries is likely to disclose whether the applicant has a disability because these inquiries seek information about the nature and duration of the broken arm (i.e., the inquiries are likely to elicit

---

[13]However, an employer may not reject the applicant because s/he is unable to perform a marginal function because of a disability.

[14]For the definition of "physical or mental impairment" under the ADA, see 29 C.F.R. § 1630.2(h).

[15]42 U.S.C. § 12102(2); 29 C.F.R. § 1630.2(g).

[16]Whether an impairment "substantially limits" a major life activity depends on the nature and severity, duration, and permanent or long-term impact of the impairment. See 29 C.F.R. § 1630.2(j)(2).

information as to whether the impairment "substantially limits" a major life activity).[17] Under these facts, this series of inquiries is prohibited at the pre-offer stage.

4. Inquiries About Ability to Perform Major Life Activities and About Substantial Limitations of Major Life Activities: Employers sometimes ask whether an applicant can perform a major life activity. The inability to perform a major life activity is often the result of a physical or mental impairment. Therefore, investigators should closely scrutinize an inquiry about whether an applicant can perform a major life activity to determine whether it is likely to elicit information about disability. If the inquiry is likely to elicit information about a disability, it is prohibited at the pre-offer stage unless it is specifically about the ability to perform job functions (as described in § IV.B.2, above). However, it is unlikely that a broad question about the ability to perform a major life activity would be considered "specifically about the ability to perform job functions."

Example 1: R asks applicants for clerical positions questions such as the following: "Can you stand?" "Can you walk?" These broad questions about the ability to perform major life activities, are likely to elicit information about disability. In addition, they are probably not specifically about an applicant's ability to perform job functions. Therefore, they are prohibited at the pre-offer stage.

Instead of asking whether an applicant can perform a major life activity, employers sometimes ask whether an applicant is substantially limited in a major life activity.[18] Since substantial limitations in a major life activity are often the result of a physical or mental impairment, investigators should closely analyze inquiries about such limitations to determine whether they are likely to elicit information about the applicant's disability. If the inquiry is likely to elicit information about a disability, the inquiry is prohibited at the pre-offer stage unless it is specifically about the ability to perform job functions (as described in § IV.B.2, above).

Example 2: R is hiring for a clerical position that requires the employee to load three-pound boxes of paper into the copy machine (among other duties). R asks applicants whether they can lift three-pound boxes. This is an inquiry concerning whether an applicant is substantially limited in the major life activity of lifting, and it is

---

[17]See 29 C.F.R. § 1630.2(j)(2).

[18]As noted above, for the definition of "substantially limits," see 29 C.F.R. § 1630.2(j). For the definition of "major life activities," see 29 C.F.R. § 1630.2(i).

likely to elicit information as to whether the applicant has a disability resulting from a physical impairment. However, this inquiry also is specifically about the ability to perform a job function. Therefore, this inquiry is permissible at the pre-offer stage.

Example 3: R is hiring for a receptionist position which requires sitting behind the lobby desk in an office suite. R asks applicants whether they can stand for short periods of time, or whether they can walk average distances. These are inquiries concerning whether an applicant is substantially limited in the major life activities of standing and walking, and are likely to elicit information as to whether the applicant has a disability resulting from a physical impairment. In addition, the inquiries are not specifically about the ability to perform job functions. Therefore, these inquiries are prohibited at the pre-offer stage.

An inquiry about an applicant's ability to achieve above-average performance in a major life activity is not a question about a substantial limitation of a major life activity.[19] Accordingly, such an inquiry is permissible at the pre-offer stage.

Example 4: R makes an inquiry about whether an applicant can walk an extreme distance, such as twenty miles, without discomfort. These inquiries are not inquiries about whether an applicant is substantially limited in a major life activity. Such inquiries are not likely to elicit information about the existence, nature, or severity of a disability. Rather, these inquiries concern whether the applicant has special abilities beyond the average person. R may therefore make such inquiries at the pre-offer stage.

5. Requests to Describe/Demonstrate Performance of Job-Related Functions: Requests to describe or demonstrate how an applicant would perform job-related functions are not considered "disability-related" because they are not likely to elicit information about a disability. Rather, such requests elicit Information about an applicant's ability to perform these functions. Accordingly, an employer may ask applicants to describe or demonstrate how they would perform essential and marginal functions, with or without reasonable accommodation.[20]

---

[19]See 29 C.F.R. pt. 1630 app. § 1630.2(j).

[20]See 29 C.F.R. pt. 1630 app. § 1630.14(a).

Example 1: R may ask applicants to demonstrate their ability to distinguish color-coded wires if distinguishing between color-coded wires is a job function.

Example 2: R may ask applicants to demonstrate their ability to lift 10-pound boxes of wood chips if such lifting is an actual job duty.

Example 3: R may ask applicants to retrieve lumber from shelves that are four feet high if this is an actual job duty.

If, in response to an employer's request to demonstrate performance, an applicant indicates that s/he will need a reasonable accommodation, the employer must either: (1) provide a reasonable accommodation that does not create an undue hardship so that the applicant can demonstrate job performance;[21] or (2) allow the applicant to simply describe how s/he would perform the job function.

a. When the Employer Could Not Reasonably Believe that Known Disability Will Interfere with Performance of Job-Related Functions: When an employer could not reasonably believe that a known disability will interfere with job-related functions, it may ask the applicant to describe or demonstrate how, with or without reasonable accommodation, s/he would perform job-related functions only if the request is made of all applicants in the same job category.[22] Such inquiries or requests are not prohibited pre-offer inquiries.

Example 4: R may ask an applicant with one leg who applies for a telephone marketing job to describe or demonstrate performance only if all applicants for the job are asked to describe or demonstrate such performance. This is because an employer could not reasonably believe that having only one leg interferes with an individual's ability to perform a telephone marketing job.

b. When the Employer Could Reasonably Believe that Known Disability Will Interfere with Performance of Job-Related Functions: When an employer could reasonably believe that an applicant's known disability will interfere with the performance of a job-related function, the employer may ask that particular applicant to describe or demonstrate how s/he would perform the

[21]See § IV.8.6 (below) for information on inquiries concerning an applicant's need for accommodation in the hiring process (which includes job demonstrations).

[22]The reason a demonstration request must be made of all applicants is to prevent discriminatory treatment of individuals who have disabilities that are unrelated to performance of the job they are seeking.

function, with or without reasonable accommodation.[23] Such inquiries or requests are not prohibited pre-offer inquiries.

> Example 5: R may ask an applicant with one leg who applies for a job as a telephone linesperson to describe or demonstrate how she would perform the duties of the job, because R may reasonably believe that having one leg interferes with the ability to climb telephone poles.

In some cases, an applicant may not have an obvious disability, but may voluntarily disclose that s/he has a hidden disability that would reasonably appear to interfere with performance of a job-related function. In such cases, the employer may ask the applicant to describe or demonstrate performance, with or without reasonable accommodation. Such inquiries or requests are not prohibited pre-offer inquiries.

> Example 6: An applicant for the job of repairing underground sewer lines voluntarily discloses that she has severe claustrophobia. R may reasonably determine that severe claustrophobia would interfere with an employee's ability to work within the confined space of an underground sewer. R may therefore ask the applicant to describe or demonstrate how she would perform the job, with or without reasonable accommodation.

6. Inquiries Concerning Need for Accommodation and Requests for Documentation If Applicant Asks for Accommodation:

a. Inquiries Regarding Need for Reasonable Accommodation During the Hiring Process or on the Job:

Accommodations for the Hiring Process: An employer may inform applicants on an application form or job advertisement that the hiring process includes a specific selection procedure (e.g., an interview, written test, or job demonstration). Applicants may be asked to inform the employer of any reasonable accommodation needed to take such a pre-offer examination, interview, or job demonstration, within a reasonable time period prior to the administration of the examination, interview, or job demonstration.[24] Such requests are not prohibited pre-offer inquiries.

---

[23]Allowing an employer to ask a particular applicant with such a known disability to describe or demonstrate performance in these circumstances is in the interest of both applicants and employers. Employers are entitled to know whether an applicant with an apparently interfering disability can perform job-related functions, with or without reasonable accommodation. It is in the interest of an applicant with such a disability to describe or demonstrate performance in order to dispel notions that s/he is unable to perform the job because of the disability.

[24]See 29 C.F.R. pt. 1630 app. § 1630.14(a).

Example 1: R may state the following on its employment application: "All applicants are required to take a 60-minute written
examination which tests reading comprehension and writing ability.
Please inform the Director of Employment within three days of your
submission of this application if, as a result of a disability, you will
need an accommodation to take this test."

Example 2: R may state the following on its employment application: "All applicants are required to demonstrate their ability to
perform the following job functions: (1) Moving 75-pound boxes
from the loading dock to the cargo elevator; and (2) Retrieving
30-pound pieces of copper pipe from shelves 15-feet high. Please
inform the Director of Employment within three days of your submission of this application if, as a result of a disability, you will
need an accommodation to perform this job demonstration."

Accommodations for the Job: An employer may ask an applicant whether
s/he can perform specified job-related functions with or without reasonable
accommodation, because these inquiries elicit information about an applicant's
ability to perform job functions, not information about an applicant's disability.
An employer also may ask an applicant to describe or demonstrate, at the pre-offer
stage, how s/he would perform job-related functions, with or without reasonable
accommodation, because these inquiries elicit information about an applicant's
ability, not information about an applicant's disability. See § IV.B.5 (above). Such
inquiries or requests are not prohibited pre-offer inquiries.

However, at the pre-offer stage, an employer may not generally inquire
whether the applicant needs reasonable accommodation for the job. For example,
an employer may not make inquiries such as, "Would you need reasonable
accommodation in this job?" or "Would you need reasonable accommodation to
perform this specific function?" Such inquiries are likely to elicit information
about the existence of a disability because, generally, only an individual with a
disability would require an accommodation. Therefore, these inquiries are
prohibited at the pre-offer stage.

If an applicant has voluntarily disclosed that s/he would need a reasonable
accommodation to perform the job, the employer still may not make inquiries at
the pre-offer stage about the type of required reasonable accommodation (except
where the applicant has requested reasonable accommodation as part of a required
pre-offer job demonstration, as described above).

Example 3: An applicant voluntarily discloses that she will need a
reasonable accommodation to perform a job function. R has not
violated the law simply because the applicant volunteers this information. However, even if R is curious about the reasonable accommodation, it may not follow up with inquiries such as, "What kind

of reasonable accommodation would you need for this job?" or "What kind of reasonable accommodation would you need to perform this specific function?" Asking about the type of required reasonable accommodation is likely to elicit information about the nature and severity of a disability. Therefore, such inquiries are prohibited at the pre-offer stage.

As the above discussion suggests, there are sometimes subtle distinctions between a permissible and a prohibited pre-offer inquiry. Therefore, in reviewing inquiries on application forms and in employment interviews, the investigator should carefully analyze the specific questions asked by the employer.

b. Requests for Documentation When Applicant Asks for Reasonable Accommodation: If an applicant requests accommodation (e.g., a request for the employer to reformat an examination, a request for a reasonable accommodation in connection with a job demonstration), an employer may require the applicant to document the fact that s/he has a disability (as defined by the ADA) and is therefore entitled to reasonable accommodation as required by the ADA. Accordingly, the applicant may be required to provide documentation from an appropriate professional (e.g., a doctor, rehabilitation counselor, etc.) stating that s/he has a disability. Such requests are not prohibited pre-offer inquiries.

Example 4: If an applicant states that s/he cannot read an employment test because of dyslexia, R may request documentation reflecting that the inability to read is the result of a physical or mental impairment that substantially limits a major life activity (e.g., as opposed to a lack of education).

The employer is entitled to such documentation because employers must provide reasonable accommodation only to individuals who are protected under the statute.

The employer also may require that such an applicant provide documentation concerning his/her functional limitations for which reasonable accommodation is requested (and which flow from the disability). Such requests are not prohibited pre-offer inquiries.

Example 5: R may require that an applicant obtain documentation from an appropriate professional stating that s/he is unable to lift a certain amount of weight due to a disability, and therefore requires a reasonable accommodation.

Requesting such documentation is consistent with the ADA's legislative history. For example, Congress specifically anticipated that when an applicant requests reasonable accommodation for the application process (or when an employee requests reasonable accommodation for the job), the employer should engage in an interactive process with the individual to determine an effective reasonable accommodation.[25]

7. Inquiries Concerning Known Disability: At the pre-offer stage, an employer may not ask an applicant with a known disability about the nature or severity of the disability, or about other disabilities.[26] These inquiries are prohibited at the pre stage even where an applicant with a known disability has been asked to demonstrate performance of job-related functions. See § IV.B.5.b (above).[27]

Example: R may not ask an applicant who uses a wheelchair questions such as, "How did you become disabled?," "What effect does being in a wheelchair have on your daily activities?," or "Do you ever expect to be able to walk again?"

8. Inquiries Concerning Attendance: An employer may state its attendance requirements and ask whether an applicant can meet them. This inquiry is not likely to elicit information about a disability because there may be many reasons unrelated to disability why someone cannot meet attendance requirements (e.g., an applicant may have to care for an elderly parent).

Example 1: R may state, "Employees regular work hours are 9:00 a.m. to 5:00 p.m. Monday through Friday. During the summer months, employees are required to work every other weekend. New employees get one week of vacation and seven sick leave days per year. Can you meet these requirements with or without reasonable accommodation?"

In addition, an employer may ask about an applicant's prior attendance record (e.g., how many days the applicant was absent from his/her last job). This inquiry is not likely to elicit information about a disability because there may be many reasons unrelated to disability why an applicant was absent for a number of days from a job (e.g., an applicant may have been involved in a lawsuit; an applicant may have been out on family leave).

---

[25]See S. Rep. No. 116, 101st Cong., 1st Sess. 34 (1989) [hereinafter Senate Report]; House Education and Labor Report at 65-66.

[26]See 29 C.F.R. pt. 1630 app. § 1630.13(a).

[27]However, in certain cases where an applicant requests reasonable accommodation, the employer may request documentation relating to the disability, as provided in § IV.B.6.b, below.

> Example 2: R may ask an applicant, "How many days were you absent from work last year?" or "Did you have any unauthorized absences from your job last year?"

However, the employer may not follow up this lawful pre-offer inquiry with an unlawful pre-offer inquiry.

> Example 3: R asks an applicant, "How many days were you absent from work last year?" The applicant answers that she was absent 30 days from work. R may not ask an unlawful pre-offer follow-up question such as, "Were you sick?"

An employer also may make inquiries designed to detect whether an applicant abused his/her leave because these inquiries are not likely to elicit information about a disability.

> Example 4: R may ask an applicant, "How many Mondays or Fridays were you absent last year on leave other than approved vacation leave?" Such inquiries are not prohibited pre-offer inquiries.

However, at the pre-offer stage, an employer may not ask how many days an applicant was sick, because such inquiries are likely to elicit information about a disability.

> Example 5: At the pre-offer stage, R may not ask an applicant questions such as, "How many days were you sick last year?" or "How many separate episodes of sickness did you have last year?"

In addition, at the pre-offer stage, an employer may not ask about how much time the applicant would need off from work on account of his/her disability because these inquiries are likely to elicit information about the nature and severity of a disability.

> Example 6: At the pre-offer stage, R may not ask, "How often will you require leave for treatment of your disability?"

9. Inquiries Concerning Workers' Compensation History: The ADA prohibits an employer from asking an applicant, at the pre-offer stage, about job-related injuries or workers' compensation history because these inquiries are likely to elicit information about an applicant's disability.[28]

---

[28]See 29 C.F.R. pt. 1630 app. § 1630.13(a). As discussed in § IV.B.1.5 (below), an employer also cannot ask these questions of third parties, such as former employers, reporting services, or state workers' compensation boards, at the pre-offer stage.

10. Inquiries Concerning Drug Use: An individual who currently engages in the illegal use of drugs is not protected under the ADA when the employer acts on the basis of the drug use.[29] Therefore, inquiries to determine the current illegal use of drugs[30] are not likely to elicit information about a covered disability, and may be made at any time, including the pre-offer stage.[31]

Example 1: R may ask, at the pre-offer stage, questions such as: "Are you currently illegally using drugs?"

However, most inquiries about current or prior lawful use of controlled substances or other medication taken under the supervision of a licensed health care professional are impermissible at the pre-offer stage. These inquiries are likely to elicit information about the existence, nature, or severity of a disability because the extent and type of medication is likely to elicit information about an individual's disability. Except as provided below, inquiries about such current or prior lawful drug use that are likely to elicit information about a disability may not be asked at the pre-offer stage.

Example 2: R may not ask, at the pre-offer stage, questions such as: "What medications are you currently taking?" or "Have you ever taken AZT?"

Example 3: During her interview an applicant volunteers to R that she is coughing and wheezing because her allergies are acting up as a result of pollen in the air. R, who also has allergies, tells applicant that he finds "Lemebreathe" (an over-the-counter antihistamine) to be effective, and asks the applicant if she has tried it. This inquiry is not prohibited at the pre-offer stage because it is not likely to elicit information about a disability.

If an applicant tests positive for illegal use of drugs (see § V.B.5 (below)), the employer may validate the test results by inquiring as to lawful drug use or other biomedical explanations for the positive result.[32] Otherwise prohibited pre-offer questions about lawful drug use may only be asked after a positive test result for illegal drug use. Such inquiries are not prohibited pre-offer inquiries.

---

[29] 42 U.S.C. § 12114(a); 29 C.F.R. § 1630.3(a).

[30] "Drug" means a controlled substance, as defined in schedules I through V of Section 202 of the Controlled Substances Act (21 U.S.C. § 81 2). 29 C.F.R. § 1630.3(a)(1).

[31] 42 U.S.C. § 12114(d); 29 C.F.R. § 1630.16(c).

[32] Employers may validate positive drug test results in this manner because Congress intended to protect individuals lawfully using drugs for treatment of a disability, and individuals who are erroneously regarded as being addicts (who are not, in fact, current illegally using drugs). See House Education and Labor Report at 77 (1990); 42, U.S.C. § 12114(b)(3); 29 C.F.R. § 1630.3(b).

Example 4: If an applicant tests positive for use of a controlled substance, R may lawfully ask, "What medications have you taken that may have resulted in a positive drug test result for this controlled substance? Are you taking this medication pursuant to a lawful prescription?"

Prior drug addiction is a disability under the ADA. However, as noted above, an individual currently engaging in the illegal use of drugs is not protected under the ADA (even if s/he is a drug addict) when a covered entity acts on the basis of such use.[33] Although an employer may ask whether an applicant has illegally used drugs in the past (e.g., "Have you ever illegally used drugs?" or "Have you used cocaine in the past two years?"),[34] an employer may not ask, at the pre-offer stage, about the extent of such prior use because this is likely to elicit information about a disability (i.e., drug addiction). Such inquiries are prohibited at the pre-offer stage.

Example 5: R may not ask an applicant, at the pre offer stage, questions such as, "How often did you use illegal drugs in the past?"; "Have you ever been addicted to drugs?"; "Have you ever been treated for drug addiction?"; or "Have you ever been treated for drug abuse?"

On the other hand, asking about an applicant's arrest/conviction record (e.g., regarding illegal drug use, possession and/or sale) would not be a prohibited medical question under the ADA. Such inquiries are not likely to elicit information as to whether an individual has a disability.[35]

11. Inquiries Concerning Certifications/Licenses: An employer may ask an applicant at the pre-offer stage whether s/he has certifications or licenses related to essential or marginal job functions. An employer also may ask an applicant whether s/he intends to get a particular job-related certification or license. Neither of these inquiries is likely to elicit information about an applicant's disability because there may be a number of reasons unrelated to disability why someone does not have, or does not intend to get, a certification/ license. Therefore, these inquiries are not prohibited pre-offer inquiries.

---

[33] 42 U.S.C. § 12114.

[34] An employer may ask such questions because prior recreational use of drugs which did not rise to the level of an addiction is not a disability.

[35] However, inquiries about arrest/conviction record must be carefully analyzed under Title VII of the Civil Rights Act of 1964, as amended. See IV.B.14 and accompanying footnote regarding questions concerning arrest/conviction records.

Example 1: R, a trucking company, may ask applicants questions such as, "Do you have Department of Transportation certification to drive a truck interstate?"; or "Do you intend to obtain such certification?"

Asking an applicant why s/he does not have a particular certification or license is not prohibited at the pre-offer stage because it is not likely to elicit information about the existence, nature, or severity of a disability. As noted above, the ADA does not prohibit inquiries that are not likely to elicit information about a disability, but that may (depending on the answer) reveal the existence, nature, or severity of a disability.

Example 2: R asks an applicant why he does not have a commercial driver's license, and the applicant states that it is because he has epilepsy. R did not make a prohibited pre-offer inquiry.

12. Inquiries Concerning Lifestyle: The ADA does not prohibit an employer from asking an applicant questions regarding such topics as eating habits, weight, and exercise habits, if these inquiries are not likely to elicit information about the existence, nature, or severity of a disability.[36]

Example 1: At the pre-offer stage, R lawfully may ask applicants questions such as: "Do you regularly eat three meals per day?"; or "How much do you weigh?" These inquiries are not likely to elicit information about a disability because there may be a number of reasons unrelated to disability why an individual does or does not regularly eat meals, or has a high or low weight.

Example 2: At the pre-offer stage, R may not lawfully ask applicants questions such as: "Do you need to eat a number of small snacks at regular intervals throughout the day in order to maintain your energy level?" These inquiries are likely to elicit information about a disability because an employer can rationally infer from an applicant's answers whether s/he has a condition likely to be a disability (e.g., diabetes).

As noted above in § IV.A, an applicant may voluntarily disclose a disability in response to a lawful pre-employment inquiry. However, at the pre-offer stage, an employer is prohibited from asking the applicant about the voluntarily disclosed disability.

---

[36]Employers ask "lifestyle" questions for a variety of reasons. For example, an employer might prefer to hire individuals who exercise regularly and who have healthy eating habits.

Example 3: At the pre-offer stage, R lawfully asks, "Do you regularly eat three meals a day?" Instead of just answering "No," an applicant answers, "No, I eat six smaller snacks to control my diabetes." At the pre-offer stage, R is prohibited from then making inquiries about the applicant's diabetes, such as, "is your diabetes under control?"; or "Does your diabetes interfere with your ability to work?"

An employer may ask an applicant whether s/he drinks alcohol. However, at the pre-offer stage, an employer may not ask an applicant about whether s/he is an alcoholic, because alcoholism is a disability. In addition, an employer may not ask an applicant about how much alcohol s/he drinks because this inquiry is likely to elicit information about the existence, nature, or severity of a disability (i.e., alcoholism). Therefore, such inquiries are prohibited at the pre-offer stage.

Example 4: R may not, at the pre-offer stage, make inquiries such as, "How much alcohol do you drink per week?"; "Do you drink every day?"; "Do you drink alone?"; "Have you ever been treated for alcoholism?"; "Are you an alcoholic?"; or "Does alcohol interfere with your daily activities?"

13. Inquiries Concerning Arrest/Conviction Record: The ADA does not prohibit an employer from asking, at the pre-offer stage, about an applicants arrest/conviction record because these inquiries are not likely to elicit information about an applicant's disability. These inquiries are not prohibited pre-offer inquiries.

Example: The ADA does not prohibit a police department from asking applicants questions such as, "Have you ever been convicted for illegal drug use?"; or "Have you ever been arrested for driving while intoxicated?[37]

However, investigators should be aware that Title VII of the Civil Rights Act of 1954, as amended, applies to such inquiries and that nothing in this Enforcement Guidance relieves an employer of its obligations to comply with Title VII. The Commission has previously provided guidance for investigators to follow concerning an employer's use of arrest/conviction records.[38]

---

[37]An employer may not, however, follow up a lawful pre-offer inquiry with an unlawful pre-offer inquiry. For example, if an applicant indicates that she has been arrested for driving under the influence of alcohol, the employer may not then ask, "Do you have a drinking problem?"

[38]With regard to questions concerning arrest and conviction records under Title VII, see Policy Guidance No. N-915-061 (9/7/90) ("Policy Guidance on the Consideration of Arrest Records in Employment Decisions under Title VII of the Civil Rights Act of 1964, as amended, 42 U.S.C. § 2000e et seq. (1982)"); EEOC Compliance Manual, Vol. II, Appendices 604-A ("Conviction Records") and 604-B ("Conviction Records-Statistics").

14. <u>Inquiries to Comply with Affirmative Action Obligations</u>: The ADA does not prohibit affirmative action for individuals with disabilities. In implementing affirmative action programs, employers sometimes invite applicants to indicate voluntarily whether and to what extent they have a disability. While such inquiries are frequently made to comply with federal, state, or local laws requiring or encouraging affirmative action, they also are made in connection with voluntary affirmative action plans that are undertaken in the absence of any such laws.

In enacting the ADA, Congress indicated that employers should be allowed to ask applicants to voluntarily self-identify as having disabilities if those employers actually provide affirmative action for such individuals.[39] At the pre-offer stage, an employer may therefore invite applicants to voluntarily supply disability-related information needed by the employer to provide affirmative action <u>if</u>:

(1) the employer is undertaking affirmative action pursuant to section 503 of the Rehabilitation Act of 1973, or any federal, state, or local law (including relevant veterans' preference laws) that requires affirmative action for individuals with disabilities (<u>i.e.</u>, require some action to be taken on behalf of individuals with disabilities); or

(2) the employer is voluntarily undertaking affirmative action for individuals with disabilities.

Therefore, an employer may always invite voluntary self-identification at the pre-offer stage when acting pursuant to a federal law requiring such voluntary self-identification. Aside from any such federal requirement, an employer also may invite voluntary self-identification: (1) when acting pursuant to any state or local law requiring affirmative action; or (2) in the absence of such a law, when actually undertaking voluntary affirmative action.

There may be instances when a law only permits/encourages (rather than requires) affirmative action, or requires collection of disability data without requiring affirmative action. In those cases, an employer may invite voluntary self-identification <u>only</u> if the employer uses the information to actually provide affirmative action for individuals with disabilities. Further, as noted above, in the absence of any such laws, an employer may invite voluntary self-identification if it is actually undertaking affirmative action.

Example 1: R is subject to a state law requiring employers to provide affirmative action (<u>e.g.</u>, goals and timetables) for individuals

---

[39]<u>See</u> House Education and Labor Report at 75-76; Senate Report at 40.

with disabilities. R may invite applicants to voluntarily self-identify in order for R to comply with this statute.

Example 2: R is subject to a state law that does not require employers to provide affirmative action, but simply encourages voluntary affirmative action plans or requires collection/monitoring of disability-related information. R has a voluntary plan that actually provides affirmative action for individuals with disabilities. R may invite applicants to voluntarily self identify in order to implement its plan.

Example 3: Same facts as Example 2, but R does not have a plan that actually provides affirmative action for individuals with disabilities. R may not invite applicants to voluntarily self-identify at the pre-offer stage.

Example 4: R asks applicants whether they were discharged from the military for a service-related disability. R uses the information to voluntarily provide affirmative action for veterans with disabilities. R may invite applicants to voluntarily self-identify in order to implement its plan.

Therefore, in cases other than voluntary self-identification that is required by a federal law, an investigator will need to analyze whether a law requires affirmative action, or whether an employer is using voluntary self-identification information to provide actual affirmative action. In making this determination, an investigator should examine whether the employer is using the information to actually benefit individuals with disabilities with respect to employment opportunities (e.g., job offers, promotions, etc.).

If the employer invites applicants to voluntarily self-identify in connection with the above-mentioned situations, the employer must take the following steps prior to inviting an applicant to voluntarily self-identify:

(1) state clearly and conspicuously on any written questionnaire used for this purpose, or state clearly orally (if no written questionnaire is used), that the specific information requested is intended for use solely in connection with its affirmative action obligations or its voluntary affirmative action efforts; and

(2) state clearly and conspicuously that the specific information is being requested on a voluntary basis, that it will be kept confidential in accordance with the ADA,[40] that refusal to provide

---

[40]See § VI.D, below, for information about the ADA's confidentiality requirements.

it will not subject the applicant to any adverse treatment, and that it will be used only in accordance with the ADA.

In order to ensure that the self-identification information is kept confidential, employers should invite such self-identification on a form separate and apart from the application, or on a sheet that will be torn off from the application.

If an employer asks applicants to self-identify at the pre-offer stage, investigators should carefully review whether the request is consistent with all of the above factors.

15. Inquiries to Third Parties Regarding an Applicant's Medical Condition: At the pre-offer stage, an employer may ask a third party (e.g., a reference) anything that it could ask the applicant directly.

Example 1: At the pre-offer stage, R may ask a third party (such as a former employer) whether the applicant currently uses illegal drugs.

However, at the pre-offer stage, an employer is prohibited from asking a third party anything that the employer is prohibited from asking the applicant directly.[41]

Example 2: At the pre-offer stage, R may not ask a third party (such as a reporting service, a state agency, or an applicant's friends, family, or former employers) questions such as, "How many days was the applicant sick last year?"; "How is the applicant's health?"; "Has the applicant ever filed a workers' compensation claim?"; or "Did this applicant have any on-the-job injuries?"

V Medical Examinations

As noted in Section III, above, an employer may not require disability related questions or conduct medical examinations before an applicant has been given a conditional offer of employment. Section IV, above, analyzed when a question is considered disability-related. This section analyzes when an examination is "medical."

A. What is a Medical Examination?

Medical examinations are procedures or tests that seek information about the existence, nature, or severity of an individual's physical or mental impairment, or that seek information regarding an individual's physical or psychological health.

---

[41]See 29 C.F.R. § 1630.13(a) (covered entity may not "make inquiries" as to whether an applicant has a disability or regarding the existence, nature, or severity of an applicant's disability).

The investigator should consider the following factors in making a recommendation concerning whether a particular test or procedure is a medical examination:

- Whether the procedure or test is one that is administered by either a health care professional[42] or someone trained by a health care professional;[43]
- Whether the results of the procedure or test are interpreted by either a health care professional or someone trained by a health care professional;
- Whether the procedure or test is designed to reveal the existence, nature, or severity of an impairment, or the subject's general physical or psychological health;
- Whether the employer is administering the procedure or test for the purpose of revealing the existence, nature, or severity of an impairment, or the subject's general physical or psychological health;
- Whether the procedure or test is invasive (e.g., whether it requires the drawing of blood, urine, breath, etc.);
- Whether the procedure or test measures physiological or psychological responses of an individual, as opposed to the individual's performance of a task;
- Whether the procedure or test would normally be administered in a medical setting (a health care professional's office, a hospital); and
- Whether medical equipment or devices are used for administering the procedure or test (e.g., medical diagnostic equipment or devices).

In many cases, a combination of factors will be relevant in the investigator's analysis of whether a procedure or test is a medical examination. In some cases, one factor may be enough for an investigator to determine that a procedure or test is medical.

> Example 1: R requires applicants to lift a thirty pound box and carry it twenty feet. This is not, in itself, a medical examination. Rather, it is simply a test of whether the applicant can perform this task. However, if R takes an applicant's blood pressure or heart rate after the lifting and carrying, the test would be a medical examination because R is measuring the applicant's physiological response to lifting and carrying, as opposed to the applicant's ability to perform the lifting and carrying.

---

[42]"Health care professional" is a broad term, and includes doctors, nurses, psychologists and other mental health professionals, physical and occupational therapy professionals, and others in the health care field.

[43]For example, in some cases, human resources personnel may be trained by health care professionals to administer blood pressure examinations, or to perform a urinalysis.

Example 2: A psychological test is designed to reveal mental illness, but R states that it does not give the test for the purpose of disclosing mental illness (e.g., R states that it uses the test to disclose merely tastes and habits). However, the test also is interpreted by a psychologist, and is routinely used in a clinical setting to provide evidence that can be used to diagnose mental health (e.g., whether an applicant has paranoid tendencies, or is depressed). Under these facts, this test would be considered a "medical examination."

When a charging party alleges that an employer has required a medical examination at the pre-offer stage, the investigator should request information relevant to the above-stated definition and factors. As noted above, if the investigator determines that a pre-offer procedure or test is a medical examination, the investigator should recommend a "cause" finding against the employer.

B. Specific Procedures/Tests

1. Physical Agility/Physical Fitness Tests: A physical agility test, in which an applicant demonstrates his/her ability to perform actual or simulated job-related tasks (essential or marginal), is not a medical examination.[44] Nor is a physical fitness test, in which an applicant's performance of physical criteria (e.g., running, strength) is measured, a prohibited medical examination. These tests do not seek information concerning the existence, nature, or severity of an individual's physical or mental impairment, or information regarding an individual's physical or psychological health. Rather, these tests measure an applicant's ability to perform a task. They may therefore be administered at the pre-offer stage.[45]

Example 1: R, a police department, tests police officer applicants' ability to run through an obstacle course designed to simulate a suspect chase in an urban setting. This is not a medical examination.

---

[44]See 29 C.F.R. pt. 1630 app. § 1630.14(a). An agility test that requires an applicant to perform actual/simulated job tasks may constitute a job demonstration. See, e.g., Evans v. City of Evanston, 695 F. Supp. 922, 928 (N.D. Ill. 1988) (firefighter physical agility test required individuals to perform "exactly the sorts of activities a firefighter performs while on duty"); Van Aken v. Young, 541 F. Supp. 448, 454 (E.D. Mich. 1982) ("[i]t is undisputed that the agility exam was related to the actual job performance").

[45]Although physical agility tests and physical fitness tests are not "medical" examinations, these tests are still subject to other parts of the ADA. For example, if a physical fitness test which requires applicants to run one mile in ten minutes screens out an applicant on the basis of disability, the employer must be prepared to demonstrate that the test is job-related and consistent with business necessity.

Example 2: R, a messenger service, tests applicants' ability to run one mile in 20 minutes. This is not a medical examination.

However, if an employer measures an applicant's physiological/biological responses to performance, the test/procedure would be considered medical.

Example 3: R, a messenger service, tests applicants' ability to run one mile in 20 minutes. At the end of the run, R takes the applicants' blood pressure and heart rate. This would be a medical procedure, and is therefore prohibited at the pre-offer stage.

Investigators should be aware that employers are frequently concerned about an applicant's ability to safely perform a physical agility/physical fitness test. As noted above, at the pre-offer stage, an employer may not make inquiries about an applicant's physical condition that are likely to elicit information about a disability. However, an employer may ask the applicant to assume responsibility and release the employer of liability for injuries resulting from any physical or mental disorders. An employer also may furnish the applicant with a description of the pre-offer agility/fitness test and ask him/her to have a private physician review the description and state whether the applicant can safely perform the test.

2. Psychological Examinations: Employers currently administer a wide variety of examinations which may be characterized as psychological[46] in nature, including various types of I.Q. tests, aptitude tests, personality tests, and honesty tests. These examinations are intended to measure an individual's capacity and propensity to successfully perform a job. For example, applicants for nuclear power plant positions are sometimes given examinations designed to reflect whether they tend to be suitable for shift work, and/or whether they are likely to respond appropriately in the event of an emergency. Applicants for cash handling positions are sometimes given written examinations designed to reflect whether they are likely to steal money from the employer.

As discussed in §§ III & IV (above), if a psychological test is considered "medical," it may not be given at the pre-offer stage,[47] but may be given at the post-offer, pre-employment stage. An investigators recommendation concerning whether a particular psychological test is a "medical examination" requires a

---

[46]The term "psychological" generally means relating to "mental functioning" and "mental processes." See Campbell, Psychiatric Dictionary (Sixth Edition) (Oxford Press 1989) at p. 583-84; Sloane, The Sloane-Dorland Annotated Medical-Legal Dictionary (West 1987) at p. 589.

[47]In the ADA's legislative history, Congress specifically noted that "[the prohibition against pre-offer medical examinations also applies to psychological examinations." H.R. Rep. No. 485 pt. 3, 101st Cong., 2d Sess. 46 (1990) [hereinafter House Judiciary Report].

case-by-case analysis, and requires the investigator to consider the relevant factors identified in § V.A (above) (e.g., the purpose of the test, the intent of the employer administering the test, the person who interprets the results of the test, etc.).

For example, psychological examinations would be considered medical examinations to the extent that they provide evidence concerning whether an applicant has a mental disorder or impairment, as categorized in the American Psychiatric Association's most recent Diagnostic and Statistical Manual of Mental Disorders (DSM).[48]

> Example 1: R gives applicants the RUOK Test (hypothetical), an examination which reflects whether applicants have excessive anxiety, depression, and certain compulsive disorders. This test is a medical examination because these conditions are evidence of mental disorders or impairments categorized under DSM. Therefore, R may not give this test at the pre-offer stage.

If a test was not designed to assess the existence, nature, or severity of an applicant's mental impairment, or an applicant's general psychological health, it still may be considered a medical examination if it is used by an employer to assess whether an applicant has a mental impairment or to assess an applicant's general psychological health.

> Example 2: R gives the RUSMART Aptitude Test (hypothetical), an examination designed to reflect whether applicants have an aptitude for mechanical operations. R, with the help of a psychologist, has determined that certain patterns of answers on the test provide evidence that an applicant may have a psychological impairment. This test, as used by R, is a medical examination. Therefore, R may not give this test at the pre-offer stage.

On the other hand, to the extent that a test is designed and used to measure only such factors as an applicant's honesty, tastes, and habits, it would not normally be considered a medical examination.

> Example 3: R gives the IFIB Personality Test (hypothetical), an examination designed and used to reflect only whether an applicant is likely to lie. This test, as used by R, is not a medical examination. Therefore, R may give this test at the pre-offer stage.

Even if a psychological test is not itself a medical examination, individual inquiries on the test that concern the existence, nature, or severity of a disability

---

[48]The International Classification of Impairments, Disabilities, and Handicaps (ICIDH), published by the World Health Organization, also categorizes mental disorders or impairments.

are prohibited at the pre-offer stage. investigators therefore should review individual test inquiries as well as the test as a whole.

> Example 4: At the pre-offer stage, R may not include questions such as the following on a psychological examination:

- Inquiries about whether an individual has sought or is currently seeking mental health services;
- Inquiries about the extent of prior illegal drug use;
- Most inquiries about prior or current lawful drug use; and
- Inquiries reflecting the extent of prior or current alcohol use.[49]

3. Polygraph Examinations: Polygraph examinations purportedly measure whether a person believes s/he is telling the truth in response to a particular inquiry.[50] The results are based on relative changes in certain physiological responses of the test taker. These examinations are not, in and of themselves, medical examinations. However, certain inquiries that are frequently made before the polygraph examination is administered, as well as certain inquiries made during the examination, are prohibited pre-offer inquiries.

For example, before a polygraph examination is administered, applicants have commonly been asked whether they have physical impairments that might be adversely affected by the emotional stress of a polygraph examination. This area of inquiry is prohibited at the pre-offer stage because it is likely to elicit information about a disability. However, an employer may ask the applicant to assume responsibility and release the employer of liability for injuries resulting from any physical or mental disorders. An employer also may furnish the applicant with a description of the polygraph examination, and ask him/her to have a private physician review the description and state whether the applicant can safely perform the examination.

Applicants who are required to take polygraph tests also are commonly asked whether they are taking medication or other substances that may skew the results of the examination (i.e., resulting in a false negative because the applicant's physiological responses are minimized because of the medication). These inquiries are prohibited at the pre-offer stage if they are likely to elicit information about a disability (see § IV.B.10 (above)). As noted above, an employer is

---

[49]As noted above in § IV.B.1 2, questions about the extent of alcohol use may disclose whether an individual is an alcoholic.

[50]Polygraph examinations aren ot widely administered by most employers. Rather, such examinations may be lawfully given by private employers only in specific types of jobs, such as security services. See Polygraph Protection Act of 1988, 29 U.S.C. § 2001 et seq. (1989) (prohibiting use of polygraph examinations in most non-governmental jobs).

permitted to make inquiries about lawful drug use at the post-offer stage. If, at that stage, an employer learns that the applicant has taken medication that would have skewed the results of a pre-offer polygraph examination in favor of the applicant, it may choose to administer the polygraph examination again at the post-offer stage.

In addition, inquiries that are prohibited at the pre-offer stage of the hiring process are prohibited during a pre-offer polygraph examination.

EMPLOYMENT POLICIES

Example 1: At the pre-offer stage, R may not make inquiries such as the following during a polygraph examination:

- Inquiries about whether an individual had sought or is currently seeking mental health services;
- Inquiries about the extent of prior illegal drug use;
- Most inquiries about prior or current lawful drug use; and Inquiries reflecting the extent of prior or current alcohol use.

Example 2: R, a police department, may not ask as part of a pre-offer polygraph examination questions such as: "Do you have any mental disorders which would hamper your performance as a police officer?" or "Have you ever been treated for drug addiction?"

4. Vision Tests: A test to diagnose an individual's ability to see may be a medical examination depending on the type of test and the circumstances in which it is given. An investigator's determination should be based on the relevant factors discussed in § V.A (above).

Evaluating an individual's ability to read labels or distinguish objects as part of a demonstration of actual job performance (see § IV.B.5 (above)) is not a medical examination. However, requiring an applicant to submit to an ophthalmologist's or optometrist's analysis of his/her vision is a prohibited pre-offer medical examination.

Example: At the pre-offer stage, R may ask an applicant for a medical laboratory helper position to distinguish between several chemicals on a shelf if distinguishing chemicals is a job function because this is a job demonstration. On the other hand, R's asking an applicant to read letters from a traditional eye chart would be a medical examination, and is therefore prohibited until a conditional employment offer is extended.

5. Drug Tests: Examinations intended or designed to determine the current illegal use of drugs are not considered medical examinations, and therefore may be administered at the pre-offer stage.[51] However, an employer may not seek information at the pre-offer stage about current or prior lawful drug use if such information could reveal the existence, nature, or severity of an impairment or disability.

Still, as discussed more fully in § IV.B.10 (above), if an applicant tests positive for illegal drug use, the employer may validate the test results by asking the applicant about lawful drug use which may have resulted in a positive test results.[52]

If an employer conducts a test solely for unlawful drug use, but receives test results indicating lawful drug use, the employer has not violated the ADA.

> Example: R tests an applicant for illegal use of controlled substances, and inadvertently receives positive test results for dilantin (a prescription drug which the applicant is lawfully using). R did not make a prohibited pre-offer disability related inquiry and has not conducted a prohibited pre-offer medical examination.

6. Alcohol Tests: Tests or procedures intended or designed to determine whether and/or how much alcohol an individual has consumed are medical examinations if they are invasive (e.g., require the drawing of blood, urine, breath). Accordingly, an employer that requires such tests during the hiring process may not administer them at the pre-offer stage.

VI Post-Offer, Pre-Employment Examinations/Inquiries

As noted above, the ADA permits employers to make disability-related inquiries and to require medical examinations after a conditional offer of employment has been extended, but before the individual has started work.

---

[51]42 U.S.C. § 12114(d); 29 C.F.R. § 1630.16(c).

[52]The ADA allows employers to exclude individuals for currently engaging in illegal drug use, 42 U.S.C. § 12114(a), and provides that tests for illegal drug use are not prohibited medical examinations. However, the ADA is not intended to exclude individuals who are not illegally using drugs, but who are erroneously regarded as being addicts and as currently using drugs illegally. See 42 U.S.C. § 12114(b)(3); 29 C.F.R. § 1630.3(b).

> Pre-offer questions about lawful drug use may only be asked after an applicant tests positive for illegal drug use. Such inquiries (i.e., in connection with test validation) are not prohibited inquiries.

A. Bona Fide Job Offers
   1. Information That Must Be Considered Prior to Offer

Job offers that are conditioned on the results of medical examinations and/or inquiries must be bona fide job offers.[53]

In order for a job offer to be considered bona fide, an employer should have evaluated all relevant non-medical information which, from a practical and legal perspective, could reasonably have been analyzed prior to extending the offer.[54]

However, investigators should recognize that there may be very limited instances when an employer may be able to show that it could not reasonably evaluate non-medical information at the pre-offer stage.

> Example 1: It may be too costly for a law enforcement employer wishing to administer a polygraph examination to administer a pre-offer examination making non-medical inquiries, and a post-offer examination making medical inquiries. In this case, the employer may be able to demonstrate that it could not reasonably evaluate the non-medical polygraph information at the pre-offer stage.

> Example 2: An applicant might state to R that his current employer should not be asked for a reference check until the potential employer makes a conditional job offer. In this case, the potential employer could not reasonably evaluate the non-medical information from the reference at the pre-offer stage.

If an employer persuades the investigator that it was reasonably necessary to give a job offer before it evaluated some non-medical information, the investigator may find that the offer was bona fide. However, investigators should

---

[53]Under general principles of contract law, an "offer" is "an act that reasonably leads the offeree to believe that a power to create a contract has been confirmed on him." Kansas Power & Light Co. v. Burlington Northern Rd. Co., 740 F.2d 780, 786 (10th Cir. 1984). Similarly, an "offer" has been defined as "an expression by one party of his assent to certain definite terms, provided that the other party involved in the bargaining transaction will likewise express his assent to the identically same terms." Corbin, Corbin on Contracts § 11 (1960 & West Supp. 1991). Invitations to deal or acts of preliminary negotiation are not offers. Id.

A valid offer must, therefore, contain the terms of the contract to be made. Id.; see also Bakaly & Grossman, Modern Law of Employment Contracts: Formation, Operation and Remedies for Breach (Prentice Hall 1988) at 29 ("terms of an employment contract must be reasonably definite"). The terms "must be of sufficient explicitness so that a court can perceive . . . the respective obligations of the parties." Soar v. National Football League Players' Association, 550 F.2d 1287, 1290 (1st Cir. 1977) (interpreting alleged contract concerning pension benefits).

[54]The ADA's legislative history reflects that, by prohibiting pre-offer medical inquiries and examinations, Congress intended to help end discrimination on the basis of "hidden" disabilities. Noting that employers used information on "hidden" disabilities "before [an applicant's] ability to perform the job was even evaluated," (Senate Report at 39; House Education and Labor Report at 72; House Judiciary Report at 42 (1990)), Congress indicated its intent to require employers to evaluate an applicant's ability to perform a job before employers could consider an applicant's medical condition.

closely scrutinize an offer that is withdrawn after a selection procedure containing both medical and non-medical components to determine whether the applicant was rejected because of a medical components.[55]

> Example 3: R administers a post-offer security clearance, as well as a post-offer medical exam. If R withdraws the offer after the post-offer medical exam, the investigator should closely scrutinize whether the withdrawal was based on the results of the medical examination. R may demonstrate to the investigator that the offer was withdrawn for non-medical-related reasons.

2. Pools
a. Whether Offers Must Be Limited to Current Vacancies

Under the ADA, bona fide job offers do not always need to be limited to currently available vacancies but also may, under certain circumstances, be given to fill reasonably anticipated openings. Investigators should be aware that an employer may be able to demonstrate that, for legitimate purposes, it must provide a specific number of job offers to fill currently available positions or reasonably anticipated vacancies. For example, an employer may demonstrate that it needs to have a pool of ready employees, and that a certain percentage of the offerees will likely be disqualified or will withdraw from the pool.

> Example 1: A police department may be able to demonstrate that it needs to make offers to 50 applicants for 25 available positions because: (1) for public safety reasons, it needs to have police officers who are ready and able to begin work when a vacancy occurs on the force; and (2) it is likely that approximately half of the offers will be revoked based on post-offer medical tests and/or the results of security checks, and because some applicants may voluntarily withdraw from consideration.

> Example 2: A maritime industry employer may be able to demonstrate that it needs to make offers to 100 applicants for 60 available positions because: (1) ships are in dock for a very short period of time and the employer must have crew members who are ready and able to fill vacancies on outbound ships; and (2) it is likely that approximately 40 of the offers will be revoked based on post-offer medical examinations or procedures.

---

[55]If an investigator determines that the offer was withdrawn based on the applicant's disability, the employer must demonstrate that the reasons for the withdrawal are job-related and consistent with business necessity. 42 U.S.C. § 12112(b)(6); 29 C.F.R. § 1630.10.

Example 3: It is unlikely that a typical law firm can demonstrate that it needs to make offers to three applicants for one available attorney position. The law firm probably cannot demonstrate that it must have a ready pool of lawyers to fill vacancies, and that offers to two of the three attorneys are likely to be revoked based on post-offer examinations or procedures.

b. Hiring Individuals From a Pool of Offerees

If more offers are made than positions exist, in order for the offers to be considered bona fide, the employer must hire individuals from the pool based on pre-established, objective standards (such as the date of application).[56] If the pre-established, objective standards have an adverse impact on a protected class, the employer must be able to justify the standards as job-related and consistent with business necessity. In relevant cases, investigators should obtain evidence of the procedures used by the employer for taking individuals from the "pool" in order to ensure that these standards are followed.

Example 1: R gives job offers to 50 applicants and places them in a pool from which employees will be hired. R legitimately withdraws the offers of some of the individuals in the pool, based on results from post-offer medical exams. In filling vacancies, R follows its pre-established procedures and takes individuals remaining in the pool based on the date of each person's application. R has made bona fide job offers for purposes of the ADA.

Example 2: R gives job offers to 50 applicants and places them in a pool from which employees will be hired. R has no pre-established, objective procedures for taking individuals from the pool to fill vacancies. Rather, R evaluates which applicant in the pool should get the job only when an opening occurs. In this case, R did not make bona fide job offers for purposes of the ADA when it placed individuals into the pool.

If an employer's pre-established, objective standard for hiring individuals from a pool includes "re-ranking" the order of the individuals in the pool based (in whole or in part) on the results of a post-offer inquiry or procedure, the employer must do the following:

- inform each individual in the hiring pool of his/her overall ranking prior to any post-offer re-ranking; and

---

[56]Such pre-established objective standards are important to ensure that the individual knows whether his/her position in the hiring priority order has changed as a result of a post-offer medical evaluation. This furthers the ADA's objective of separating an evaluation of an individual's qualifications from his/her disability.

- inform each individual of any change in his/her overall ranking after any post-offer re-ranking.

> Example 3: A police department gives a post-offer psychological examination, which is designed to analyze an individual's mental stability and is therefore a medical examination. The department re-ranks the individuals in its pool based on scores on this examination, placing those individuals who score most favorably at the top of the hiring priority list. In this case, the department must inform individuals in the hiring pool of their initially-determined hiring rank order; after the post-offer medical examination, the department must inform the individuals in the hiring pool whether their rank has changed based (in whole or in part) on the post-offer medical examination.

This procedure furthers the ADA's goal of isolating the employer's consideration of an individual's non-medical qualifications from any consideration of his/her medical condition. It also ensures that an individual knows whether, and to what extent, his/her physical or mental disability has affected his/her hiring priority.

If an employer lowers the rank of an individual in a pool based on disability, the employer must demonstrate to the investigator that the standard used to lower the rank is job-related and consistent with business necessity. See Section III, above.

B. General Rules Regarding Post-Offer Medical Examinations/Inquiries

After an applicant has been offered employment, but before employment has begun, an employer may require medical examinations and may inquire regarding the existence, nature, or severity of a disability. Employer may condition the employment offer on the results of an examination/inquiry, as long as:

- all entering employees[57] in the same job category are subjected to the examination/inquiry, regardless of disability; and
- the information obtained is kept confidential (as explained in § VI.D (below)).[58]

Accordingly, at the post-offer stage, an employer may ask about an individual's workers' compensation history, prior sick leave usage, illnesses/diseases, and general physical and mental health. Medical examinations and inquiries that are

---

[57]An entering employee is someone who has been given a conditional job offer.

[58]42 U.S.C. § 12112(d)(3); 29 C.F.R. (185) 1630.14(b)(1), (2).

required of all entering employees in a job category at the post-offer stage do not have to be related to the job in question.[59]

If an employer administers a medical examination or makes disability-related inquiries at the post-offer stage, all entering employees in the job category must be given an initial examination or asked the initial disability related questions.[60]

In some cases, medical information obtained in response to an initial medical examination or disability-related inquiry may indicate that additional information is needed. An employer may subject specific entering employees to follow-up medical examinations or follow-up disability-related inquiries, if the follow-up examinations/inquiries are medically related to the previously obtained medical information.

> Example: At the post-offer stage, R asks entering employees whether they have had back injuries, and learns that some of the individuals have had such injuries. R may give medical examinations designed to diagnose back impairments to persons who stated that they had prior back injuries, as long as the follow-up medical examinations are medically related to those injuries.

If an examination or inquiry is used to screen out an individual with a disability as a result of the disability, the exclusionary criteria must be job-related and consistent with business necessity, and the employer must demonstrate to the investigator that the essential job functions could not be performed with reasonable accommodation.[61] Where safety considerations are implicated, the individual can only be screened out because s/he poses a "direct threat." Employers must present evidence to the investigator that this determination was based on objective, factual evidence that this particular individual poses a significant risk of substantial harm to him/herself or others, and that this risk cannot be reduced below the level of a direct threat through reasonable accommodation.[62] As more fully explained in the Commission's regulations and the accompanying Appendix,

---

[59]Although the ADA allows post-offer medical examinations/disability-related inquiries that are not job-related, employers may, as a practical matter, find it desirable to avoid requiring such examinations/inquiries. This is so because an employer's obtaining information unrelated to the job can be probative of an employer's knowledge of an individual's disability if discrimination is alleged at a later time.

[60]42 U.S.C. § 12112(d)(3)(A); 29 C.F.R. § 1630.14(b).

[61]29 C.F.R. pt. 1630 app. § 1630.10.

[62]See 29 C.F.R. pt. 1630 app. § 1630.2(r); House Education and Labor Report at 56-57; House Judiciary Report at 45; Senate Report at 27.

the direct threat standard is a stringent one, requiring an assessment of risk based on individualized, objective evidence.[63]

C. Requesting Documentation of the Need for Reasonable Accommodation

When an individual, at the post-offer stage, requests accommodation to actually perform a job, the employer may require documentation of the individual's need for, and entitlement to, reasonable accommodation. Documentation may be required concerning both the individual's status as an individual with a disability and his/her functional limitations. Such requests are not prohibited inquiries.

> Example: An entering employee states that she will need a 15 minute break every two hours to eat a snack in order to maintain her blood sugar level. R may ask the entering employee to provide documentation from her doctor reflecting that: (1) she has insulin-dependent diabetes which substantially limits a major life activity; and (2) she actually needs the breaks she has requested because of the diabetes.

Requesting documentation concerning both an individual's status as an individual with a disability and his/her functional limitations is consistent with the ADA and the statute's legislative history. Requesting documentation concerning a person's status as an individual with a disability is consistent with an employer's obligation to provide reasonable accommodation only to protected individuals.[64] Accordingly, when an individual requests reasonable accommodation to actually perform his/her job, an employer may request documentation from an appropriate professional concerning whether that individual is protected by the statute. See § IV.B.6.b (above). An employer is entitled to request documentation concerning an individual's functional limitations in order to: (1) ascertain whether the functional limitations for which reasonable accommodation is sought result from the disability; and (2) engage in the intended interactive process to determine an appropriate reasonable accommodation.[65]

---

[63]For example, if an employer learns that an entering employee for a job operating heavy machinery has insulin-dependent diabetes, the employer might have some fear that the individual will lose consciousness because of a hypoglycemic reaction and thereby cause an accident. The employer may withdraw the offer because of the diabetes only if the direct threat standard is satisfied. In addition, even if the individual poses a direct threat (i.e., based on an objective, individualized assessment), the employer must determine whether the risk of substantial harm can be reduced below the direct threat level through some reasonable accommodation. In this case, it might be a reasonable accommodation for the employer to install some type of safety device on the machine, or to provide the employee with work breaks so that s/he can eat a snack and/or take medication to control the diabetes.

[64]See 42 U.S.C. § 12112(b)(5)(A) (employer must make reasonable accommodations "to the known physical or mental limitations of an otherwise qualified individual with a disability").

[65]See Senate Report at 34; House Education and Labor Report at 65-66.

D. Confidentiality

Medical information obtained in the course of a post-offer medical examination or inquiry may be provided to and used by appropriate decisionmakers involved in the hiring process in order to make employment decisions consistent with the ADA. For example, the employer may use the information to determine whether a reasonable accommodation is possible for a particular applicant with a disability.

> Example 1: R has extended a job offer to an applicant with paraplegia. The individual requests reasonable accommodation so that she can perform the job. R may consult with an occupational health professional, as R's agent, concerning possible reasonable accommodations. Such consultation does not violate the confidentiality restrictions of the ADA.

The employer may only share the medical information with individuals involved in the hiring process who need to know the information. It is not always appropriate for every person involved in the decision-making process to be informed about an applicant's medical-related information. For example, in some cases, a number of people may be involved in evaluating an applicant; some individuals may simply be responsible for evaluating an applicant's references. These individuals may have no need to know an applicant's medical condition and, therefore, should not have access to the information.

Once the selection decision is made, the medical information must be kept confidential.[66] However, the ADA does not prohibit an individual with a disability from voluntarily disclosing his/her own medical information to persons beyond those to whom an employer can disclose such information. If an individual voluntarily discloses such information, the employer has not violated the law. Still, the employer may not request, persuade, coerce, or otherwise pressure the individual to disclose such information.

The ADA requires that the information be collected and maintained on separate forms and in separate medical files.[67]

Thus, an employer should not place any medical-related material in an employee's non-medical personnel file.[68]

The ADA prohibits an employer from disclosing confidential medical information to anyone, including co-workers, except as expressly provided in the

---

[66] 42 U.S.C. § 12112(d)(3); 29 C.F.R. § 1630.14(b).

[67] 42 U.S.C. § 12112(d)(3)(B).

[68] Of course, if an employer wishes to place a document containing some medical information in a personnel file, the employer must simply remove the medical information from the document before placing it in the personnel file.

law. The ADA allows disclosure of this information only in the following circumstances:[69]

> (1) supervisors and managers may be informed regarding necessary restrictions on the work or duties of the employee and necessary accommodations;[70]
>
> (2) first aid and safety personnel may be informed, when appropriate, if the disability might require emergency treatment;[71]
>
> (3) government officials investigating compliance with the ADA shall be provided relevant information on request;[72]
>
> (4) employers may submit information to state workers' compensation offices, state second injury funds or workers' compensation insurance carriers in accordance with state workers' compensation laws;[73] and
>
> (5) employers may use the information for insurance purposes.[74]

The fact that an applicant was not hired or that an employee no longer works for the employer does not terminate the employer's obligation to maintain the confidentiality of medical information regarding the individual.[75]

> Example 2: R gives an applicant an offer of employment, conditioned on a post-offer medical examination. After the medical examination, R withdraws the conditional offer for reasons that are job-related and consistent with business necessity. R must continue to maintain the confidentiality of the applicant's medical information even though the applicant was not hired.

---

[69]These confidentiality provisions apply to medical information obtained at both the pre-employment and post-employment stages. See 42 U.S.C. §§ 12112(d)(3)(B), (4)(C).

[70]29 C.F.R. § 1630.14(b)(1)(i).

[71]29 C.F.R. § 1630.14(b)(1)(ii).

[72]29 C.F.R. § 1630.14(b)(1)(iii).

[73]See 42 U.S.C. § 12201(b); 29 C.F.R. pt. 1630 app. § 1630.14(b).

[74]See 42 U.S.C. § 12201(c); 29 C.F.R. pt. 1630 app. § 1630.14(b). For example, an employer may submit medical information to the company's health insurance carrier if the information is needed to administer a health insurance plan in accordance with § 501(c) of the ADA.

[75]The ADA's confidentiality obligation applies regardless of whether the individual becomes or remains an employee. Section 102(c)(3) of the ADA expressly protects "information obtained" concerning an applicant's medical condition or history. 42 U.S.C. § 12112(d)(3)(B). See also House Judiciary Report at 43 ("information obtained" during pre-employment, post-offer examination must be kept confidential). "Nothing in the statute or the legislative history limits an employer's confidentiality obligation with regard to such information to the duration of an actual or potential employment relationships.

Information obtained by a covered entity before the effective date of the ADA is not restricted by the ADA's confidentiality provisions. However, information obtained by a covered entity after the effective date is restricted by the ADA.

> Example 3: Employer A obtained medical information from employees before it became covered by the ADA. Employer A is not required to segregate this medical information pursuant to the ADA, and is not required by the ADA to keep this information confidential.

> Example 4: Same facts as the previous example. A former employee of Employer A now applies for a job with Employer B, an employer covered by the ADA. At the post-offer stage, Employer B lawfully obtains from Employer A CP's medical records (which Employer A obtained before it was covered by the ADA). Employer A has not violated the ADA by disclosing CP's medical records because Employer A was not restricted by the ADA concerning these records (i.e., because they were obtained pre-ADA). However, because Employer B is covered by the ADA at the time it obtains the medical records, Employer B must keep the records segregated/ confidential in accordance with the ADA.

If an individual reveals medical information in response to a nonmedical inquiry, the information obtained still must be kept confidential.[76] An employer must ensure that medical information is not included in any personnel documents that are to be distributed to individuals beyond those permitted under the ADA to receive an individual's medical information.

| Date | Tony Gallegos |
| | Chairman |

---

[76]Cf. 42 U.S.C. § 12112(d)(3)(B) ("information obtained regarding the medical condition or history of the applicant" must be kept confidential). Therefore, medical information voluntarily disclosed by an individual would be confidential information because the information was lawfully obtained under the ADA.

Appendix B

Equal Employment Opportunities Commission's (EEOC's) Enforcement Guidance: Reasonable Accommodation and Undue Hardship Under the Americans with Disabilities Act (ADA) (March 1, 1999)

TABLE OF CONTENTS

INTRODUCTION

This Enforcement Guidance clarifies the rights and responsibilities of employers and individuals with disabilities regarding reasonable accommodation and undue hardship. Title I of the ADA requires an employer to provide reasonable accommodation to qualified individuals with disabilities who are employees or applicants for employment, except when such accommodation would cause an undue hardship. This Guidance sets forth an employer's legal obligations regarding reasonable accommodation; however, employers may provide more than the law requires.

This Guidance examines what "reasonable accommodation" means and who is entitled to receive it. The Guidance addresses what constitutes a request for reasonable accommodation, the form and substance of the request, and an employer's ability to ask questions and seek documentation after a request has been made.

The Guidance discusses reasonable accommodations applicable to the hiring process and to the benefits and privileges of employment. The Guidance also covers different types of reasonable accommodations related to job performance, including job restructuring, leave, modified or part-time schedules, modified workplace policies, and reassignment. Questions concerning the relationship between the ADA and the Family and Medical Leave Act (FMLA) are examined as they affect leave and modified schedules. Reassignment issues addressed include who is entitled to reassignment and the extent to which an employer must search for a vacant position. The Guidance also examines issues concerning the interplay between reasonable accommodations and conduct rules.

The final section of this Guidance discusses undue hardship, including when requests for schedule modifications and leave may be denied.

GENERAL PRINCIPLES

Reasonable Accommodation

Title I of the Americans with Disabilities Act of 1990 (the "ADA")[1] requires an employer[2] to provide reasonable accommodation to qualified individuals with disabilities who are employees or applicants for employment, unless to do so would cause undue hardship. "In general, an accommodation is any change in the work environment or in the way things are customarily done that enables an individual with a disability to enjoy equal employment opportunities."[3] There are three categories of "reasonable accommodations":

> "(i) modifications or adjustments to a **job application process** that enable a qualified applicant with a disability to be considered for the position such qualified applicant desires; or

(ii) modifications or adjustments to the **work environment,** or to the **manner** or **circumstances under which the position held or desired is customarily performed,** that enable a qualified individual with a disability to perform the essential functions of that position; or

(iii) modifications or adjustments that enable a covered entity's employee with a disability to enjoy **equal benefits and privileges of employment** as are enjoyed by its other similarly situated employees without disabilities."[4]

The duty to provide reasonable accommodation is a fundamental statutory requirement because of the nature of discrimination faced by individuals with disabilities. Although many individuals with disabilities can apply for and perform jobs without any reasonable accommodations, there are workplace barriers that keep others from performing jobs which they could do with some form of accommodation. These barriers may be physical obstacles (such as inaccessible facilities or equipment), or they may be procedures or rules (such as rules concerning when work is performed, when breaks are taken, or how essential or marginal functions are performed). Reasonable accommodation removes workplace barriers for individuals with disabilities.

Reasonable accommodation is available to qualified applicants and employees with disabilities.[5] Reasonable accommodations must be provided to qualified employees regardless of whether they work part-time or full-time, or are considered "probationary." Generally, the individual with a disability must inform the employer that an accommodation is needed.[6]

There are a number of possible reasonable accommodations that an employer may have to provide in connection with modifications to the work environment or adjustments in how and when a job is performed. These include:

* making existing facilities accessible;
* job restructuring;
* part-time or modified work schedules;
* acquiring or modifying equipment;
* changing tests, training materials, or policies;
* providing qualified readers or interpreters; and
* reassignment to a vacant position.[7]

There are several **modifications or adjustments that are not considered forms of reasonable accommodation.** An employer does not have to eliminate an essential function, i.e., a fundamental duty of the position. This is because a person with a disability who is unable to perform the essential functions, with or without reasonable accommodation,[8] is not a "qualified" individual with a disability within the meaning of the ADA. Nor is an employer required to lower production standards — whether qualitative or quantitative[9] — that are applied uniformly to employees with and without disabilities. However, an employer may have to provide reasonable accommodation to enable an employee with a disability to meet the production standard. While an employer is not required to eliminate an essential function or lower a production standard, it may do so if it wishes.

An employer does not have to provide as reasonable accommodations personal use items needed in accomplishing daily activities both on and off the job. Thus, an employer is not required to provide an employee with a prosthetic limb, a wheelchair, eyeglasses, hearing aids, or similar devices if they are also needed off the job. Furthermore, an employer is not required to provide personal use amenities, such as a hot pot or refrigerator, if those items are not provided to employees without disabilities. However, items that might otherwise be considered personal may be required as reasonable accommodations where they are specifically designed or required to meet job-related rather than personal needs.[10]

A modification or adjustment satisfies the reasonable accommodation obligation if it is "effective."[11] In the context of job performance, this means that a reasonable accommodation enables the individual to perform the essential functions of the position. Similarly, an effective accommodation will enable an applicant with a disability to have an equal opportunity to participate in the application process and to be considered for a job. Finally, a reasonable accommodation will be effective if it allows an employee with a disability an equal opportunity to enjoy the benefits and privileges of employment that employees without disabilities enjoy.

> Example A: An employee with a hearing disability must be able to contact the public by telephone. The employee proposes that he use a TTY[12] to call a relay service operator who can then place the telephone call and relay the conversation between the parties. This is a reasonable accommodation because it is effective. It enables the employee to communicate with the public.

> Example B: A cashier easily becomes fatigued because of lupus and, as a result, has difficulty making it through her shift, The employee requests a stool because sitting greatly reduces the fatigue. This reasonable accommodation is effective because it removes a workplace barrier — being required to stand — and thus gives the employee the opportunity to perform as well as any other cashier.

The term "reasonable accommodation" is a term of art that Congress defined only through examples of changes or modifications to be made, or items to be provided, to a qualified individual with a disability. The statutory definition of "reasonable accommodation" does not include any quantitative, financial, or other limitations regarding the extent of the obligation to make changes to a job or work environment.[13] **The only statutory limitation on an employer's obligation to provide "reasonable accommodation" is that no such change or modification is required if it would cause "undue hardship" on the employer.**[14] Undue hardship addresses quantitative, financial, or other limitations on an employer's ability to provide reasonable accommodation.

Undue Hardship

"Undue hardship" means significant difficulty or expense and focuses on the resources and circumstances of the particular employer in relationship to the cost or difficulty of providing a specific accommodation. Undue hardship refers not only to financial difficulty, but to reasonable accommodations that are unduly extensive, substantial, or disruptive, or those that would fundamentally alter the nature or operation of the business.[15] An employer must assess on a case-by-case basis whether a particular reasonable accommodation would cause undue hardship. The ADA's "undue hardship" standard is different from that applied by courts under Title VII of the Civil Rights Act of 1964 for religious accommodation.[16]

REQUESTING REASONABLE ACCOMMODATION

1. **How must an individual** request a reasonable accommodation?

   When an individual decides to request accommodation, the individual or his/her representative must let the employer know that s/he needs an adjustment or change at work for a reason related to a medical condition. To request accommodation, an individual may use "plain English" and need not mention the ADA or use the phrase "reasonable accommodation."[17]

   Example A: An employee tells her supervisor, "I'm having trouble getting to work at my scheduled starting time because of medical treatments I'm undergoing." This is a request for a reasonable accommodation.

   Example B: An employee tells his supervisor, "I need six weeks off to get treatment for a back problem." This is a request for a reasonable accommodation.

Example C: A new employee, who uses a wheelchair, informs the employer that her wheelchair cannot fit under the desk in her office. This is a request for reasonable accommodation.

Example D: An employee tells his supervisor that he would like a new chair because his present one is uncomfortable. Although this is a request for a change at work, his statement is insufficient to put the employer on notice that he is requesting reasonable accommodation. He does not link his need for the new chair with a medical condition.

While an individual with a disability may request a change due to a medical condition, **this request does not necessarily mean that the employer is required to provide the change. A request for reasonable accommodation is the first step** in an informal, interactive process between the individual and the employer. In some instances, before addressing the merits of the accommodation request, the employer needs to determine if the individual's medical condition meets the ADA definition of "disability,"[18] a prerequisite for the individual to be entitled to a reasonable accommodation.

2. May someone **other than the individual with a disability request a reasonable accommodation** on behalf of the individual?

Yes, a family member, friend, health professional, or other representative may request a reasonable accommodation on behalf of an individual with a disability.[19] Of course, the individual with a disability may refuse to accept an accommodation that is not needed.

Example A: An employee's spouse phones the employee's supervisor on Monday morning to inform her that the employee had a medical emergency due to multiple sclerosis, needed to be hospitalized, and thus requires time off. This discussion constitutes a request for reasonable accommodation.

Example B: An employee has been out of work for six months with a workers' compensation injury. The employee's doctor sends the employer a letter, stating that the employee is released to return to work, but with certain work restrictions. (Alternatively, the letter may state that the employee is released to return to a light duty position.) The letter constitutes a request for reasonable accommodation.

3. Do requests for reasonable accommodation need to be **in writing?**

No. Requests for reasonable accommodation do not need to be in writing. Individuals may request accommodations in conversation or may use any other mode of communication.[20] An employer may choose to write a memorandum or letter confirming the individual's request. Alternatively, an employer may ask the individual to fill out a form or submit the request in written form, but the employer cannot ignore the initial request. An employer also may request reasonable documentation that the individual has an ADA disability and needs a reasonable accommodation. (See Question 6).

4. When should an individual with a disability **request a reasonable accommodation?**

An individual with a disability may request a reasonable accommodation at any time during the application process or during the period of employment. The ADA does not preclude an employee with a disability from requesting a reasonable accommodation because s/he did not ask for one when applying for a job or after receiving a job offer. Rather, an individual with a disability should request a reasonable accommodation when s/he knows that there is a workplace barrier that is preventing him/her, due to a disability, from effectively competing for a position, performing a job, or gaining equal access to a benefit of employment.[21] As a practical matter, it may be in an employee's interest to request a reasonable accommodation before performance suffers or conduct problems occur.

5. What must an employer do **after receiving a request for reasonable accommodation?**

The employer and the individual with a disability should **engage in an informal process** to clarify what the individual needs and identify the appropriate reasonable accommodation.[22] The employer may ask the individual relevant questions that will enable it to make an informed decision about the request. This includes asking what type of reasonable accommodation is needed.

The exact nature of the dialogue will vary. In many instances, both the disability and the type of accommodation required will be obvious, and thus there may be little or no need to engage in any discussion. In other situations, the employer may need to ask questions concerning the nature of the disability and the individual's functional limitations in order to identify an effective accommodation. While the individual with a disability does not have to be able to specify the precise accommodation, s/he does need to describe the problems posed by the workplace barrier. Additionally, suggestions from the individual with a disability may assist the employer in determining the type of reasonable accommodation to provide. Where the individual or the employer are not familiar with possible accommodations, there are extensive public and private resources to help the employer identify reasonable accommodations once the specific limitations and workplace barriers have been ascertained.[23]

6. May an employer ask an individual for **documentation** when the individual requests reasonable accommodation?

Yes. When the **disability and/or the need for accommodation is not obvious,** the employer may ask the individual for **reasonable documentation** about his/her disability and functional limitations.[24] The employer is entitled to know that the individual has a covered disability for which s/he needs a reasonable accommodation.

Reasonable documentation means that the employer may require only the documentation that is needed to establish that a person has an ADA disability, and that the disability necessitates a reasonable accommodation. Thus, an employer, in response to a request for reasonable accommodation, cannot ask for documentation that is unrelated to determining the existence of a disability and the necessity for an accommodation. This means that in most situations an employer cannot request a person's complete medical records because they are likely to contain information unrelated to the disability at issue and the need for accommodation. If an individual has more than one disability, an employer can request information pertaining only to the disability that requires a reasonable accommodation.

An employer may require that the documentation about the disability and the functional limitations come from an appropriate health care or rehabilitation professional. The appropriate professional in any particular situation will depend on the disability and the type of functional limitation it imposes. Appropriate professionals include, but are not limited to, doctors (including psychiatrists), psychologists, nurses, physical therapists, occupational therapists, speech therapists, vocational rehabilitation specialists, and licensed mental health professionals.

In requesting documentation, employers should specify what types of information they are seeking regarding the disability, its functional limitations, and the need for reasonable accommodation. The individual can be asked to sign a limited release allowing the employer to submit a list of specific questions to the health care or vocational professional.[25]

As an alternative to requesting documentation, an employer may simply discuss with the person the nature of his/her disability and functional limitations. It would be useful for the employer to make clear to the individual why it is requesting information, i.e., to verify the existence of an ADA disability and the need for a reasonable accommodation.

Example A: An employee says to an employer, "I'm having trouble reaching tools because of my shoulder injury." The employer may ask the employee for documentation describing the impairment; the nature, severity, and duration of the impairment; the activity or activities that the impairment limits; and the extent to which the impairment limits the employee's ability to perform the activity or activities (i.e., the employer is seeking information as to whether the employee has an ADA disability).

Example B: A marketing employee has a severe learning disability. He attends numerous meetings to plan marketing strategies. In order to remember what is discussed at these meetings he must take detailed notes but, due to his disability, he has great difficulty writing. The employee tells his supervisor about his disability and requests a laptop computer to use in the meetings. Since neither the disability nor the need for accommodation are obvious, the supervisor may ask the employee for reasonable documentation about his impairment; the nature, severity, and duration of the impairment; the activity or activities that the impairment limits; and the extent to which the impairment limits the employee's ability to perform the activity or activities. The employer also may ask why the disability necessitates use of a laptop computer (or any other type of reasonable accommodation, such as a tape recorder) to help the employee retain the information from the meetings.[26]

Example C: An employee's spouse phones the employee's supervisor on Monday morning to inform her that the employee had a medical emergency due to multiple sclerosis, needed to be hospitalized, and thus requires time off. The supervisor can ask the spouse to send in documentation from the employee's treating physician that confirms that the hospitalization was related to the multiple sclerosis and provides information on how long an absence may be required from work.[27]

If an individual's disability or need for reasonable accommodation is not obvious, and s/he refuses to provide the reasonable documentation requested by the employer, then s/he is not entitled to reasonable accommodation.[28] On the other hand, failure by the employer to initiate or participate in an informal dialogue with the individual after receiving a request for reasonable accommodation could result in liability for failure to provide a reasonable accommodation.[29]

7. May an employer require an individual to go to a health care professional of the **employer's (rather than the employee's) choice** for purposes of documenting need for accommodation and disability?

The ADA does not prevent an employer from requiring an individual to go to an appropriate health professional of the employer's choice if the individual provides insufficient information from his/her treating physician (or other health care professional) to substantiate that s/he has an ADA disability and needs a reasonable accommodation. However, if an individual provides insufficient documentation in response to the employer's initial request, the employer should explain why the documentation is insufficient and allow the individual an opportunity to provide the missing information in a timely manner. Documentation is insufficient if it does not specify the existence of an ADA disability and explain the need for reasonable accommodation.[30]

Any medical examination conducted by the employer's health professional must be job-related and consistent with business necessity. This means that the examination must be limited to determining the existence of an ADA disability and the functional limitations that require reasonable accommodation.[31] If an employer requires an employee to go to a health professional of the employer's choice, the employer must pay all costs associated with the visit(s).

8. Are there situations in which an employer **cannot ask for documentation** in response to a request for reasonable accommodation?

Yes. An employer cannot ask for documentation when: (1) both the disability and the need for reasonable accommodation are obvious, or (2) the individual has already provided the employer with sufficient information to substantiate that s/he has an ADA disability and needs the reasonable accommodation requested.

> Example A: An employee brings a note from her treating physician explaining that she has diabetes and that, as a result, she must test her blood sugar several times a day to ensure that her insulin level is safe in order to avoid a hyperglycemic reaction. The note explains that a hyperglycemic reaction can include extreme thirst, heavy breathing, drowsiness, and flushed skin, and eventually would result in unconsciousness. Depending on the results of the blood test, the employee might have to take insulin. The note requests that the employee be allowed three or four 10-minute breaks each day to test her blood, and if necessary, to take insulin. The doctor's note constitutes sufficient documentation that the person has an ADA disability because it describes a substantially limiting

impairment and the reasonable accommodation needed as a result. The employer cannot ask for additional documentation.

Example B: One year ago, an employer learned that an employee had bipolar disorder after he requested a reasonable accommodation. The documentation provided at that time from the employee's psychiatrist indicated that this was a permanent condition which would always involve periods in which the disability would remit and then intensify. The psychiatrist's letter explained that during periods when the condition flared up, the person's manic moods or depressive episodes could be severe enough to create serious problems for the individual in caring for himself or working, and that medication controlled the frequency and severity of these episodes.

Now, one year later, the employee again requests a reasonable accommodation related to his bipolar disorder. Under these facts, the employer may ask for reasonable documentation on the need for the accommodation (if the need is not obvious), but it cannot ask for documentation that the person has an ADA disability. The medical information provided one year ago established the existence of a long-term impairment that substantially limits a major life activity.

Example C: An employee gives her employer a letter from her doctor, stating that the employee has asthma and needs the employer to provide her with an air filter. This letter contains insufficient information as to whether the asthma is an ADA disability because it does not provide any information as to its severity (i.e., whether it substantially limits a major life activity). Furthermore, the letter does not identify precisely what problem exists in the workplace that requires an air filter or any other reasonable accommodation. Therefore, the employer can request additional documentation.

9. Is an employer required to provide the reasonable accommodation **that the individual wants?**

The employer may choose among reasonable accommodations as long as the chosen accommodation is effective.[32] Thus, as part of the interactive process, the employer may offer alternative suggestions for reasonable accommodations and discuss their effectiveness in removing the workplace barrier that is impeding the individual with a disability.

If there are two possible reasonable accommodations, and one costs more or is more burdensome than the other, the employer may choose the less expensive or burdensome accommodation as long as it is effective (i.e., it would remove a workplace barrier, thereby providing the individual with an equal opportunity to apply for a position, to perform the essential functions of a position, or to gain equal access to a benefit or privilege of employment). Similarly, when there are two or more effective accommodations, the employer may choose the one that is easier to provide. In either situation, the employer does not have to show that it is an undue hardship to provide the more expensive or more difficult accommodation. If more than one accommodation is effective, "the preference of the individual with a disability should be given primary consideration. However, the employer providing the accommodation has the ultimate discretion to choose between effective accommodations."[33]

> Example A: An employee with a severe learning disability has great difficulty reading. His supervisor sends him many detailed memoranda which he often has trouble understanding. However, he has no difficulty understanding oral communication. The employee requests that the employer install a computer with speech output and that his supervisor send all memoranda through electronic mail which the computer can then read to him. The supervisor asks whether a tape recorded message would accomplish the same objective and the employee agrees that it would. Since both accommodations are effective, the employer may choose to provide the supervisor and employee with a tape recorder so that the supervisor can record her memoranda and the employee can listen to them.

> Example B: An attorney with a severe vision disability requests that her employer provide someone to read printed materials that she needs to review daily. The attorney explains that a reader enables her to review substantial amounts of written materials in an efficient manner. Believing that this reasonable accommodation would be too costly, the employer instead provides the attorney with a device that allows her to magnify print so that she can read it herself. The attorney can read print using this device, but with such great difficulty it significantly slows down her ability to review written materials. The magnifying device is ineffective as a reasonable accommodation because it does not provide the attorney with an equal opportunity to attain the same level of performance as her colleagues. Without an equal opportunity to attain the same level of performance, this attorney is denied an equal opportunity to compete for promotions. In this instance, failure to provide the reader, absent undue hardship, would violate the ADA.

10. **How quickly must an employer respond** to a request for reasonable accommodation?

An employer should respond expeditiously to a request for reasonable accommodation. If the employer and the individual with a disability need to engage in an interactive process, this too should proceed as quickly as possible.[34] Similarly, the employer should act promptly to provide the reasonable accommodation. Unnecessary delays can result in a violation of the ADA.[35]

> Example A: An employer provides parking for all employees. An employee who uses a wheelchair requests from his supervisor an accessible parking space, explaining that the spaces are so narrow that there is insufficient room for his van to extend the ramp that allows him to get in and out. The supervisor does not act on the request and does not forward it to someone with authority to respond. The employee makes a second request to the supervisor. Yet, two months after the initial request, nothing has been done. Although the supervisor never definitively denies the request, the lack of action under these circumstances amounts to a denial, and thus violates the ADA.

> Example B: An employee who is blind requests adaptive equipment for her computer as a reasonable accommodation. The employer must order this equipment and is informed that it will take three months to receive delivery. No other company sells the adaptive equipment the employee needs. The employer notifies the employee of the results of its investigation and that it has ordered the equipment. Although it will take three months to receive the equipment, the employer has moved as quickly as it can to obtain it and thus there is no ADA violation resulting from the delay. The employer and employee should determine what can be done so that the employee can perform his/her job as effectively as possible while waiting for the equipment.

11. May an employer **require an individual with a disability to accept a reasonable accommodation that s/he does not want?**

No. An employer may not require a qualified individual with a disability to accept an accommodation. If, however, an employee needs a reasonable accommodation to perform an essential function or to eliminate a direct threat, and refuses to accept an effective accommodation, s/he may not be qualified to remain in the job.[36]

REASONABLE ACCOMMODATION AND JOB APPLICANTS

12. **May** an employer ask whether a reasonable accommodation is needed when **an applicant has not asked for one?**

An employer may tell applicants what the hiring process involves (e.g., an interview, timed written test, or job demonstration), and may ask applicants whether they will need a reasonable accommodation for this process.

During the hiring process and before a conditional offer is made, an employer generally may not ask an applicant whether s/he needs a reasonable accommodation for the job, except when the employer knows that an applicant has a disability — either because it is obvious or the applicant has voluntarily disclosed the information — and could reasonably believe that the applicant will **need a reasonable accommodation to perform specific job functions.** If the applicant replies that s/he needs a reasonable accommodation, the employer may inquire as to what type.[37]

After a conditional offer of employment is extended, an employer may inquire whether applicants will **need reasonable accommodations related to anything connected with the job** (i.e., job performance or access to benefits/privileges of the job) as long as all entering employees in the same job category are asked this question. Alternatively, an employer may ask a specific applicant if s/he needs a reasonable accommodation if the employer knows that this applicant has a disability — either because it is obvious or the applicant has voluntarily disclosed the information — and could reasonably believe that the applicant will need a reasonable accommodation. If the applicant replies that s/he needs a reasonable accommodation, the employer may inquire as to what type.[38]

13. Does an employer have to provide a reasonable accommodation to an applicant with a disability even **if it believes that it will be unable to provide this individual with a reasonable accommodation on the job?**

Yes. An employer must provide a reasonable accommodation to a **qualified applicant with a disability** that will enable the individual to have an equal opportunity to participate in the application process and to be considered for a job (unless it can show undue hardship). Thus, individuals with disabilities who meet initial requirements to be considered for a job should not be excluded from the application process because the employer speculates, based on a request for reasonable accommodation for the application process, that it will be unable to provide the individual with reasonable accommodation to perform the job. In many instances, employers will be unable to determine whether an individual needs reasonable accommodation to perform a job based solely on a request for accommodation during the application process. And even if an individual will need reasonable accommodation to perform the job, it may not be the same type or degree of accommodation that is needed for the application process. Thus, an employer should assess the need for accommodations for the application process separately from those that **may** be needed to perform the job.[39]

> Example A: An employer is impressed with an applicant's resume and contacts the individual to come in for an interview. The applicant, who is deaf, requests a sign language interpreter for the interview. The employer cancels the interview and refuses to consider further this applicant because it believes it would have to hire a full-time interpreter. The employer has violated the ADA. The employer should have proceeded with the interview, using a sign language interpreter (absent undue hardship), and at the interview inquired to what extent the individual would need a sign language interpreter to perform any essential functions requiring communication with other people.

> Example B: An individual who has paraplegia applies for a secretarial position. Because the office has two steps at the entrance, the employer arranges for the applicant to take a typing test, a requirement of the application process, at a different location. The applicant fails the test. The employer does not have to provide any further reasonable accommodations for this individual because she is no longer qualified to continue with the application process.

REASONABLE ACCOMMODATION RELATED TO THE BENEFITS AND PRIVILEGES OF EMPLOYMENT[40]

The ADA requires employers to provide reasonable accommodations so that employees with disabilities can enjoy the "benefits and privileges of employment" equal to those enjoyed by similarly-situated employees without disabilities. Benefits and privileges of employment include, but are not limited to, employer-sponsored: (1) training, (2) services (e.g., employee assistance programs (EAP's), credit unions, cafeterias, lounges, gymnasiums, auditoriums, transportation), and (3) parties or other social functions (e.g., parties to celebrate retirements and birthdays, and company outings).[41] If an employee with a disability needs a reasonable accommodation in order to gain access to, and have an equal opportunity to participate in, these benefits and privileges, then the employer must provide the accommodation unless it can show undue hardship.

14. Does an employer have to provide reasonable accommodation **to enable an employee with a disability to have equal access to information communicated in the workplace to non-disabled employees?**

Yes. Employers provide information to employees through different means, including computers, bulletin boards, mailboxes, posters, and public address systems. Employers must ensure that employees with disabilities have access to information that is provided to other similarly-situated employees without disabilities, regardless of whether they need it to perform their jobs.

Example A: An employee who is blind has adaptive equipment for his computer that integrates him into the network with other employees, thus allowing communication via electronic mail and access to the computer bulletin board. When the employer installs upgraded computer equipment, it must provide new adaptive equipment in order for the employee to be integrated into the new networks, absent undue hardship. Alternative methods of communication (e.g., sending written or telephone messages to the employee instead of electronic mail) are likely to be ineffective substitutes since electronic mail is used by every employee and there is no effective way to ensure that each one will always use alternative measures to ensure that the blind employee receives the same information that is being transmitted via computer.

Example B: An employer authorizes the Human Resources Director to use a public address system to remind employees about special meetings and to make certain announcements. In order to make this information accessible to a deaf employee, the Human Resources Director arranges to send in advance an electronic mail message to the deaf employee conveying the information that will be broadcast. The Human Resources Director is the only person who uses the public address system; therefore, the employer can ensure that all public address messages are sent, via electronic mail, to the deaf employee. Thus, the employer is providing this employee with equal access to office communications.

15. Must an employer provide reasonable accommodation so that **an employee may attend training programs?**

Yes. Employers must provide reasonable accommodation (e.g., sign language interpreters; written materials produced in alternative formats, such as braille, large print, or on audio-cassette) that will provide employees with disabilities with an equal opportunity to participate in employer-sponsored training, absent undue hardship. This obligation extends to in-house training, as well as to training provided by an outside entity. Similarly, the employer has an obligation to provide reasonable accommodation whether the training occurs on the employer's premises or elsewhere.

Example A: XYZ Corp. has signed a contract with Super Trainers, Inc., to provide mediation training at its facility to all of XYZ's Human Resources staff. One staff member is blind and requests that materials be provided in braille. Super Trainers refuses to provide the materials in braille. XYZ maintains that it is the responsibility of Super Trainers and sees no reason why it should have to arrange and pay for the braille copy.

Both XYZ (as an employer covered under Title I of the ADA) and Super Trainers (as a public accommodation covered under Title III of the ADA[42]) have obligations to provide materials in alternative formats. This fact, however, does not excuse either one from their respective obligations. If Super Trainers refuses to provide the braille version, despite its Title III obligations, XYZ still retains its obligation to provide it as a reasonable accommodation, absent undue hardship.

Employers arranging with an outside entity to provide training may wish to avoid such problems by specifying in the contract who has the responsibility to provide appropriate reasonable accommodations. Similarly, employers should ensure that any offsite training will be held in an accessible facility if they have an employee who, because of a disability, requires such an accommodation.

Example B: XYZ Corp. arranges for one of its employees to provide CPR training. This three-hour program is optional. A deaf employee wishes to take the training and requests a sign language interpreter. XYZ must provide the interpreter because the CPR training is a benefit that XYZ offers all employees, even though it is optional.

TYPES OF REASONABLE ACCOMMODATIONS RELATED TO JOB PERFORMANCE[43]

Below are discussed certain types of reasonable accommodations related to job performance.

Job Restructuring

Job restructuring includes modifications such as:

- reallocating or redistributing marginal job functions that an employee is unable to perform because of a disability; and
- altering when and/or how a function, essential or marginal, is performed.[44]

An employer never has to reallocate essential functions as a reasonable accommodation, but can do so if it wishes.

16. If, as a reasonable accommodation, an employer restructures an employee's job to eliminate some marginal functions, **may the employer require the employee to take on other marginal functions** that s/he can perform?

Yes. An employer may switch the marginal functions of two (or more) employees in order to restructure a job as a reasonable accommodation.

> Example A: A cleaning crew works in an office building. One member of the crew wears a prosthetic leg which enables him to walk very well, but climbing steps is painful and difficult. Although he can perform his essential functions without problems, he cannot perform the marginal function of sweeping the steps located throughout the building. The marginal functions of a second crew member include cleaning the small kitchen in the employee's lounge, which is something the first crew member can perform. The employer can switch the marginal functions performed by these two employees.

Leave

Permitting the use of accrued paid leave, or unpaid leave, is a form of reasonable accommodation when necessitated by an employee's disability.[45] **An employer does not have to provide paid leave beyond that which is provided to similarly-situated employees.** Employers should allow an employee with a disability to exhaust accrued paid leave first and then provide unpaid leave.[46] For example, if employees get 10 days of paid leave, and an employee with a disability needs 15 days of leave, the employer should allow the individual to use 10 days of paid leave and 5 days of unpaid leave.

An employee with a disability may need leave for a number of reasons related to the disability, including, but not limited to:

- obtaining medical treatment (e.g., surgery, psychotherapy, substance abuse treatment, or dialysis); rehabilitation services; or physical or occupational therapy;
- recuperating from an illness or an episodic manifestation of the disability;
- obtaining repairs on a wheelchair, accessible van, or prosthetic device;
- avoiding temporary adverse conditions in the work environment (for example, an air-conditioning breakdown causing unusually warm temperatures that could seriously harm an employee with multiple sclerosis);
- training a service animal (e.g., a guide dog); or
- receiving training in the use of braille or to learn sign language.

17. May an employer apply a **"no-fault" leave policy,** under which employees are automatically terminated after they have been on leave for a certain period of time, to an employee with a disability who needs leave beyond the set period?

No. If an employee with a disability needs additional unpaid leave as a reasonable accommodation, the employer must modify its "no-fault" leave policy to provide the employee with the additional leave, unless it can show that: (1) there is another effective accommodation that would enable the person to perform the essential functions of his/her position, or (2) granting additional leave would cause an undue hardship. Modifying workplace policies, including leave policies, is a form of reasonable accommodation.[47]

18. Does an employer have to **hold open an employee's job** as a reasonable accommodation?

Yes. An employee with a disability who is granted leave as a reasonable accommodation is entitled to return to his/her same position unless the employer demonstrates that holding open the position would impose an undue hardship.[48]

If an employer cannot hold a position open during the entire leave period without incurring undue hardship, the employer must consider whether it has a vacant, equivalent position for which the employee is qualified and to which the employee can be reassigned to continue his/her leave for a specific period of time and then, at the conclusion of the leave, can be returned to this new position.[49]

> Example: An employee needs eight months of leave for treatment and recuperation related to a disability. The employer grants the request, but after four months the employer determines that it can no longer hold open the position for the remaining four months without incurring undue hardship. The employer must consider whether it has a vacant, equivalent position to which the employee can be reassigned for the remaining four months of leave, at the end of which time the employee would return to work in that new position. If an equivalent position is not available, the employer must look for a vacant position at a lower level. Continued leave is not required as a reasonable accommodation if a vacant position at a lower level is also unavailable.

19. Can an employer **penalize an employee for work missed during leave** taken as a reasonable accommodation?

No. To do so would be retaliation for the employee's use of a reasonable accommodation to which s/he is entitled under the law.[50] Moreover, such punishment would make the leave an ineffective accommodation, thus making an employer liable for failing to provide a reasonable accommodation.[51]

Example A: A salesperson took five months of leave as a reasonable accommodation. The company compares the sales records of all salespeople over a one-year period, and any employee whose sales fall more than 25% below the median sales performance of all employees is automatically terminated. The employer terminates the salesperson because she had fallen below the required performance standard. The company did not consider that the reason for her lower sales performance was her five-month leave of absence; nor did it assess her productivity during the period she did work (i.e., prorate her productivity).

Penalizing the salesperson in this manner constitutes retaliation and a denial of reasonable accommodation.

Example B: Company X is having a reduction-in-force. The company decides that any employee who has missed more than four weeks in the past year will be terminated. An employee took five weeks of leave for treatment of his disability. The company cannot count those five weeks in determining whether to terminate this employee.[52]

20. When an employee requests leave as a reasonable accommodation, may an employer provide an accommodation that **requires him/her to remain on the job** instead?

Yes, if the employer's reasonable accommodation would be effective and eliminate the need for leave.[53] An employer need not provide an employee's preferred accommodation as long as the employer provides an effective accommodation.[54] Accordingly, in lieu of providing leave, an employer may provide a reasonable accommodation that requires an employee to remain on the job (e.g., reallocation of marginal functions or temporary transfer) as long as it does not interfere with the employee's ability to address his/her medical needs. The employer is obligated, however, to restore the employee's full duties or to return the employee to his/her original position once s/he no longer needs the reasonable accommodation.

Example A: An employee with emphysema requests ten weeks of leave for surgery and recuperation related to his disability. In discussing this request with the employer, the employee states that he could return to work after seven weeks if, during his first three weeks back, he could work part-time and eliminate two marginal functions that require lots of walking. If the employer provides these accommodations, then it can require the employee to return to work after seven weeks.

Example B: An employee's disability is getting more severe and her doctor recommends surgery to counteract some of the effects. After receiving the employee's request for leave for the surgery, the employer proposes that it provide certain equipment which it believes will mitigate the effects of the disability and delay the need for leave to get surgery. The employer's proposed accommodation is not effective because it interferes with the employee's ability to get medical treatment.

21. **How should an employer handle leave for an employee covered by both the ADA and the Family and Medical Leave Act (FMLA)?**[55]

An employer should determine an employee's rights under each statute separately, and then consider whether the two statutes overlap regarding the appropriate actions to take.[56]

Under the ADA, an employee who needs leave related to his/her disability is entitled to such leave if there is no other effective accommodation and the leave will not cause undue hardship. An employer must allow the individual to use any accrued paid leave first, but, if that is insufficient to cover the entire period, then the employer should grant unpaid leave. An employer must continue an employee's health insurance benefits during his/her leave period only if it does so for other employees in a similar leave status. As for the employee's position, the ADA requires that the employer hold it open while the employee is on leave unless it can show that doing so causes undue hardship. When the employee is ready to return to work, the employer must allow the individual to return to the same position (assuming that there was no undue hardship in holding it open) if the employee is still qualified (i.e., the employee can perform the essential functions of the position with or without reasonable accommodation).

If it is an undue hardship under the ADA to hold open an employee's position during a period of leave, or an employee is no longer qualified to return to his/her original position, then the employer must reassign the employee (absent undue hardship) to a vacant position for which s/he is qualified.

Under the FMLA, an eligible employee is entitled to a maximum of 12 weeks of leave per 12 month period. The FMLA guarantees the right of the employee to return to the same position or to an equivalent one.[57] An employer must allow the individual to use any accrued paid leave first, but if that is insufficient to cover the entire period, then the employer should grant unpaid leave. The FMLA requires an employer to continue the employee's health insurance coverage during the leave period, provided the employee pays his/her share of the premiums.

Example A: An employee with an ADA disability needs 13 weeks of leave for treatment related to the disability. The employee is eligible under the FMLA for 12 weeks of leave (the maximum available), so this period of leave constitutes both FMLA leave and a reasonable accommodation. Under the FMLA, the employer could deny the employee the thirteenth week of leave. But, because the employee is also covered under the ADA, the employer cannot deny the request for the thirteenth week of leave unless it can show undue hardship. The employer may consider the impact on its operations caused by the initial 12-week absence, along with other undue hardship factors.[58]

Example B: An employee with an ADA disability has taken 10 weeks of FMLA leave and is preparing to return to work. The employer wants to put her in an equivalent position rather than her original one. Although this is permissible under the FMLA, the ADA requires that the employer return the employee to her original position. Unless the employer can show that this would cause an undue hardship, or that the employee is no longer qualified for her original position (with or without reasonable accommodation), the employer must reinstate the employee to her original position.

Example C: An employee with an ADA disability has taken 12 weeks of FMLA leave. He notifies his employer that he is ready to return to work, but he no longer is able to perform the essential functions of his position or an equivalent position. Under the FMLA, the employer could terminate his employment,[59] but under the ADA the employer must consider whether the employee could perform the essential functions with reasonable accommodation (e.g., additional leave, part-time schedule, job restructuring, or use of specialized equipment). If not, the ADA requires the employer to reassign the employee if there is a vacant position available for which he is qualified, with or without reasonable accommodation, and there is no undue hardship.

Modified or Part-Time Schedule

22. Must an employer allow an **employee with a disability to work a modified or part-time schedule** as a reasonable accommodation, absent undue hardship?

Yes.[60] A modified schedule may involve adjusting arrival or departure times, providing periodic breaks, altering when certain functions are performed, allowing an employee to use accrued paid leave, or providing additional unpaid leave. An employer must provide a modified or part-time schedule when required as a reasonable accommodation, absent undue hardship, even if it does not provide such schedules for other employees.

> Example A: An employee with HIV infection must take medication on a strict schedule. The medication causes extreme nausea about one hour after ingestion, and generally lasts about 45 minutes. The employee asks that he be allowed to take a daily 45-minute break when the nausea occurs. The employer must grant this request absent undue hardship.

For certain positions, **the time during which an essential function is performed may be critical.** This could affect whether an employer can grant a request to modify an employee's schedule.[61] Employers should carefully assess whether modifying the hours could **significantly disrupt** their operations — that is, cause undue hardship — or whether the essential functions may be performed at different times with **little or no impact** on the operations or the ability of other employees to perform their jobs.

If modifying an employee's schedule poses an undue hardship, an employer must consider reassignment to a vacant position that would enable the employee to work during the hours requested.[62]

> Example B: A day care worker requests that she be allowed to change her hours from 7:00 a.m. - 3:00 p.m. to 10:00 a.m. - 6:00 p.m. because of her disability. The day care center is open from 7:00 a.m. - 7:00 p.m. and it will still have sufficient coverage at the beginning of the morning if it grants the change in hours. In this situation, the employer must provide the reasonable accommodation.

> Example C: An employee works for a morning newspaper, operating the printing presses which run between 10 p.m. and 3 a.m. Due to her disability, she needs to work in the daytime. The essential function of

her position, operating the printing presses, requires that she work at night because the newspaper cannot be printed during the daytime hours. Since the employer cannot modify her hours, it must consider whether it can reassign her to a different position.

23. How should an employer handle requests for modified or part-time schedules for an **employee covered by both the ADA and the Family and Medical Leave Act (FMLA)**.[63]

An employer should determine an employee's rights under each statute separately, and then consider whether the two statutes overlap regarding the appropriate actions to take.

Under the ADA, an employee who needs a modified or part-time schedule because of his/her disability is entitled to such a schedule if there is no other effective accommodation and it will not cause undue hardship. If there is undue hardship, the employer must reassign the employee if there is a vacant position for which s/he is qualified and which would allow the employer to grant the modified or part-time schedule (absent undue hardship).[64] An employee receiving a part-time schedule as a reasonable accommodation is entitled only to the benefits, including health insurance, that other part-time employees receive. Thus, if non-disabled part-time workers are not provided with health insurance, then the employer does not have to provide such coverage to an employee with a disability who is given a part-time schedule as a reasonable accommodation.

Under the FMLA, an eligible employee is entitled to take leave intermittently or on a part-time basis, when medically necessary, until s/he has used up the equivalent of 12 workweeks in a 12-month period. When such leave is foreseeable based on planned medical treatment, an employer may require the employee to temporarily transfer (for the duration of the leave) to an available alternative position, with equivalent pay and benefits, for which the employee is qualified and which better suits his/her reduced hours.[65] An employer always must maintain the employee's existing level of coverage under a group health plan during the period of FMLA leave, provided the employee pays his/her share of the premium.[66]

Example: An employee with an ADA disability requests that she be excused from work one day a week for the next six months because of her disability. If this employee is eligible for a modified schedule under the FMLA, the employer must provide the requested leave under that statute if it is medically necessary, even if the leave would be an undue hardship under the ADA.

Modified Workplace Policies

24. Is it a reasonable accommodation to **modify a workplace policy?**

Yes. It is a reasonable accommodation to modify a workplace policy when necessitated by an individual's disability-related limitations,[67] absent undue hardship. But, reasonable accommodation only requires that the employer modify the policy for an employee who requires such action because of a disability; therefore, the employer may continue to apply the policy to all other employees.

Example: An employer has a policy prohibiting employees from eating or drinking at their workstations. An employee with insulin-dependent diabetes explains to her employer that she may occasionally take too much insulin and, in order to avoid going into insulin shock, she must immediately eat a candy bar or drink fruit juice. The employee requests permission to keep such food at her workstation and to eat or drink when her insulin level necessitates. The employer must modify its policy to grant this request, absent undue hardship. Similarly, an employer might have to modify a policy to allow an employee with a disability to bring in a small refrigerator, or to use the employer's refrigerator, to store medication that must be taken during working hours.

Granting an employee time off from work or an adjusted work schedule as a reasonable accommodation may involve modifying leave or attendance procedures or policies. For example, it would be a reasonable accommodation to modify a policy requiring employees to schedule vacation time in advance if an otherwise qualified individual with a disability needed to use accrued vacation time on an unscheduled basis because of disability-related medical problems, barring undue hardship.[68] Furthermore, an employer may be required to provide additional leave to an employee with a disability as a reasonable accommodation in spite of a "no-fault" leave policy, unless the provision of such leave would impose an undue hardship.[69]

In some instances, an employer's refusal to modify a workplace policy, such as a leave or attendance policy, could constitute disparate treatment as well as a failure to provide a reasonable accommodation. For example, an employer may have a policy requiring employees to notify supervisors before 9:00 a.m. if they are unable to report to work. If an employer would excuse an employee from complying with this policy because of emergency hospitalization due to a car accident, then the employer must do the same thing when the emergency hospitalization is due to a disability.[70]

Reassignment[71]

The ADA specifically lists "reassignment to a vacant position" as a form of reasonable accommodation.[72] This type of reasonable accommodation must be provided to an employee who, because of a disability, can no longer perform the essential functions of his/her current position, with or without reasonable accommodation, unless the employer can show that it would be an undue hardship.[73]

An employee must be "qualified" for the new position. An employee is "qualified" for a position if s/he: (1) satisfies the requisite skill, experience, education, and other job-related requirements of the position, and (2) can perform the essential functions of the new position, with or without reasonable accommodation.[74] The employee does not need to be the best qualified individual for the position in order to obtain it as a reassignment.

There is no obligation for the employer to assist the individual to become qualified. Thus, the employer does not have to provide training so that the employee acquires necessary skills to take a job.[75] The employer, however, would have to provide an employee with a disability who is being reassigned with any training that is normally provided to anyone hired for or transferred to the position.

> Example A: An employer is considering reassigning an employee with a disability to a position which requires the ability to speak Spanish in order to perform an essential function. The employee never learned Spanish and wants the employer to send him to a course to learn Spanish. The employer is not required to provide this training as part of the obligation to make a reassignment. Therefore, the employee is not qualified for this position.

> Example B: An employer is considering reassigning an employee with a disability to a position in which she will contract for goods and services. The employee is qualified for the position. The employer has its own specialized rules regarding contracting that necessitate training all individuals hired for these positions. In this situation, the employer must provide the employee with this specialized training.

Before considering reassignment as a reasonable accommodation, employers should first consider those accommodations that would enable an employee to remain in his/her current position. Reassignment is the reasonable accommodation of last resort and is required only after it has been determined that: (1) there are no effective accommodations that will enable the employee to perform the essential functions of his/her current position, or (2) all other reasonable accommodations would impose an undue hardship.[76] However, if both the employer and the employee **voluntarily** agree that transfer is preferable to remaining in the current position with some form of reasonable accommodation, then the employer may transfer the employee.

"Vacant" means that the position is available when the employee asks for reasonable accommodation, or that the employer knows that it will become available within a reasonable amount of time. A "reasonable amount of time" should be determined on a case-by-case basis considering relevant facts, such as whether the employer, based on experience, can anticipate that an appropriate position will become vacant within a short period of time.[77] A position is considered vacant even if an employer has posted a notice or announcement seeking applications for that position. The employer does not have to bump an employee from a job in order to create a vacancy, nor does it have to create a new position.[78]

> Example C: An employer is seeking a reassignment for an employee with a disability. There are no vacant positions today, but the employer has just learned that another employee resigned and that that position will become vacant in four weeks. The impending vacancy is equivalent to the position currently held by the employee with a disability. If the employee is qualified for that position, the employer must offer it to him.

> Example D: An employer is seeking a reassignment for an employee with a disability. There are no vacant positions today, but the employer has just learned that an employee in an equivalent position plans to retire in six months. Although the employer knows that the employee with a disability is qualified for this position, the employer does not have to offer this position to her because six months is beyond a "reasonable amount of time." (If, six months from now, the employer decides to advertise the position, it must allow the individual to apply for that position and give the application the consideration it deserves.)

The employer must reassign the individual to a vacant position that is equivalent in terms of pay, status, or other relevant factors (e.g., benefits, geographical location) if the employee is qualified for the position. If there is no vacant equivalent position, the employer must reassign the employee to a vacant lower level position for which the individual is qualified. Assuming there is more than one vacancy for which the employee is qualified, the employer must place the individual in the position that comes closest to the employee's current position in terms of pay, status, etc.[79] If it is unclear which position comes closest, the employer should consult with the employee about his/her preference before determining the position to which the employee will be reassigned. **Reassignment does not include giving an employee a promotion. Thus, an employee must compete for any vacant position that would constitute a promotion.**

25. Is a **probationary employee** entitled to reassignment?

Employers cannot deny a reassignment to an employee solely because s/he is designated as "probationary."[80] An employee with a disability is eligible for reassignment to a new position, regardless of whether s/he is considered "probationary," as long as the employee adequately performed the essential functions of the position, with or without reasonable accommodation, before the need for a reassignment arose.

The longer the period of time in which an employee has adequately performed the essential functions, with or without reasonable accommodation, the more likely it is that reassignment is appropriate if the employee becomes unable to continue performing the essential functions of the current position due to a disability. If, however, the probationary employee has **never** adequately performed the essential functions, with or without reasonable accommodation, then s/he is not entitled to reassignment because s/he was never "qualified" for the original position. In this situation, the employee is similar to an applicant who applies for a job for which s/he is not qualified, and then requests reassignment. Applicants are not entitled to reassignment.

Example A: An employer designates all new employees as "probationary" for one year. An employee has been working successfully for nine months when she becomes disabled in a car accident. The employee, due to her disability, is unable to continue performing the essential functions of her current position, with or without reasonable accommodation, and seeks a reassignment. She is entitled to a reassignment if there is a vacant position for which she is qualified and it would not pose an undue hardship.

Example B: A probationary employee has been working two weeks, but has been unable to perform the essential functions of the job because of his disability. There are no reasonable accommodations that would permit the individual to perform the essential functions of the position, so the individual requests a reassignment. The employer does not have to provide a reassignment (even if there is a vacant position) because, as it turns out, the individual was never qualified — i.e., the individual was never able to perform the essential functions of the position, with or without reasonable accommodation, for which he was hired.

26. Must an employer offer reassignment as a reasonable accommodation **if it does not allow any of its employees to transfer** from one position to another?

Yes. The ADA requires employers to provide reasonable accommodations to individuals with disabilities, including reassignment, even though they are not available to others. Therefore, an employer who does not normally transfer employees would still have to reassign an employee with a disability, unless it could show that the reassignment caused an undue hardship. And, if an employer has a policy prohibiting transfers, it would have to modify that policy in order to reassign an employee with a disability, unless it could show undue hardship.[81]

27. Is an employer's obligation to offer reassignment to a vacant position **limited to those vacancies within an employee's office, branch, agency, department, facility, personnel system** (if the employer has more than a single personnel system), **or geographical area?**

No. This is true even if the employer has a policy prohibiting transfers from one office, branch, agency, department, facility, personnel system, or geographical area to another. The ADA contains no language limiting the obligation to reassign only to positions within an office, branch, agency, etc.[82] Rather, the extent to which an employer must search for a vacant position will be an issue of undue hardship.[83] If an employee is being reassigned to a different geographical area, the employee must pay for any relocation expenses unless the employer routinely pays such expenses when granting voluntary transfers to other employees.

28. Does an employer have **to notify an employee with a disability about vacant positions,** or is it the employee's responsibility to learn what jobs are vacant?

The employer is in the best position to know which jobs are vacant or will become vacant within a reasonable period of time.[84] In order to narrow the search for potential vacancies, the employer, as part of the interactive process, should ask the employee about his/her qualifications and interests. Based on this information, the employer is obligated to inform an employee about vacant positions for which s/he may be eligible as a reassignment. However, an employee should assist the employer in identifying appropriate vacancies to the extent that the employee has access to information about them. If the employer does not know whether the employee is qualified for a specific position, the employer can discuss with the employee his/her qualifications.[85]

An employer should proceed as expeditiously as possible in determining whether there are appropriate vacancies. The length of this process will vary depending on how quickly an employer can search for and identify whether an appropriate vacant position exists. For a very small employer, this process may take one day; for other employers this process may take several weeks.[86] When an employer has completed its search, identified whether there are any vacancies (including any positions that will become vacant in a reasonable amount of time), notified the employee of the results, and either offered an appropriate vacancy to the employee or informed him/her that no appropriate vacancies are available, the employer will have fulfilled its obligation.

29. Does **reassignment** mean that the employee **is permitted to compete** for a vacant position?

No. Reassignment means that the employee gets the vacant position **if s/he is qualified for it.** Otherwise, reassignment would be of little value and would not be implemented as Congress intended.[87]

30. If an employee is reassigned to a lower level position, **must an employer maintain his/her salary** from the higher level position?

No, unless the employer transfers employees without disabilities to lower level positions and maintains their original salaries.[88]

OTHER REASONABLE ACCOMMODATION ISSUES[89]

31. If an employer has provided one reasonable accommodation, does it have to **provide additional reasonable accommodations** requested by an individual with a disability?

The duty to provide reasonable accommodation is an ongoing one.[90] Certain individuals require only one reasonable accommodation, while others may need more than one. Still others may need one reasonable accommodation for a period of time, and then at a later date, require another type of reasonable accommodation. If an individual requests multiple reasonable accommodations, s/he is entitled only to those accommodations that are necessitated by a disability and that will provide an equal employment opportunity.

An employer must consider each request for reasonable accommodation and determine: (1) whether the accommodation is needed, (2) if needed, whether the accommodation would be effective, and (3) if effective, whether providing the reasonable accommodation would impose an undue hardship. If a reasonable accommodation turns out to be ineffective and the employee with a disability remains unable to perform an essential function, the employer must consider whether there would be an alternative reasonable accommodation that would not pose an undue hardship. If there is no alternative accommodation, then the employer must attempt to reassign the employee to a vacant position for which s/he is qualified, unless to do so would cause an undue hardship.

32. Does an employer have to **change a person's supervisor** as a form of reasonable accommodation?

No. An employer does not have to provide an employee with a new supervisor as a reasonable accommodation. Nothing in the ADA, however, prohibits an employer from doing so. Furthermore, although an employer is not required to change supervisors, the ADA may require that supervisory methods be altered as a form of reasonable accommodations.[91] Also, an employee with a disability is protected from disability-based discrimination by a supervisor, including disability-based harassment.

> Example: A supervisor frequently schedules team meetings on a day's notice — often notifying staff in the afternoon that a meeting will be held on the following morning. An employee with a disability has missed several meetings because they have conflicted with previously-scheduled physical therapy sessions. The employee asks that the supervisor give her two to three days' notice of team meetings so that, if necessary, she can reschedule the physical therapy sessions. Assuming no undue hardship would result, the supervisor must make this reasonable accommodation.

33. Does an employer have to allow an employee with a disability to **work at home** as a reasonable accommodation?

An employer must modify its policy concerning where work is performed if such a change is needed as a reasonable accommodation, but **only if this accommodation would be effective and would not cause an undue hardship.**[92] Whether this accommodation is effective will depend on whether the essential functions of the position can be performed at home. There are certain jobs in which the essential functions can only be performed at the work site — e.g., food server, cashier in a store. For such jobs, allowing an employee to work at home is not effective because it does not enable an employee to perform his/her essential functions. Certain considerations may be critical in determining whether a job can be effectively performed at home, including (but not limited to) the employer's ability to adequately supervise the employee and the employee's need to work with certain equipment or tools that cannot be replicated at home. In contrast, employees may be able to perform the essential functions of certain types of jobs at home (e.g., telemarketer, proofreader).[93] For these types of jobs, an employer may deny a request to work at home if it can show that another accommodation would be effective or if working at home will cause undue hardship.

34. Must an employer **withhold discipline or termination of an employee who, because of a disability, violated a conduct rule** that is job-related for the position in question and consistent with business necessity?

No. An employer never has to excuse a violation of a uniformly applied conduct rule that is job-related and consistent with business necessity. This means, for example, that an employer never has to tolerate or excuse violence, threats of violence, stealing, or destruction of property. An employer may discipline an employee with a disability for engaging in such misconduct if it would impose the same discipline on an employee without a disability.

35. Must an employer provide a **reasonable accommodation for an employee with a disability who violated a conduct rule that is job-related for the position in question and consistent with business necessity?**

An employer must make reasonable accommodation to enable **an otherwise qualified employee with a disability** to meet such a conduct standard **in the future,** barring undue hardship, except where the punishment for the violation is termination.[94] Since reasonable accommodation is always **prospective,** an employer is not required to excuse past misconduct even if it is the result of the individual's disability.[95] Possible reasonable accommodations could include adjustments to starting times, specified breaks, and leave if these accommodations will enable an employee to comply with conduct rules.[96]

> Example: An employee with major depression is often late for work because of medication side-effects that make him extremely groggy in the morning. His scheduled hours are 9:00 a.m. to 5:30 p.m., but he arrives at 9:00, 9:30, 10:00, or even 10:30 on any given day. His job responsibilities involve telephone contact with the company's traveling sales representatives, who depend on him to answer urgent marketing questions and expedite special orders. The employer disciplines him for tardiness, stating that continued failure to arrive promptly during the next

month will result in termination of his employment. The individual then explains that he was late because of a disability and needs to work on a later schedule. In this situation, the employer may discipline the employee because he violated a conduct standard addressing tardiness that is job-related for the position in question and consistent with business necessity. The employer, however, must consider reasonable accommodation, barring undue hardship, to enable this individual to meet this standard in the future. For example, if this individual can serve the company's sales representatives by regularly working a schedule of 10:00 a.m. to 6:30 p.m., a reasonable accommodation would be to modify his schedule so that he is not required to report for work until 10:00 a.m.

36. Is it a reasonable accommodation to **make sure that an employee takes medication** as prescribed?

No. Medication monitoring is not a reasonable accommodation. Employers have no obligation to monitor medication because doing so does not remove a workplace barrier. Similarly, an employer has no responsibility to monitor an employee's medical treatment or ensure that s/he is receiving appropriate treatment because such treatment does not involve modifying workplace barriers.[97]

It may be a form of reasonable accommodation, however, to give an employee a break in order that s/he may take medication, or to grant leave so that an employee may obtain treatment.

37. Is an employer **relieved of its obligation to provide reasonable accommodation** for an employee with a disability who **fails to take medication,** to obtain medical treatment, or to use an assistive device (such as a hearing aid)?

No. The ADA requires an employer to provide reasonable accommodation to remove workplace barriers, regardless of what effect medication, other medical treatment, or assistive devices may have on an employee's ability to perform the job.[98]

However, if an employee with a disability, with or without reasonable accommodation, cannot perform the essential functions of the position or poses a direct threat in the absence of medication, treatment, or an assistive device, then s/he is unqualified.

38. Must an employer provide a reasonable accommodation that is needed because of the **side effects of medication or treatment related to the**

disability, or because of symptoms or other medical conditions resulting from the underlying disability?

Yes. The side effects caused by the medication that an employee must take because of the disability are limitations resulting from the disability. Reasonable accommodation extends to all limitations resulting from a disability.

> Example A: An employee with cancer undergoes chemotherapy twice a week, which causes her to be quite ill afterwards. The employee requests a modified schedule — leave for the two days a week of chemotherapy. The treatment will last six weeks. Unless it can show undue hardship, the employer must grant this request.

Similarly, any symptoms or related medical conditions resulting from the disability that cause limitations may also require reasonable accommodation.[99]

> Example B: An employee, as a result of insulin-dependent diabetes, has developed background retinopathy (a vision impairment). The employee, who already has provided documentation showing his diabetes is a disability, requests a device to enlarge the text on his computer screen. The employer can request documentation that the retinopathy is related to the diabetes but the employee does not have to show that the retinopathy is an independent disability under the ADA. Since the retinopathy is a consequence of the diabetes (an ADA disability), the request must be granted unless undue hardship can be shown.

39. **Must** an employer ask whether a reasonable accommodation is needed when **an employee has not asked for one?**

Generally, no. As a general rule, the individual with a disability — who has the most knowledge about the need for reasonable accommodation — must inform the employer that an accommodation is needed.[100]

However, **an employer should initiate the reasonable accommodation interactive process**[101] **without being asked if** the employer: (1) knows that the employee has a disability, (2) knows, or has reason to know, that the employee is experiencing workplace problems because of the disability, and (3) knows, or has reason to know, that the disability prevents the employee from requesting a reasonable accommodation. If the individual with a disability states that s/he does not need a reasonable accommodation, the employer will have fulfilled its obligation.

Example: An employee with mental retardation delivers messages at a law firm. He frequently mixes up messages for "R. Miller" and "T. Miller." The employer knows about the disability, suspects that the performance problem is a result of the disability, and knows that this employee is unable to ask for a reasonable accommodation because of his mental retardation. The employer asks the employee about mixing up the two names and asks if it would be helpful to spell the first name of each person. When the employee says that would be better, the employer, as a reasonable accommodation, instructs the receptionist to write the full first name when messages are left for one of the Messrs. Miller.

40. **May an employer ask whether a reasonable accommodation is needed when an employee with a disability has not asked for one?**

An employer may ask an employee with a known disability whether s/he needs a reasonable accommodation when it reasonably believes that the employee may need an accommodation. For example, an employer could ask a deaf employee who is being sent on a business trip if s/he needs reasonable accommodation. Or, if an employer is scheduling a luncheon at a restaurant and is uncertain about what questions it should ask to ensure that the restaurant is accessible for an employee who uses a wheelchair, the employer may first ask the employee. An employer also may ask an employee with a disability who is having performance or conduct problems if s/he needs reasonable accommodation.[102]

41. May an employer **tell other employees that an individual is receiving a reasonable accommodation** when employees ask questions about a coworker with a disability?

No. An employer may not disclose that an employee is receiving a reasonable accommodation because this usually amounts to a disclosure that the individual has a disability. The ADA specifically prohibits the disclosure of medical information except in certain limited situations, which do not include disclosure to coworkers.[103]

An employer may certainly respond to a question from an employee about why a coworker is receiving what is perceived as "different" or "special" treatment by emphasizing its policy of assisting any employee who encounters difficulties in the workplace. The employer also may find it helpful to point out that many of the workplace issues encountered by employees are personal, and that, in these circumstances, it is the employer's policy to respect employee privacy. An employer may be able to make this point effectively by reassuring the employee asking the question that his/her privacy would similarly be respected if s/he found it necessary to ask the employer for some kind of workplace change for personal reasons.

Since responding to specific coworker questions may be difficult, employers might find it helpful before such questions are raised to provide all employees with information about various laws that require employers to meet certain employee needs (e.g., the ADA and the Family and Medical Leave Act), while also requiring them to protect the privacy of employees. In providing general ADA information to employees, an employer may wish to highlight the obligation to provide reasonable accommodation, including the interactive process and different types of reasonable accommodations, and the statute's confidentiality protections. Such information could be delivered in orientation materials, employee handbooks, notices accompanying paystubs, and posted flyers. Employers may wish to explore these and other alternatives with unions because they too are bound by the ADA's confidentiality provisions. Union meetings and bulletin boards may be further avenues for such educational efforts.

As long as there is no coercion by an employer, an employee with a disability may **voluntarily** choose to disclose to coworkers his/her disability and/or the fact that s/he is receiving a reasonable accommodation.

UNDUE HARDSHIP ISSUES[104]

An employer does not have to provide a reasonable accommodation that would cause an "undue hardship" to the employer. Generalized conclusions will not suffice to support a claim of undue hardship. Instead, undue hardship must be based on an individualized assessment of current circumstances that show that a specific reasonable accommodation would cause significant difficulty or expense.[105] A determination of undue hardship should be based on several factors, including:

- the nature and cost of the accommodation needed;
- the overall financial resources of the facility making the reasonable accommodation; the number of persons employed at this facility; the effect on expenses and resources of the facility;
- the overall financial resources, size, number of employees, and type and location of facilities of the employer (if the facility involved in the reasonable accommodation is part of a larger entity);
- the type of operation of the employer, including the structure and functions of the workforce, the geographic separateness, and the administrative or fiscal

relationship of the facility involved in making the accommodation to the employer;

- the impact of the accommodation on the operation of the facility.[106]

The ADA's legislative history indicates that Congress wanted employers to consider all possible sources of outside funding when assessing whether a particular accommodation would be too costly.[107] Undue hardship is determined based on the **net cost** to the employer. Thus, an employer should determine whether funding is available from an outside source, such as a state rehabilitation agency, to pay for all or part of the accommodation. In addition, the employer should determine whether it is eligible for certain tax credits or deductions to offset the cost of the accommodation.[108] Also, to the extent that a portion of the cost of an accommodation causes undue hardship, the employer should ask the individual with a disability if s/he will pay the difference.

If an employer determines that one particular reasonable accommodation will cause undue hardship, but a second type of reasonable accommodation will be effective and will not cause an undue hardship, then the employer must provide the second accommodation.

An employer cannot claim undue hardship based on employees' (or customers') fears or prejudices toward the individual's disability.[109] Nor can undue hardship be based on the fact that provision of a reasonable accommodation might have a negative impact on the morale of other employees. Employers, however, may be able to show undue hardship where provision of a reasonable accommodation would be unduly disruptive to other employees' ability to work.

> Example A: An employee with breast cancer is undergoing chemotherapy. As a consequence of the treatment, the employee is subject to fatigue and finds it difficult to keep up with her regular workload. So that she may focus her reduced energy on performing her essential functions, the employer transfers three of her marginal functions to another employee for the duration of the chemotherapy treatments. The second employee is unhappy at being given extra assignments, but the employer determines that the employee can absorb the new assignments with little effect on his ability to perform his own assignments in a timely manner. Since the employer cannot show significant disruption to its operation, there is no undue hardship.[110]

> Example B: A convenience store clerk with multiple sclerosis requests that he be allowed to go from working full-time to part-time as a reasonable accommodation because of his disability. The store assigns two clerks per shift, and if the first clerk's hours are reduced, the second

clerk's workload will increase significantly beyond his ability to handle his responsibilities. The store determines that such an arrangement will result in inadequate coverage to serve customers in a timely manner, keep the shelves stocked, and maintain store security. Thus, the employer can show undue hardship based on the significant disruption to its operations and, therefore, can refuse to reduce the employee's hours. The employer, however, should explore whether any other reasonable accommodation will assist the store clerk without causing undue hardship.

42. Must an employer modify the work hours of an employee with a disability if doing so **would prevent other employees from performing their jobs?**

No. If the result of modifying one employee's work hours (or granting leave) is to prevent other employees from doing their jobs, then the significant disruption to the operations of the employer constitutes an undue hardship.

Example A: A crane operator, due to his disability, requests an adjustment in his work schedule so that he starts work at 8:00 a.m. rather than 7:00 a.m., and finishes one hour later in the evening. The crane operator works with three other employees who cannot perform their jobs without the crane operator. As a result, if the employer grants this requested accommodation, it would have to require the other three workers to adjust their hours, find other work for them to do from 7:00 to 8:00, or have the workers do nothing. The ADA does not require the employer to take any of these actions because they all significantly disrupt the operations of the business. Thus, the employer can deny the requested accommodation, but should discuss with the employee if there are other possible accommodations that would not result in undue hardship.

Example B: A computer programmer works with a group of people to develop new software. There are certain tasks that the entire group must perform together, but each person also has individual assignments. It is through habit, not necessity, that they have often worked together first thing in the morning.

The programmer, due to her disability, requests an adjustment in her work schedule so that she works from 10:00 a.m. - 7:00 p.m. rather than 9:00 a.m. - 6:00 p.m. In this situation, the employer could grant the adjustment in hours because it would not significantly disrupt the operations of the business. The effect of the reasonable accommodation would be to alter when the group worked together and when they performed their individual assignments.

43. Can an employer deny a request for leave when **an employee cannot provide a fixed date of return?**

Providing leave to an employee who is unable to provide a fixed date of return is a form of reasonable accommodation. However, if an employer is able to show that the lack of a fixed return date causes an undue hardship, then it can deny the leave. In certain circumstances, undue hardship will derive from the disruption to the operations of the entity that occurs because the employer can neither plan for the employee's return nor permanently fill the position. If an employee cannot provide a fixed date of return, and an employer determines that it can grant such leave at that time without causing undue hardship, the employer has the right to require, as part of the interactive process, that the employee provide periodic updates on his/her condition and possible date of return. After receiving these updates, employers may reevaluate whether continued leave constitutes an undue hardship.

In certain situations, an employee may be able to provide only an **approximate date of return.** Treatment and recuperation do not always permit exact timetables. Thus, an employer cannot claim undue hardship solely because an employee can provide only an approximate date of return.[111] In such situations, or in situations in which a return date must be postponed because of unforeseen medical developments, employees should stay in regular communication with their employers to inform them of their progress and discuss, if necessary, the need for continued leave beyond what might have been granted originally.[112]

> Example A: An experienced chef at a top restaurant requests leave for treatment of her disability but cannot provide a fixed date of return. The restaurant can show that this request constitutes undue hardship because of the difficulty of replacing, even temporarily, a chef of this caliber. Moreover, it leaves the employer unable to determine how long it must hold open the position or to plan for the chef's absence. Therefore, the restaurant can deny the request for leave as a reasonable accommodation.

> Example B: An employee requests eight weeks of leave for surgery for his disability. The employer grants the request. During surgery, serious complications arise that require a lengthier period of recuperation than originally anticipated, as well as additional surgery. The employee contacts the employer after three weeks of leave to ask for an additional ten to fourteen weeks of leave (i.e., a total of 18 to 22 weeks of leave). The employer must assess whether granting additional leave causes an undue hardship.

44. Does a **cost-benefit analysis** determine whether a reasonable accommodation will cause undue hardship?

No. A cost-benefit analysis assesses the cost of a reasonable accommodation in relation to the perceived benefit to the employer and the employee. Neither the statute nor the legislative history supports a cost-benefit analysis to determine whether a specific accommodation causes an undue hardship.[113] Whether the cost of a reasonable accommodation imposes an undue hardship depends on the employer's resources, not on the individual's salary, position, or status (e.g., full-time versus part-time, salary versus hourly wage, permanent versus temporary).

45. Can an employer claim that a reasonable accommodation imposes an undue hardship simply because it **violates a collective bargaining agreement (CBA)?**[114]

No. First, an employer should determine if it could provide a reasonable accommodation that would remove the workplace barrier without violating the CBA. If no reasonable accommodation exists that avoids violating the CBA, then the ADA requires an employer and a union, as a collective bargaining representative, to negotiate in good faith a variance to the CBA so that the employer may provide a reasonable accommodation, except if the proposed accommodation unduly burdens the expectations of other workers (i.e., causes undue hardship). Undue hardship must be assessed on a case-by-case basis to determine the extent to which the proposed accommodation would affect the expectations of other employees. Among the relevant factors to assess would be the duration and severity of any adverse effects caused by granting a variance and the number of employees whose employment opportunities would be affected by the variance.[115]

46. Can an employer claim undue hardship **solely** because a reasonable accommodation would require it to make **changes to property owned by someone else?**

No, an employer cannot claim undue hardship **solely** because a reasonable accommodation would require it to make changes to property owned by someone else. In some situations, an employer will have the right under a lease or other contractual relationship with the property owner to make the type of changes that are needed. If this is the case, the employer should make the changes, assuming no other factors exist that would make the changes too difficult or costly. If the contractual relationship between the employer and property owner requires the owner's consent to the kinds of changes that are required, or prohibits them from being made, then the employer must make good faith efforts either to obtain the owner's permission or to negotiate an exception to the terms of the contract. If the owner refuses to allow the employer to make the modifications, the employer may claim undue hardship. Even in this situation, however, the employer must still provide another reasonable accommodation, if one exists, that would not cause undue hardship.

> Example A: X Corp., a travel agency, leases space in a building owned by Z Co. One of X Corp.'s employees becomes disabled and needs to use a wheelchair. The employee requests as a reasonable accommodation that several room dividers be moved to make his work space easily accessible. X Corp.'s lease specifically allows it to make these kinds of physical changes, and they are otherwise easy and inexpensive to make. The fact that X Corp. does not own the property does not create an undue hardship and therefore it must make the requested accommodation.

> Example B: Same as Example A, except that X Corp.'s lease requires it to seek Z Co.'s permission before making any physical changes that would involve reconfiguring office space. X Corp. requests that Z Co. allow it to make the changes, but Z Co. denies the request, X Corp. can claim that making the physical changes would constitute an undue hardship. However, it must provide any other type of reasonable accommodation that would not involve making physical changes to the facility, such as finding a different location within the office that would be accessible to the employee.

An employer should remember its obligation to make reasonable accommodation when it is negotiating contracts with property owners.[116] Similarly, a property owner should carefully assess a request from an employer to make physical changes that are needed as a reasonable accommodation because failure to permit the modification might constitute "interference" with the rights of an employee with a disability.[117] In addition, other ADA provisions may require the property owner to make the modifications.[118]

INSTRUCTIONS FOR INVESTIGATORS

When assessing whether a Respondent has violated the ADA by denying a reasonable accommodation to a Charging Party, investigators should consider the following:

- **Is the Charging Party "otherwise qualified"** (i.e., is the Charging Party qualified for the job except that, because of disability, s/he needs a reasonable accommodation to perform the position's essential functions)?

- **Did the Charging Party, or a representative, request a reasonable accommodation** (i.e., did the Charging Party let the employer know that s/he needed an adjustment or change at work for a reason related to a medical condition)? [see Questions 1-4]

  - Did the Respondent request **documentation** of the Charging Party's disability and/or functional limitations? If yes, was the documentation provided? Did the Respondent have a legitimate reason for requesting documentation? [see Questions 6-8]
  - What **specific type of reasonable accommodation,** if any, did the Charging Party request?
  - Was there a **nexus** between the reasonable accommodation requested and the functional limitations resulting from the Charging Party's disability? [see Question 6]
  - Was the need for reasonable accommodation related to the **use of medication, side effects from treatment, or symptoms related to a disability?** [see Questions 36-38]

- **For what purpose did the Charging Party request a reasonable accommodation:**

  - for the application process? [see Questions 12-13]
  - in connection with aspects of job performance? [see Questions 16-24, 32-33]
  - in order to enjoy the benefits and privileges of employment? [see Questions 14-15]

- Should the **Respondent have initiated the interactive process, or provided a reasonable accommodation, even if the Charging Party did not ask** for an accommodation? [see Questions 11, 39]

- What did the Respondent do in response to the Charging Party's request for reasonable accommodation (i.e., did the Respondent engage in an **interactive process** with the Charging Party and if so, describe both the Respondent's and the Charging Party's actions/statements during this process)? [see Questions 5-11]

- If the Charging Party asked the Respondent for a particular reasonable accommodation, and the Respondent provided a different accommodation, **why did the Respondent provide a different reasonable accommodation than the one requested by the Charging Party?** Why does the Respondent believe that the reasonable accommodation it provided was effective in eliminating the workplace barrier at issue, thus providing the Charging Party with an equal employment opportunity? Why does the Charging Party believe that the reasonable accommodation provided by the Respondent was ineffective? [see Question 9]

- **What type of reasonable accommodation** could the Respondent have provided that would have been **effective** in eliminating the workplace barrier at issue, thus providing the Charging Party with an equal employment opportunity?

- Does the charge involve allegations concerning reasonable accommodation and violations of any **conduct rules?** [see Questions 34-35]

- If the Charging Party alleges that the Respondent failed to provide a **reassignment** as a reasonable accommodation [see generally Questions 25-30 and accompanying text]:

  - did the Respondent and the Charging Party first discuss other forms of reasonable accommodation that would enable the Charging Party to remain in his/her current position before discussing reassignment?
  - did the Respondent have any vacant positions? [see Question 27]
  - did the Respondent notify the Charging Party about possible vacant positions? [see Question 28]
  - was the Charging Party qualified for a vacant position?
  - if there was more than one vacant position, did the Respondent place the Charging Party in the one that was most closely equivalent to the Charging Party's original position?

- If the Respondent is claiming **undue hardship** [see generally Questions 42-46 and accompanying text]:

  - what evidence has the Respondent produced showing that providing a specific reasonable accommodation would entail significant difficulty or expense?
  - if a modified schedule or leave is the reasonable accommodation, is undue hardship based on the impact on the ability of other employees to do their jobs? [see Question 42]
  - if leave is the reasonable accommodation, is undue hardship based on the amount of leave requested? [see Question 43]
  - is undue hardship based on a conflict between the reasonable accommodation and the provisions of a collective bargaining agreement? [see Question 45]
  - is undue hardship based on the fact that providing the reasonable accommodation requires changes to property owned by an entity other than the Respondent? [see Question 46]

- if the Respondent claims that a particular reasonable accommodation would result in undue hardship, is there another reasonable accommodation that Respondent could have provided that would not have resulted in undue hardship?

- Based on the evidence obtained in answers to the questions above, is the Charging Party a **qualified** individual with a disability (i.e., can the Charging Party perform the essential functions of the position with or without reasonable accommodation)?

APPENDIX

Resources For Locating Reasonable Accommodations

U.S. Equal Employment Opportunity Commission
1-800-669-3362 (Voice) 1-800-800-3302 (TT)

The EEOC's Publication Center has many free documents on the Title I employment provisions of the ADA, including both the statute, 42 U.S.C. 12101 et seq. (1994), and the regulations, 29 C.F.R. 1630 (1997). In addition, the EEOC has published a great deal of basic information about reasonable accommodation and undue hardship. The two main sources of interpretive information are: (1) the Interpretive Guidance accompanying the Title I regulations (also known as the "Appendix" to the regulations), 29 C.F.R. pt. 1630 app. 1630.2(o), (p), 1630.9 (1997), and (2) A Technical Assistance Manual on the Employment Provisions (Title 1) of the Americans with Disabilities Act III, 8 FEP Manual (BNA) 405:6981, 6998-7018 (1992). The Manual includes a 200-page Resource Directory, including federal and state agencies, and disability organizations that can provide assistance in identifying and locating reasonable accommodations.

The EEOC also has discussed issues involving reasonable accommodation in the following guidances and documents: (1) Enforcement Guidance: Preemployment Disability-Related Questions and Medical Examinations at 5, 6-8, 20, 21-22, 8 FEP Manual (BNA) 405:7191, 7192-94, 7201 (1995); (2) Enforcement Guidance: Workers' Compensation and the ADA at 15-20, 8 FEP Manual (BNA) 405:7391, 7398-7401 (1996); (3) Enforcement Guidance: The Americans with Disabilities Act and Psychiatric Disabilities at 19-28, 8 FEP Manual (BNA) 405:7461, 7470-76 (1997); and (4) Fact Sheet on the Family and Medical Leave Act, the Americans with Disabilities Act, and Title VII of the Civil Rights Act of 1964 at 6-9, 8 FEP Manual (BNA) 405:7371, 7374-76 (1996).

Finally, the EEOC has a poster that employers and labor unions may use to fulfill the ADA's posting requirement.

All of the above-listed documents, with the exception of the <u>ADA Technical Assistance Manual and Resource Director</u> and the poster, are also available through the Internet at http://www.eeoc.gov.

U.S. Department of Labor (To obtain information on the Family and Medical Leave Act)

To request written materials: 1-800-959-3652 (Voice) 1-800-326-2577 (TT)

To ask questions: (202) 219-8412 (Voice)

Internal Revenue Service (For information on tax credits and deductions for providing certain reasonable accommodations)

(202) 622-6060 (Voice)

Job Accommodation Network (JAN)
1-800-232-9675 (Voice/TT)
http://janweb.icdi.wvu.edu/

A service of the President's Committee on Employment of People with Disabilities. JAN can provide information, free-of-charge, about many types of reasonable accommodations.

ADA Disability and Business Technical Assistance Centers (DBTACS)
1-800-949-4232 (Voice/TT)

The DBTACs consist of 10 federally funded regional centers that provide information, training, and technical assistance on the ADA. Each center works with local business, disability, governmental, rehabilitation, and other professional networks to provide current ADA information and assistance, and places special emphasis on meeting the needs of small businesses. The DBTACs can make referrals to local sources of expertise in reasonable accommodations.

Registry of Interpreters for the Deaf
(301) 608-0050 (Voice/TT)

The Registry offers information on locating and using interpreters and transliteration services.

RESNA Technical Assistance Project
(703) 524-6686 (Voice) (703) 524-6639 (TT)
http://www.resna.org/hometal.htm

RESNA, the Rehabilitation Engineering and Assistive Technology Society of North America, can refer individuals to projects in all 50 states and the six territories offering technical assistance on technology-related services for individuals with disabilities. Services may include:

- information and referral centers to help determine what devices may assist a person with a disability (including access to large data bases containing information on thousands of commercially available assistive technology products),
- centers where individuals can try out devices and equipment,
- assistance in obtaining funding for and repairing devices, and
- equipment exchange and recycling programs.

INDEX

Note: Page numbering and references removed for on-line version.

Footnotes

1. 42 U.S.C. 12101-12117, 12201-12213 (1994) (codified as amended).

The analysis in this guidance applies to federal sector complaints of non-affirmative action employment discrimination arising under section 501 of the Rehabilitation Act of 1973. 29 U.S.C. 791(g) (1994). It also applies to complaints of non-affirmative action employment discrimination arising under section 503 and employment discrimination under section 504 of the Rehabilitation Act. 29 U.S.C. 793(d), 794(d) (1994).

The ADA's requirements regarding reasonable accommodation and undue hardship supersede any state or local disability antidiscrimination laws to the extent that they offer less protection than the ADA. See 29 C.F.R. 1630.1(c)(2) (1997).

2. In addition to employers, the ADA requires employment agencies, labor organizations, and joint labor-management committees to provide reasonable accommodations. See 42 U.S.C. 12112(a), (b)(5)(A) (1994).

3. 29 C.F.R. pt. 1630 app. 1630.2(o) (1997).

4. 29 C.F.R. 1630.2(o)(1)(i-iii) (1997) (emphasis added). The notices that employers and labor unions must post informing applicants, employees, and members of labor organizations of their ADA rights must include a description of

the reasonable accommodation requirement. These notices, which must be in an accessible format, are available from the EEOC. See the Appendix.

5. All examples used in this document assume that the applicant or employee has an ADA "disability."

Individuals with a relationship or association with a person with a disability are not entitled to receive reasonable accommodations. See Den Hartog v. Wasatch Academy, 129 F.3d 1076, 1084, 7 AD Cas. (BNA) 764, 772 (10th Cir. 1997).

6. See 29 C.F.R. pt. 1630 app. 1630.9 (1997); see also H.R. Rep. No. 101-485, pt. 3, at 39 (1990) [hereinafter House Judiciary Report]; H.R. Rep. No. 101-485, pt. 2, at 65 (1990) [hereinafter House Education and Labor Report]; S. Rep. No. 101-116, at 34 (1989) [hereinafter Senate Report].

For more information concerning requests for a reasonable accommodation, see Questions 1-4, infra. For a discussion of the limited circumstance under which an employer would be required to ask an individual with a disability whether s/he needed a reasonable accommodation, see Question 39, infra.

7. 42 U.S.C. 12111(9) (1994); 29 C.F.R. 1630.2(o)(2)(i-ii) (1997).

8. "[W]ith or without reasonable accommodation" includes, if necessary, reassignment to a vacant position. Thus, if an employee is no longer qualified because of a disability to continue in his/her present position, an employer must reassign him/her as a reasonable accommodation. See the section on "Reassignment," infra pp. 37-38 and n. 73.

9. 29 C.F.R. pt. 1630 app. 1630.2(n) (1997).

10. 29 C.F.R. pt. 1630 app. 1630.9 (1997).

11. See 29 C.F.R. pt. 1630 app. 1630.9 (1997); Senate Report, supra note 6, at 35 ("reasonableness" of an accommodation is assessed "in terms of effectiveness and equal opportunity"); House Education and Labor Report, supra note 6, at 66 ("[a] reasonable accommodation should be effective for the employee"); see also Bryant v. Better Business Bureau of Greater Maryland, 923 F. Supp. 720, 736, 5 AD Cas. (BNA) 625, 634-35 (D. Md. 1996); Dutton v. Johnson County Bd. of Comm'rs, 859 F. Supp. 498, 507, 3 AD Cas. (BNA) 808, 815 (D. Kan. 1994); Davis v. York Int'l, Inc., 2 AD Cas. (BNA) 1810, 1816 (D. Md. 1993).

Some courts have said that in determining whether an accommodation is "reasonable," one must look at the costs of the accommodation in relation to its benefits. See, e.g., Monette v. Electronic Data Sys. Corp., 90 F.3d 1173, 1184 n. 10, 5 AD Cas. (BNA) 1326, 1335 n. 10 (6th Cir. 1996); Vande Zande v. Wisconsin Dept. of Admin., 44 F.3d 538, 543, 3 AD Cas. (BNA) 1636, 1638-39 (7th Cir, 1995). This "cost/benefit" analysis has no foundation in the statute, regulations, or legislative history of the ADA. See 42 U.S.C. 12111(9), (10) (1994); 29 C.F.R. 1630.2(o), (p) (1997); see also Senate Report, supra, at 31-35; House Education and Labor Report, supra, at 57-58.

12. A TTY is a device that permits individuals with hearing and speech impairments to communicate by telephone.

13. 42 U.S.C. 12111(9) (1994) ("The term 'reasonable accommodation' may include — (A) making existing facilities . . . readily accessible . . . ; and (B) job restructuring; part-time or modified work schedules, reassignment to a vacant position; acquisition or modification of equipment or devices, . . .").

14. See 42 U.S.C. 12112 (b)(5)(A) (1994) (it is a form of discrimination to fail to provide a reasonable accommodation "unless such covered entity can demonstrate that the accommodation would impose an undue hardship . . . "); see also 42 U.S.C. 12111(10) (1994) (defining "undue hardship" based on factors assessing cost and difficulty).

The legislative history discusses financial, administrative, and operational limitations on providing reasonable accommodations only in the context of defining "undue hardship." Compare Senate Report, supra note 6, at 31-34 with 35-36; House Education and Labor Report, supra note 6, at 57-58 with 67-70.

15. See 42 U.S.C. 12111(10) (1994); 29 C.F.R. 1630.2(p) (1997); 29 C.F.R. pt. 1630 app. 1630.2(p) (1997).

16. See 29 C.F.R. pt. 1630 app. 1630.15(d) (1997). See also Eckles v. Consolidated Rail Corp., 94 F.3d 1041, 1048-49, 5 AD Cas. (BNA) 1367, 1372-73 (7th Cir, 1996); Bryant v. Better Business Bureau of Maryland, 923 F. Supp. 720, 740, 5 AD Cas. (BNA) 625, 638 (D. Md. 1996).

17. See, e.g., Schmidt v. Safeway Inc., 864 F. Supp. 991, 997, 3 AD Cas. (BNA) 1141, 1146-47 (D. Or. 1994) ("statute does not require the plaintiff to speak any magic words. . . . The employee need not mention the ADA or even the term 'accommodation.' "). See also Hendricks-Robinson v. Excel Corp., 154 F.3d 685, 694, 8 AD Cas. (BNA) 875, 882 (7th Cir. 1998) ("[a] request as straightforward as asking for continued employment is a sufficient request for accommodation"); Bultemeyer v. Ft. Wayne Community Schs., 100 F.3d 1281, 1285, 6 AD Cas. (BNA) 67, 71 (7th Cir. 1996) (an employee with a known psychiatric disability

requested reasonable accommodation by stating that he could not do a particular job and by submitting a note from his psychiatrist); McGinnis v. Wonder Chemical Co., 5 AD Cas. (BNA) 219 (E.D. Pa. 1995) (employer on notice that accommodation had been requested because: (1) employee told supervisor that his pain prevented him from working and (2) employee had requested leave under the Family and Medical Leave Act).

Nothing in the ADA requires an individual to use legal terms or to anticipate all of the possible information an employer may need in order to provide a reasonable accommodation. The ADA avoids a formulistic approach in favor of an interactive discussion between the employer and the individual with a disability, after the individual has requested a change due to a medical condition. Nevertheless, some courts have required that individuals initially provide detailed information in order to trigger the employer's duty to investigate whether reasonable accommodation is required. See, e.g., Taylor v. Principal Fin. Group, Inc., 93 F.3d 155, 165, 5 AD Cas. (BNA) 1653, 1660 (5th Cir. 1996); Miller v. Nat'l Cas. Co., 61 F.3d 627, 629-30, 4 AD Cas. (BNA) 1089, 1090-91 (8th Cir. 1995).

18. See Questions 5-7, infra, for a further discussion on when an employer may request reasonable documentation about a person's "disability" and the need for reasonable accommodation.

19. Cf. Beck v. Univ. of Wis. Bd. of Regents, 75 F.3d 1130, 5 AD Cas. (BNA) 304 (7th Cir. 1996); Schmidt v. Safeway Inc., 864 F. Supp. 991, 997, 3 AD Cas. (BNA) 1141, 1146 (D. Or. 1994). But see Miller v. Nat'l Casualty Co., 61 F.3d 627, 630, 4 AD Cas. (BNA) 1089, 1091 (8th Cir. 1995) (employer had no duty to investigate reasonable accommodation despite the fact that the employee's sister notified the employer that the employee "was mentally falling apart and the family was trying to get her into the hospital").

The employer should be receptive to any relevant information or requests it receives from a third party acting on the individual's behalf because the reasonable accommodation process presumes open communication in order to help the employer make an informed decision. See 29 C.F.R. 1630.2(o), 1630.9 (1997); 29 C.F.R. pt. 1630 app. 1630.2(o), 1630.9 (1997).

20. Although individuals with disabilities are not required to keep records, they may find it useful to document requests for reasonable accommodation in the event there is a dispute about whether or when they requested accommodation. Employers, however, **must** keep all employment records, including records of requests for reasonable accommodation, for one year from the making of the record or the personnel action involved, whichever occurs later. If a charge is

filed, records must be preserved until the charge is resolved. 29 C.F.R. 1602.14 (1997).

21. Cf. Masterson v. Yellow Freight Sys., Inc., Nos. 98-6126, 98-6025, 1998 WL 856143 (10th Cir. Dec. 11, 1998) (fact that an employee with a disability does not need a reasonable accommodation all the time does not relieve employer from providing an accommodation for the period when he does need one).

22. See 29 C.F.R. 1630.2(o)(3) (1997); 29 C.F.R. pt. 1630 app. 1630.2(o), 1630.9 (1997); see also Haschmann v. Time Warner Entertainment Co., 151 F.3d 591, 601, 8 AD Cas. (BNA) 692, 700 (7th Cir. 1998); Dalton v. Subaru-Isuzu, 141 F.3d 667, 677, 7 AD Cas. (BNA) 1872, 1880-81 (7th Cir. 1998). The appendix to the regulations at 1630.9 provides a detailed discussion of the reasonable accommodation process.

Engaging in an interactive process helps employers to discover and provide reasonable accommodation. Moreover, in situations where an employer fails to provide a reasonable accommodation (and undue hardship would not be a valid defense), evidence that the employer engaged in an interactive process can demonstrate a "good faith" effort which can protect an employer from having to pay punitive and certain compensatory damages. See 42 U.S.C. 1981a(a)(3) (1994).

23. See 29 C.F.R. pt. 1630 app. 1630.9 (1997). The Appendix to this Guidance provides a list of resources to identify possible accommodations.

24. 29 C.F.R. pt. 1630 app. 1630.9 (1997); see also EEOC Enforcement Guidance: Preemployment Disability-Related Questions and Medical Examinations at 6, 8 FEP Manual (BNA) 405:7191, 7193 (1995) [hereinafter Preemployment Questions and Medical Examinations]; EEOC Enforcement Guidance: The Americans with Disabilities Act and Psychiatric Disabilities at 22-23, 8 FEP Manual (BNA) 405:7461, 7472-73 (1997) [hereinafter ADA and Psychiatric Disabilities]. Although the latter Enforcement Guidance focuses on psychiatric disabilities, the legal standard under which an employer may request documentation applies to disabilities generally.

When an employee seeks leave as a reasonable accommodation, an employer's request for documentation about disability and the need for leave may overlap with the certification requirements of the Family and Medical Leave Act (FMLA), 29 C.F.R. 825.305-.306, 825.310-.311 (1997).

25. Since a doctor cannot disclose information about a patient without his/her permission, an employer must obtain a release from the individual that will permit

his/her doctor to answer questions. The release should be clear as to what information will be requested. Employers must maintain the confidentiality of all medical information collected during this process, regardless of where the information comes from. See Question 41 and note 103, infra.

26. See Question 9, infra, for information on choosing between two or more effective accommodations.

27. This employee also might be covered under the Family and Medical Leave Act, and if so, the employer would need to comply with the requirements of that statute.

28. See Templeton v. Neodata Servs., Inc., No. 98-1106, 1998 WL 852516 (10th Cir. Dec. 10, 1998); Beck v. Univ. of Wis. Bd. of Regents,, 75 F.3d 1130, 1134, 5 AD Cas. (BNA) 304, 307 (7th Cir. 1996); McAlpin v. National Semiconductor Corp., 921 F. Supp. 1518, 1525, 5 AD Cas. (BNA) 1047, 1052 (N.D. Tex. 1996).

29. See Hendricks-Robinson v. Excel Corp., 154 F.3d 685, 700, 8 AD Cas. (BNA) 875, 887 (7th Cir. 1998).

30. If an individual provides sufficient documentation to show the existence of an ADA disability and the need for reasonable accommodation, continued efforts by the employer to require that the individual see the employer's health professional could be considered retaliation.

31. Employers also may consider alternatives like having their health professional consult with the individual's health professional, with the employee's consent.

32. See 29 C.F.R. pt. 1630 app. 1630.9 (1997); see also Stewart v. Happy Herman's Cheshire Bridge Inc., 117 F.3d 1278, 1285-86, 6 AD Cas. (BNA) 1834, 1839 (11th Cir. 1997); Hankins v. The Gap Inc., 84 F.3d 797, 800, 5 AD Cas. (BNA) 924, 926-27 (6th Cir. 1996); Gile v. United Airlines, Inc., 95 F.3d 492, 499, 5 AD Cas. (BNA) 1466, 1471 (7th Cir. 1996).

33. 29 C.F.R. pt. 1630 app. 1630.9 (1997).

34. See Dalton v. Subaru-Isuzu Automotive, Inc., 141 F.3d 667, 677, 7 AD Cas. (BNA) 1872, 1880 (7th Cir. 1998).

35. In determining whether there has been an unnecessary delay in responding to a request for reasonable accommodation, relevant factors would include: (1) the reason(s) for the delay, (2) the length of the delay, (3) how much the individual

with a disability and the employer each contributed to the delay, (4) what the employer was doing during the delay, and (5) whether the required accommodation was simple or complex to provide.

36. See 29 C.F.R. pt. 1630 app. 1630.9 (1997); see also Hankins v. The Gap, Inc., 84 F.3d 797, 801, 5 AD Cas. (BNA) 924, 927 (6th Cir. 1996).

37. 42 U.S.C. 12112(d)(2)(A) (1994); 29 C.F.R. 1630.13(a) (1997). For a thorough discussion of these requirements, see Preemployment Questions and Medical Examinations, supra note 24, at 6-8, 8 FEP Manual (BNA) 405: 7193-94.

38. 42 U.S.C. 12112(d)(3) (1994); 29 C.F.R. 1630.14(b) (1997); see also Preemployment Questions and Medical Examinations, supra note 24, at 20, 8 FEP Manual (BNA) 405:7201.

39. See Question 12, supra, for the circumstances under which an employer may ask an applicant whether s/he will need reasonable accommodation to perform specific job functions.

40. The discussions and examples in this section assume that there is only one effective accommodation and that the reasonable accommodation will not cause undue hardship.

41. See 29 C.F.R. pt. 1630 app, 1630.9 (1997).

42. 42 U.S.C. 12181(7), 12182(1)(A), (2)(A)(iii) (1994).

43. The discussions and examples in this section assume that there is only one effective accommodation and that the reasonable accommodation will not cause undue hardship.

The types of reasonable accommodations discussed in this section are not exhaustive. For example, employees with disabilities may request reasonable accommodations to modify the work environment, such as changes to the ventilation system or relocation of a work space.

See the Appendix for additional resources to identify other possible reasonable accommodations.

44. 42 U.S.C. 12111(9)(B) (1994); 29 C.F.R. pt. 1630 app. 1630.2(o), 1630.9 (1997); see Benson v. Northwest Airlines, Inc., 62 F.3d 1108, 1112-13, 4 AD Cas. (BNA) 1234, 1236-37 (8th Cir. 1995).

45. 29 C.F.R. pt. 1630 app. 1630.2(o) (1997). See Cehrs v. Northeast Ohio Alzheimer's, 155 F.3d 775, 782, 8 AD Cas. (BNA) 825, 830-31 (6th Cir. 1998).

An employee who needs leave, or a part-time or modified schedule, as a reasonable accommodation also may be entitled to leave under the Family and Medical Leave Act. See Questions 21 and 23, infra.

46. See A Technical Assistance Manual on the Employment Provisions (Title I) of the Americans with Disabilities Act, at 3.10(4), 8 FEP Manual (BNA) 405:6981, 7011 (1992) [hereinafter TAM].

47. 42 U.S.C. 12111(9)(B) (1994); 29 C.F.R. 1630.2(o)(2)(ii) (1997). See also Question 24, infra. While undue hardship cannot be based solely on the existence of a no-fault leave policy, the employer may be able to show undue hardship based on an individualized assessment showing the disruption to the employer's operations if additional leave is granted beyond the period allowed by the policy. In determining whether undue hardship exists, the employer should consider how much additional leave is needed (e.g., two weeks, six months, one year?).

48. See Schmidt v. Safeway Inc., 864 F. Supp. 991, 996-97, 3 AD Cas. (BNA) 1141, 1145-46 (D. Or. 1994); Corbett v. National Products Co., 4 AD Cas. (BNA) 987, 990 (E.D. Pa. 1995).

49. See EEOC Enforcement Guidance: Workers' Compensation and the ADA at 16, 8 FEP Manual (BNA) 405:7391, 7399 (1996) [hereinafter Workers' Compensation and the ADA]. See also pp. 37-45, infra, for information on reassignment as a reasonable accommodation.

50. Cf. Kiel v. Select Artificials, 142 F.3d 1077, 1080, 8 AD Cas. (BNA) 43, 44 (8th Cir. 1998).

51. See Criado v. IBM, 145 F.3d 437, 444-45, 8 AD Cas. (BNA) 336, 341 (1st Cir, 1998).

52. But see Matthews v. Commonwealth Edison Co., 128 F.3d 1194,1197-98, 7 AD Cas. (BNA) 1651, 1653-54 (7th Cir. 1997) (an employee who, because of a heart attack, missed several months of work and returned on a part-time basis until health permitted him to work full-time, could be terminated during a RIF based on his lower productivity). In reaching this decision, the Seventh Circuit failed to consider that the employee needed leave and a modified schedule as reasonable accommodations for his disability, and that the accommodations became meaningless when he was penalized for using them.

53. If an employee, however, qualifies for leave under the Family and Medical Leave Act, an employer **may not** require him/her to remain on the job with an adjustment in lieu of taking leave. See 29 C.F.R. 825.702(d)(1) (1997).

54. See Question 9, supra.

55. For more detailed information on issues raised by the interplay between these statutes, refer to the FMLA/ADA Fact Sheet listed in the Appendix.

56. Employers should remember that many employees eligible for FMLA leave will not be entitled to leave as a reasonable accommodation under the ADA, either because they do not meet the ADA's definition of disability or, if they do have an ADA disability, the need for leave is unrelated to that disability.

57. 29 C.F.R. 825.214(a), 825.215 (1997).

58. For further information on the undue hardship factors, see infra p. 54.

59. 29 C.F.R. 825.702(c)(4) (1997).

60. See Ralph v. Lucent Technologies, Inc., 135 F.3d 166, 172, 7 AD Cas. (BNA) 1345, 1349 (1st Cir. 1998) (a modified schedule is a form of reasonable accommodation).

61. Certain courts have characterized attendance as an "essential function." See, e.g., Carr v. Reno, 23 F.3d 525, 530, 3 AD Cas. (BNA) 434, 438 (D.C. Cir, 1994); Jackson v. Department of Veterans Admin., 22 F.3d 277, 278-79, 3 AD Cas. (BNA) 483, 484 (11th Cir. 1994). Attendance, however, is not an essential function as defined by the ADA because it is not one of "the fundamental **job duties** of the employment position." 29 C.F.R. 1630.2(n)(1) (1997) (emphasis added). As the regulations make clear, essential functions are duties to be performed. 29 C.F.R. 1630.2(n)(2) (1997). See Haschmann v. Time Warner Entertainment Co., 151 F.3d 591, 602, 8 AD Cas. (BNA) 692, 701 (7th Cir. 1998); Cehrs v. Northeast Ohio Alzheimer's, 155 F.3d 775, 782-83, 8 AD Cas. (BNA) 825, 830-31 (6th Cir. 1998).

On the other hand, attendance is **relevant to job performance** and employers need not grant all requests for a modified schedule. To the contrary, if the time during which an essential function is performed is **integral to its successful completion,** then an employer may deny a request to modify an employee's schedule as an undue hardship.

62. Employers covered under the Family and Medical Leave Act (FMLA) should determine whether any denial of leave or a modified schedule is also permissible under that law. See 29 C.F.R. 825.203 (1997).

63. For more detailed information on issues raised by the interplay between these statutes, refer to the FMLA/ADA Fact Sheet listed in the Appendix.

64. See infra pp. 37-45 for more information on reassignment, including under what circumstances an employer and employee may voluntarily agree that a transfer is preferable to having the employee remain in his/her current position.

65. 29 C.F.R. 825.204 (1997); see also special rules governing intermittent leave for instructional employees at 825.601, 825.602.

66. 29 C.F.R. 825.209, 825.210 (1997).

67. 42 U.S.C. 12111(9)(B) (1994); 29 C.F.R. 1630.2(o)(2)(ii) (1997).

68. See Dutton v. Johnson County Bd. of Comm'rs, 868 F. Supp. 1260, 1264-65, 3 AD Cas. (BNA) 1614, 1618 (D. Kan. 1994).

69. See 29 C.F.R. pt. 1630 app. 1630.15(b), (c) (1997). See also Question 17, supra.

70. But cf. Miller v. Nat'l Casualty Co., 61 F.3d 627, 629-30, 4 AD Cas. (BNA) 1089, 1090 (8th Cir. 1995) (court refuses to find that employee's sister had requested reasonable accommodation despite the fact that the sister informed the employer that the employee was having a medical crisis necessitating emergency hospitalization).

71. Pursuant to the Rehabilitation Act Amendment of 1992, the ADAs employment standards apply to all non-affirmative action employment discrimination claims filed by federal applicants or employees with disabilities under section 501 of the Rehabilitation Act. Pub. L. No. 102-569, 503(b), 106 Stat. 4344 (1992) (codified as amended at 29 U.S.C. 791(g) (1994)). The Rehabilitation Act regulations governing reassignment of federal employees with disabilities, which were promulgated several months prior to the enactment of the Rehabilitation Act Amendment, differ in several respects from the ADA's requirements. See 29 C.F.R. 1614.203(g) (1997). For non-discrimination purposes, federal agencies must follow the ADA standards.

For information on how reassignment may apply to employers who provide light duty positions, see Workers' Compensation and the ADA, supra note 49, at 20-23, 8 FEP Manual (BNA) 405:7401-03.

72. 42 U.S.C. 12111(9)(B) (1994); 29 C.F.R. 1630.2(o)(2)(ii) (1997). See Benson v. Northwest Airlines, Inc., 62 F.3d 1108, 1114, 4 AD Cas. (BNA) 1234, 1238 (8th Cir. 1995); Monette v. Electronic Data Sys. Corp., 90 F.3d 1173, 1187, 5 AD Cas. (BNA) 1326, 1338 (6th Cir. 1996); Gile v. United Airlines, Inc., 95 F.3d 492, 498, 5 AD Cas. (BNA) 1466, 1471 (7th Cir. 1996).

Reassignment is available only to employees, not to applicants. 29 C.F.R. pt. 1630 app. 1630.2(o) (1997).

73. 29 C.F.R. pt. 1630 app. 1630.2(o) (1997); see Haysman v. Food Lion, Inc., 893 F. Supp. 1092, 1104, 4 AD Cas. (BNA) 1297, 1305 (S.D. Ga. 1995).

Some courts have found that an employee who is unable to perform the essential functions of his/her **current position** is unqualified to receive a reassignment. See, e.g., Schmidt v. Methodist Hosp. of Indiana Inc., 89 F.3d 342, 345, 5 AD Cas. (BNA) 1340, 1342 (7th Cir. 1996); Pangalos v. Prudential Ins. Co. of Am., 5 AD Cas. (BNA) 1825, 1826 (E.D. Pa. 1996). These decisions, however, nullify Congress' inclusion of reassignment in the ADA. An employee requires a reassignment **only if** s/he is unable to continue performing the essential functions of his/her current position, with or without reasonable accommodation. Thus, an employer must provide reassignment either when reasonable accommodation in an employee's current job would cause undue hardship or when it would not be possible. See Aka v. Washington Hosp. Ctr., 156 F.3d 1284, 1300-01, 8 AD Cas. (BNA) 1093, 1107-08 (D.C. Cir. 1998); Dalton v. Subaru-Isuzu Automotive, Inc., 141 F.3d 667, 678, 7 AD Cas. (BNA) 1872, 1880 (7th Cir. 1998); see also ADA and Psychiatric Disabilities, supra note 24, at 28, 8 FEP Manual (BNA) 405:7476; Workers'Compensation and the ADA, supra note 49, at 17-18, 8 FEP Manual (BNA) 405:7399-7400.

74. 29 C.F.R. 1630.2(m) (1997); 29 C.F.R. pt. 1630 app. 1630.2(m), 1630.2(o) (1997). See Stone v. Mount Vernon, 118 F.3d 92, 100-01, 6 AD Cas. (BNA) 1685, 1693 (2d Cir, 1997).

75. See Quintana v. Sound Distribution Corp., 6 AD Cas. (BNA) 842, 846 (S.D.N.Y. 1997).

76. See 29 C.F.R. pt. 1630 app. 1630.2(o) (1997); Senate Report, supra note 6, at 31; House Education and Labor Report, supra note 6, at 63.

77. For suggestions on what the employee can do while waiting for a position to become vacant within a reasonable amount of time, see note 86, infra.

78. See 29 C.F.R. pt. 1630 app. 1630.2(o) (1997); see also White v. York Int'l Corp., 45 F.3d 357, 362, 3 AD Cas. (BNA) 1746, 1750 (10th Cir. 1995).

79. See 29 C.F.R. pt. 1630 app. 1630.2(o) (1997).

80. The current regulation governing reassignment of federal employees states that reassignment is available to "nonprobationary" employees. See 29 C.F.R. 1614.203(g) (1997). This regulation does not state the applicable ADA non-discrimination standard. See note 71, supra.

81. See Aka v. Washington Hosp. Ctr., 156 F.3d 1284, 1304-05, 8 AD Cas. (BNA) 1093, 1110-11 (D.C. Cir. 1998); United States v. Denver, 943 F. Supp. 1304, 1312, 6 AD Cas. (BNA) 245, 252 (D. Colo. 1996). See also Question 24, supra.

82. 42 U.S.C. 12111(9)(B) (1994); 29 C.F.R. 1630.2(o)(2)(ii) (1997); see Hendricks-Robinson v. Excel Corp., 154 F.3d 685, 695, 8 AD Cas. (BNA) 875, 883 (7th Cir. 1998); see generally Dalton v. Subaru-Isuzu Automotive, Inc., 141 F.3d 667, 677-78, 7 AD Cas. (BNA) 1872, 1880-81 (7th Cir. 1998).

83. See Gile v. United Airlines, Inc., 95 F.3d 492, 499, 5 AD Cas. (BNA) 1466, 1472 (7th Cir. 1996); see generally United States v. Denver, 943 F. Supp. 1304, 1311-13, 6 AD Cas. (BNA) 245, 251-52 (D. Colo. 1996).

Some courts have limited the obligation to provide a reassignment to positions within the same department or facility in which the employee currently works, except when the employer's standard practice is to provide inter-department or inter-facility transfers for all employees. See, e.g., Emrick v. Libbey-Owens-Ford Co., 875 F. Supp. 393, 398, 4 AD Cas. (BNA) 1, 4-5 (E.D. Tex. 1995). However, the ADA requires modification of workplace policies, such as transfer policies, as a form of reasonable accommodation. See Question 24, supra. Therefore, policies limiting transfers cannot be a *per se* bar to reassigning someone outside his/her department or facility. Furthermore, the ADA requires employers to provide reasonable accommodations, including reassignment, regardless of whether such accommodations are routinely granted to non-disabled employees. See Question 26, supra.

84. See Hendricks-Robinson v. Excel Corp., 154 F.3d 685, 695-96, 697-98, 8 AD Cas. (BNA) 875, 883, 884 (7th Cir. 1998) (employer cannot mislead disabled employees who need reassignment about full range of vacant positions; nor can it post vacant positions for such a short period of time that disabled employees on medical leave have no realistic chance to learn about them); Mengine v. Runyon, 114 F.3d 415, 420, 6 AD Cas. (BNA) 1530, 1534 (3d Cir. 1997) (an employer has a duty to make reasonable efforts to assist an employee in identifying a vacancy because an employee will not have the ability or resources to identify a vacant position absent participation by the employer); Woodman v. Runyon, 132 F.3d

1330, 1344, 7 AD Cas. (BNA) 1189, 1199 (10th Cir. 1997) (federal employers are far better placed than employees to investigate in good faith the availability of vacant positions).

85. See Dalton v. Subaru-Isuzu Automotive, Inc., 141 F.3d 667, 678, 7 AD Cas. (BNA) 1872, 1881 (7th Cir. 1998) (employer must first identify full range of alternative positions and then determine which ones employee qualified to perform, with or without reasonable accommodation); Hendricks-Robinson v. Excel Corp., 154 F.3d 685, 700, 8 AD Cas. (BNA) 875, 886-87 (7th Cir. 1998) (employer's methodology to determine if reassignment is appropriate does not constitute the "interactive process" contemplated by the ADA if it is directive rather than interactive); Mengine v. Runyon, 114 F.3d 415, 419-20, 6 AD Cas. (BNA) 1530, 1534 (3d Cir. 1997) (once an employer has identified possible vacancies, an employee has a duty to identify which one he is capable of performing).

86. If it will take several weeks to determine whether an appropriate vacant position exists, the employer and employee should discuss the employee's status during that period. There are different possibilities depending on the circumstances, but they may include: use of accumulated paid leave, use of unpaid leave, or a temporary assignment to a light duty position. Employers also may choose to take actions that go beyond the ADA's requirements, such as eliminating an essential function of the employee's current position, to enable an employee to continue working while a reassignment is sought.

87. 42 U.S.C. 12111(9)(b) (1994); 29 C.F.R. pt. 1630 app. 1630.2(o) (1997). See Senate Report, supra note 6, at 31 ("If an employee, because of disability, can no longer perform the essential functions of the job that she or he has held, a transfer to another vacant job for which the person is qualified may prevent the employee from being out of work and the employer from losing a valuable worker."). See Wood v. County of Alameda, 5 AD Cas. (BNA) 173, 184 (N.D. Cal. 1995) (when employee could no longer perform job because of disability, she was entitled to reassignment to a vacant position, not simply an opportunity to "compete"); cf. Aka v. Washington Hosp. Ctr., 156 F.3d 1284, 1304-05, 8 AD Cas. (BNA) 1093, 1110-11 (D.C. Cir. 1998) (the court, in interpreting a collective bargaining agreement provision authorizing reassignment of disabled employees, states that "[a]n employee who is allowed to compete for jobs precisely like any other applicant has not been 'reassigned' "); United States v. Denver, 943 F. Supp. 1304, 1310-11, 6 AD Cas. (BNA) 245, 250 (D. Colo. 1996) (the ADA requires employers to move beyond traditional analysis and consider reassignment as a method of enabling a disabled worker to do a job).

Some courts have suggested that reassignment means simply an opportunity to compete for a vacant position. See, e.g., Daugherty v. City of El Paso, 56 F.3d 695, 700, 4 AD Cas. (BNA) 993, 997 (5th Cir. 1995). Such an interpretation nullifies the clear statutory language stating that reassignment is a form of reasonable accommodation. Even without the ADA, an employee with a disability may have the right to compete for a vacant position.

88. 29 C.F.R. pt. 1630 app. 1630.2(o) (1997).

89. The discussions and examples in this section assume that there is only one effective accommodation and that the reasonable accommodation will not cause an undue hardship.

90. See Ralph v. Lucent Technologies, Inc., 135 F.3d 166, 171, 7 AD Cas. (BNA) 1345, 1349 (1st Cir. 1998).

91. For a discussion on ways to modify supervisory methods, see ADA and Psychiatric Disabilities, supra note 24, at 26-27, 8 FEP Manual (BNA) 405:7475.

92. See 29 C.F.R. 1630.2(o)(1)(ii), (2)(ii) (1997) (modifications or adjustments to the manner or circumstances under which the position held or desired is customarily performed that enable a qualified individual with a disability to perform the essential functions).

93. Courts have differed regarding whether "work-at-home" can be a reasonable accommodation. Compare Langon v. Department of Health and Human Servs., 959 F.2d 1053, 1060, 2 AD Cas. (BNA) 152, 159 (D.C. Cir. 1992); Anzalone v. Allstate Insurance Co., 5 AD Cas. (BNA) 455, 458 (E.D. La. 1995); Carr v. Reno, 23 F.3d 525, 530, 3 AD Cas. (BNA) 434, 437-38 (D.D.C. 1994), with Vande Zande v. Wisconsin Dep't of Admin., 44 F.3d 538, 545, 3 AD Cas. (BNA) 1636, 1640 (7th Cir. 1995). Courts that have rejected working at home as a reasonable accommodation focus on evidence that personal contact, interaction, and coordination are needed for a specific position. See, e.g., Whillock v. Delta Air Lines, 926 F. Supp. 1555, 1564, 5 AD Cas. (BNA) 1027 (N.D. Ga. 1995), aff'd, 86 F.3d 1171, 7 AD Cas. (BNA) 1267 (11th Cir. 1996); Misek-Falkoff v. IBM Corp., 854 F. Supp. 215, 227-28, 3 AD Cas. (BNA) 449, 457-58 (S.D.N.Y. 1994), aff'd, 60 F.3d 811, 6 AD Cas. (BNA) 576 (2d Cir. 1995).

94. See 29 C.F.R. 1630.15(d) (1997).

95. See Siefken v. Arlington Heights, 65 F.3d 664, 666, 4 AD Cas. (BNA) 1441, 1442 (7th Cir. 1995). Therefore, it may be in the employee's interest to request a reasonable accommodation **before** performance suffers or conduct problems

occur. For more information on conduct standards, including when they are job-related and consistent with business necessity, see ADA and Psychiatric Disabilities, supra note 24, at 29-32, 8 FEP Manual (BNA) 405:7476-78.

An employer does not have to offer a "firm choice" or a "last chance agreement" to an employee who performs poorly or who has engaged in misconduct because of alcoholism. "Firm choice" or "last chance agreements" involve excusing past performance or conduct problems resulting from alcoholism in exchange for an employee's receiving substance abuse treatment and refraining from further use of alcohol. Violation of such an agreement generally warrants termination. Since the ADA does not require employers to excuse poor performance or violation of conduct standards that are job-related and consistent with business necessity, an employer has no obligation to provide "firm choice" or a "last chance agreement" as a reasonable accommodation. See Johnson v. Babbitt, EEOC Docket No. 03940100 (March 28, 1996). However, an employer may choose to offer an employee a "firm choice" or a "last chance agreement."

96. See ADA and Psychiatric Disabilities, supra note 24, at 31-32, 8 FEP Manual (BNA) 405:7477-78.

97. See Robertson v. The Neuromedical Ctr., 161 F.3d 292, 296 (5th Cir. 1998); see also ADA and Psychiatric Disabilities, supra note 24, at 27-28, 8 FEP Manual (BNA) 405:7475.

98. While from an employer's perspective it may appear that an employee is "failing" to use medication or follow a certain treatment, such questions can be complex. There are many reasons why a person would choose to forgo treatment, including expense and serious side effects.

99. See Vande Zande v. Wisconsin Dep't of Admin., 44 F.3d 538, 544, 3 AD Cas. (BNA) 1636, 1639 (7th Cir. 1995).

100. See 29 C.F.R. pt. 1630 app. 1630.9 (1997); see also House Judiciary Report, supra note 6, at 39; House Education and Labor Report, supra note 6, at 65; Senate Report, supra note 6, at 34.

See, e.g., Taylor v. Principal Fin. Group, Inc., 93 F.3d 155, 165, 5 AD Cas. (BNA) 1653, 1659 (5th Cir. 1996); Tips v. Regents of Texas Tech Univ., 921 F. Supp. 1515, 1518 (N.D. Tex. 1996); Cheatwood v. Roanoke Indus, 891 F. Supp. 1528, 1538, 5 AD Cas. (BNA) 141, 147 (N.D. Ala. 1995); Mears v. Gulfstream Aerospace Corp., 905 F. Supp. 1075, 1080, 5 AD Cas. (BNA) 1295, 1300 (S.D. Ga. 1995), aff'd, 87 F.3d 1331, 6 AD Cas. (BNA) 1152 (11th Cir. 1996). But see Schmidt v. Safeway Inc., 864 F. Supp. 991, 997, 3 AD Cas. (BNA) 1141, 1146-47

(D. Or. 1994) (employer had obligation to provide reasonable accommodation because it knew of the employee's alcohol problem and had reason to believe that an accommodation would permit the employee to perform the job).

An employer may not assert that it never received a request for reasonable accommodation, as a defense to a claim of failure to provide reasonable accommodation, if it actively discouraged an individual from making such a request.

For more information about an individual requesting reasonable accommodation, see Questions 1-4, supra.

101. See Question 5, supra, for information on the interactive process.

102. 29 C.F.R. pt. 1630 app. 1630.9 (1997).

103. 42 U.S.C. 12112(d)(3)(B), (d)(4)(C) (1994); 29 C.F.R. 1630.14(b)(1) (1997). The limited exceptions to the ADA confidentiality requirements are:

(1) supervisors and managers may be told about necessary restrictions on the work or duties of the employee and about necessary accommodations; (2) first aid and safety personnel may be told if the disability might require emergency treatment; and

(3) government officials investigating compliance with the ADA must be given relevant information on request. In addition, the Commission has interpreted the ADA to allow employers to disclose medical information in the following circumstances: (1) in accordance with state workers' compensation laws, employers may disclose information to state workers' compensation offices, state second injury funds, or workers' compensation insurance carriers; and (2) employers are permitted to use medical information for insurance purposes. See 29 C.F.R. pt. 1630 app. 1630.14(b) (1997); Preemployment Questions and Medical Examinations, supra note 24, at 23, 8 FEP Manual (BNA) 405:7201; Workers' Compensation and the ADA, supra note 49, at 7, 8 FEP Manual (BNA) 405:7394.

104. The discussions and examples in this section assume that there is only one effective accommodation.

105. See 29 C.F.R. pt. 1630 app. 1630.15(d) (1996); see also Stone v. Mount Vernon, 118 F.3d 92, 101, 6 AD Cas. (BNA) 1685, 1693 (2d Cir. 1997) (an employer who has not hired any persons with disabilities cannot claim undue hardship based on speculation that if it were to hire several people with disabilities it may not have sufficient staff to perform certain tasks), Bryant v. Better Business Bureau of Greater Maryland, 923 F. Supp. 720, 735, 5 AD Cas. (BNA) 625, 634 (D. Md. 1996).

106. See 42 U.S.C. 12111(10)(B) (1994); 29 C.F.R. 1630.2(p)(2) (1997); 29 C.F.R. pt. 1630 app. 1630.2(p) (1997); TAM, supra note 46, at 3.9, 8 FEP Manual (BNA) 405:7005-07.

107. See Senate Report, supra note 6, at 36; House Education and Labor Report, supra note 6, at 69. See also 29 C.F.R. pt. 1630 app. 1630.2(p) (1997).

108. See the Appendix on how to obtain information about the tax credit and deductions.

109. See 29 C.F.R. pt. 1630 app. 1630.15(d) (1997).

110. Failure to transfer marginal functions because of its negative impact on the morale of other employees also could constitute disparate treatment when similar morale problems do not stop an employer from reassigning tasks in other situations.

111. See Haschmann v. Time Warner Entertainment Co., 151 F.3d 591, 600-02, 8 AD Cas. (BNA) 692, 699-701 (7th Cir, 1998).

112. See Criado v. IBM, 145 F.3d 437, 444-45, 8 AD Cas. (BNA) 336, 341 (1st Cir. 1998).

113. The ADA's definition of undue hardship does not include any consideration of a cost-benefit analysis. See 42 U.S.C. 12111(10) (1994); see also House Education and Labor Report, supra note 6, at 69 ("[T]he committee wishes to make clear that the fact that an accommodation is used by only one employee should not be used as a negative factor counting in favor of a finding of undue hardship.").

Furthermore, the House of Representatives rejected a cost-benefit approach by defeating an amendment which would have presumed undue hardship if a reasonable accommodation cost more than 10% of the employee's annual salary. See 136 Cong. Rec. H2475 (1990), see also House Judiciary Report, supra note 6, at 41; 29 C.F.R. pt. 1630 app. 1630.15(d) (1997).

Despite the statutory language and legislative history, some courts have applied a cost-benefit analysis. See, e.g., Monette v. Electronic Data Sys. Corp., 90 F.3d 1173, 1184 n. 10, 5 AD Cas. (BNA) 1326, 1335 n. 10 (6th Cir. 1996); Vande Zande v. Wisconsin Dep't of Admin., 44 F.3d 538, 543, 3 AD Cas. (BNA) 1636, 1638-39 (7th Cir. 1995).

114. The current regulation governing reassignment of federal employees states that Postal Service workers with disabilities shall not be considered qualified for a reassignment to the extent that it would be inconsistent with the terms of a

collective bargaining agreement. See 29 C.F.R. 1614.203(g) (1997). This regulation does not state the applicable ADA non-discrimination standard when there is a conflict between a collective bargaining agreement and the need to provide a reassignment to an employee with a disability.

115. See 42 U.S.C. 12111(10) (1994). Certain circuits have held that it is an undue hardship to provide a reasonable accommodation when doing so will violate the seniority provisions of a collective bargaining agreement. See Eckles v. Consolidated Rail Corp., 94 F.3d 1041, 1048, 5 AD Cas. (BNA) 1367, 1372 (7th Cir. 1996); Kralik v. Durbin, 130 F.3d 76, 83, 7 AD Cas. (BNA) 1040, 1045-46 (3d Cir. 1997). These decisions create a virtual *per se* rule that the ADA does not mandate as a reasonable accommodation an action that infringes on the seniority rights of another employee in a collective bargaining agreement. In the EEOC's view, such a *per se* rule nullifies Congress' intent that undue hardship always be determined on a case-by-case basis. See House Judiciary Report, supra note 6, at 42. Indeed, Congress believed employers could consider the terms of a collective bargaining agreement as one factor, but not the determining factor, in assessing undue hardship. See Senate Report, supra note 6, at 32; House Education and Labor Report, supra note 6, at 63. Finally, both Eckles and Kralik rely heavily upon pre-ADA Rehabilitation Act case law, despite the fact that Congress amended that statute by incorporating the ADA's employment discrimination provisions. See 29 U.S.C. 791(g), 793(d), 794(d) (1994).

116. See 42 U.S.C. 12112(b)(2) (1994); 29 C.F.R. 1630.6 (1997) (prohibiting an employer from participating in a contractual relationship that has the effect of subjecting qualified applicants or employees with disabilities to discrimination).

117. See 42 U.S.C. 12203(b) (1994); 29 C.F.R. 1630.12(b) (1997).

118. For example, under Title III of the ADA a private entity that owns a building in which goods and services are offered to the public has an obligation, subject to certain limitations, to remove architectural barriers so that people with disabilities have equal access to these goods and services. 42 U.S.C. 12182(b)(2)(A)(iv) (1994). Thus, the requested modification may be something that the property owner should have done to comply with Title III.

Appendix C

Equal Employment Opportunities Commission's (EEOC's) Uniform Guidelines on Employee Selection Procedures: A Summary

Federal regulations contain uniform guidelines on employee selection procedures adopted by the Equal Employment Opportunity Commission (EEOC), U.S. Civil Service Commission, U.S. Department of Justice, and U.S. Department of Labor. [29 C.F.R. Part 1607 (1999).] The guidelines incorporate a single set of principles which are designed to assist employers, labor organizations, and others, to comply with the requirements of federal law prohibiting employment practices which discriminate on the grounds of race, color, religion, sex, and national origin. They are designed to form a framework for determining the proper use of tests and other selection procedures.

The guidelines apply only to persons subject to the Civil Rights Act of 1964 (Title VII), Executive Order 11246, or other equal employment opportunity requirements of federal law. These guidelines do not apply to responsibilities under the Age Discrimination in Employment Act (ADEA), the Americans With Disabilities Act (ADA), or the Rehabilitation Act, which forbid discrimination on the basis of handicap.

Record Keeping:

The guidelines require each employer to keep records which will disclose whether or not its selection procedures may have an adverse impact on race, sex, or ethnic groups.

Records should be maintained by sex, and by the following races and ethnic groups: Blacks (African-Americans), American Indians (including Alaskan natives), Asians (including Pacific Islanders), Hispanic (including Mexican, Puerto Rican, Cuban, Central or South American, or other Spanish origin or culture, regardless of race), Whites (Caucasians) other than Hispanic, and totals.

Adverse Impact

Employer policies or practices which have an adverse impact on employment opportunities of any race, sex, or ethnic group, are illegal under Title VII and the Executive order, unless justified by business necessity.

Validation of Selection Procedures

For purposes of satisfying these guidelines, employers may rely upon:

1. Criterion-related validity studies
2. Content validity studies or
3. Construct validity studies.

Evidence of a test's validity or other selection procedures by a criterion-related validity study should consist of empirical data demonstrating that the selection procedure is predictive or significantly correlated with important elements of job performance.

Evidence of a test's validity or other selection procedures by a content validity study should consist of data showing that the content of the selection procedure is representative of the important aspects of performance on the job for which the candidate(s) is to be evaluated.

Evidence of a test's validity or other selection procedures through a construct validity study should consist of data showing that the procedure measures the degree to which candidates have identifiable characteristics which have been determined to be important in successful performance in the job for which the candidate(s) is to be evaluated.

Detailed Information on Record-Keeping, Adverse Impact, and Validation of Selection Procedures

The above discussion has been condensed for this text. For complete information and interpretation of the Uniform Guidelines on Employee Selection Procedures, it is advisable to consult 29 C.F.R. Part 1607 and legal counsel.

Table of Cases

Index

About The Author

Kurt H. Decker is a partner with the 150 attorney law firm of Stevens & Lee of Allentown, Harrisburg, Lancaster, Philadelphia, Reading, Scranton, Valley Forge, and Wilkes-Barre, Pennsylvania; Wilmington, Delaware; and Cherry Hill, New Jersey. He received a B.A. degree from Thiel College, an M.P.A. from the Pennsylvania State University, his J.D. from the School of Law at Vanderbilt University, and an L.L.M. in labor from the School of Law at Temple University. He serves as an adjunct professor of law with Widener University School of Law (Harrisburg, Pennsylvania) and as an adjunct professor with the Graduate School of Human Resource Management and Industrial Relations at Saint Francis College in Loretto, Pennsylvania. Mr. Decker is the author of over 150 books and articles on employment law that have been referenced in various federal and state court decisions, including the following books: *Employee Privacy Law and Practice* (1987), *Employee Privacy Forms and Procedures* (1988); *A Manager's Guide to Employee Privacy Law, Procedures, and Policies* (1989); *The Individual Employment Rights Primer* (1991), *Covenants Not to Compete* (1993), *Drafting and Revising Employment Policies and Handbooks* (1994), *Privacy in the Workplace* (1994); and *Family and Medical Leave in a Nutshell* (1999). He is also the co-author with H. Thomas Felix, Esquire of *Drafting and Revising Employment Contracts* (1991) and *Drafting and Revising Employment Handbooks* (1991) and the co-author with Robert N. Covington of *Individual Employee Rights in a Nutshell* (1995). He is co-editor of the *Journal of Individual Employment Rights.* Mr. Decker is a member of the American and Pennsylvania Bar Associations and their respective labor and employment law sections.

For Product Safety Concerns and Information please contact our EU
representative GPSR@taylorandfrancis.com
Taylor & Francis Verlag GmbH, Kaufingerstraße 24, 80331 München, Germany

www.ingramcontent.com/pod-product-compliance
Ingram Content Group UK Ltd.
Pitfield, Milton Keynes, MK11 3LW, UK
UKHW021825240425
457818UK00006B/72